Product Management

by Brian Lawley and Pamela Schure

for dummies®
A Wiley Brand

Product Management For Dummies®

Published by: **John Wiley & Sons, Inc.**, 111 River Street, Hoboken, NJ 07030-5774, www.wiley.com

Copyright © 2017 by John Wiley & Sons, Inc., Hoboken, New Jersey

Media and software compilation copyright © 2017 by John Wiley & Sons, Inc. All rights reserved.

Published simultaneously in Canada

For general information on our other products and services, please contact our Customer Care Department within the U.S. at 877-762-2974, outside the U.S. at 317-572-3993, or fax 317-572-4002. For technical support, please visit https://hub.wiley.com/community/support/dummies

Wiley publishes in a variety of print and electronic formats and by print-on-demand. Some material included with standard print versions of this book may not be included in e-books or in print-on-demand. If this book refers to media such as a CD or DVD that is not included in the version you purchased, you may download this material at http://booksupport.wiley.com. For more information about Wiley products, visit www.wiley.com.

Library of Congress Control Number: 2016962002

ISBN 978-1-119-26402-6 (pbk); ISBN 978-1-119-26403-3 (ebk); ISBN 978-1-119-26404-0 (ebk)

Manufactured in the United States of America

10 9 8 7 6 5 4 3 2 1

Contents at a Glance

Table of Contents

Introduction

Product management is a critical strategic driver in a company. It can make a huge impact in terms of whether products, as well as the entire company, succeed or fail in both the short and long term. It's the only role in a company that grasps all aspects of the business, including customers, the market, competition, trends, strategy, business models, and more. As such, great product management makes great companies.

While writing *Product Management For Dummies*, we tapped into our combined 60 years of hands-on product management experience. We also took advantage of the methodology and learning we've discovered working with tens of thousands of clients and individual product managers over the past 20 years in the product management consulting and training business. The resulting book, we hope, will allow you to discover and apply great product management concepts to your business and products to create massive success.

Product management has grown tremendously in importance in the corporate world in the past 10 years, as have the resources available to learn about it. As authors, we can sincerely say that we wish there had been a book like this when we were just starting in the profession. We had to learn much of what is in this book by trial and error. We owe a great debt to our mentors and the organizations we've had the privilege of working for.

If you're looking for the link to the downloadable Product Management LifeCycle Toolkit, jump to the "Beyond the Book" section later in this Introduction. We wish you tremendous success in delivering products that truly delight your customers!

About This Book

Product management as a topic is vast. The breadth of knowledge you need to be an effective product manager is very complex. The best answer to a question that arises is "It depends." As such, covering concepts from all angles was a challenge. We have done our best to provide a well-rounded look at the product management profession.

One of the beauties of a product management career is that you can make how you perform your job unique to who you are. Rather than envisioning this book as a prescriptive set of rules, imagine it as a starting point in your own career. Understand why a concept is important and then pretend you are playing a jazz score. You find yourself improvising actions while keeping the end goal in mind. This is the true fascination of this work: It is endlessly different while retaining core principles.

Product Management For Dummies is intended for all product management audiences: new product managers, those who are looking to enter the field, and business-people and entrepreneurs who want to apply product management best practices in their companies. We give you guidelines as to what you should be doing given your situation at any particular time; share when you're likely to be thrown off track; and provide handy lists, tables, and figures for reference. For those with more experience in product management, the book no doubt has some concepts you've never experienced and can serve as a good refresher on other things you have picked up along the way. Because product managers are by and large self-taught, for certain topics, you can at least take comfort in that you're on the right track. We also hope that you can use the book to review, enhance, and extend the excellent work you're already doing. With more information and preparation, you'll have more confidence in reining in a difficult situation and the ability to keep the project and your product headed in a good direction.

Here are a few conventions we use throughout the book:

>> Info in the shaded sidebars or marked with Technical Stuff icons is text you can skip if you're short on time. It's good information, but it's nonessential to the main concept.

>> We often use the term *product* to refer to both products and services even though a *product* is typically an actual physical good and a *service* refers to the work done by individuals and companies for customers. In any case, the basic concepts of product management are all highly applicable to products, services, and hybrid offerings.

>> *Product marketing* is a term that you may have heard interchangeably or in conjunction with *product management*. Its focus is typically responsible for making sure that the marketing, messaging, pricing, and other critical marketing success factors are in place.

Some companies have a dedicated product management group. Some companies have a dedicated product marketing group, and some companies have both product management and product marketing groups. And some companies have groups (called either of these terms) where the individuals perform all of the responsibilities for both.

In this book, we refer to both product management and product marketing using the term *product management* only. In this context it covers all activities in a product's life from conception of the initial idea to when the product is retired. The only exception occurs when we're discussing the difference between these roles.

Foolish Assumptions

In writing this book, we made a few assumptions about you. We assume that you have some business knowledge but not necessarily any particular technical knowledge of a subject or product area. We assume that if you need to have this technical knowledge, you have acquired or will acquire it elsewhere (and we let you know when you'll likely need to get outside information).

In an ideal world, product managers would all be deep technical experts and have MBAs and business backgrounds. However, that isn't the real world. We assume that as you grow as a product manager, you'll develop your own philosophy of product management, create your own versions of our tools, and innovate and share with others in the profession. Ultimately, you may aspire to help grow the next generation of product managers, resulting in more great products available in the world.

Icons Used in This Book

Throughout this book, you find icons that alert you to information that you need to know:

REMEMBER

Product management definitions vary widely. This icon calls out key terms and concepts that you'd be wise to file away.

TECHNICAL STUFF

This icon means we're providing some technical information that may or may not interest you. You can skip this paragraph if you want without missing any important information.

TIP

The Tip icon flags quick tricks to make your job easier and ideas to help you apply the techniques and approaches discussed. If there's an easier way to get through your workload, this is where you'll find it.

WARNING

You can easily run into trouble in product management. This icon marks hidden traps and difficult situations.

Beyond the Book

Downloading the Product Management LifeCycle Toolkit: In addition to the great content in the book you're reading right now, the 280 Group has included with your purchase a single-user license for the Product Management LifeCycle Toolkit at no extra charge. This collection of templates and tools goes along with the book and allows you to produce more effective documents more quickly. In addition, there are completed sample versions of these documents that you can use as a guideline for how to actually complete them. Go to `www.280group.com/toolkit` and use the coupon code PMDUMMIES to get your complimentary copy.

Also available online are some quick answers to some basic product management elements. To view this book's Cheat Sheet, simply go to `www.dummies.com` and search for "Product Management For Dummies Cheat Sheet" in the Search box.

Where to Go from Here

If you are new to product management or investigating it for the first time, the best place to start is in Part 1 of the book. Read it from start to finish.

If you already have some experience in product management, we still recommend starting at Part 1 to refresh what you have learned and to find information that may be new to you. If you are facing immediate challenges, find the chapter that most closely addresses your issue.

1

Getting Started with Product Management

Discover what product management is all about and what critical role it takes in delivering successful products to market.

Find out about the wide range of job functions you'll be working with and bring to your team.

Understand the complete process of bringing a product to market.

Determine what information you need to compile to keep a product on track to achieve market success.

Chapter 1

Welcome to the World of Product Management

As a product manager, you have one of the most rewarding, challenging, interesting, difficult, and important jobs in the business industry. You get to step up and be a product leader for everyone on your team and throughout your company while learning how to influence and lead usually without any formal authority or people reporting to you directly. You get to be responsible for every aspect of the product offering and for the overall success and failure of your product. This position provides one of the best training grounds for moving onward and upward into roles like vice president, general manager, and CEO. And if you're lucky and choose carefully, you get to work with some pretty talented engineering and development teams to create products that delight your customers, make a huge difference in your customers' lives, and help achieve profits and strategic objectives that propel your company to success.

Understanding the Need for Product Management

The corporate world has recently gained a deep understanding about why product management is the best choice for driving products strategically to ensure companies' customers are delighted and their businesses are growing. According to Aegis Resources companies that empower product managers are shown to be 50 percent faster to market. And in a 2013 CBS News *MoneyWatch* article, product management was listed as the fourth most important role in corporations, behind only the CEO, general managers, and senior executives. You're part of a select and important crowd.

The benefits of having a great product management organization are hard to ignore:

>> Delivering products that better meet customer needs

>> Increasing revenues and profitability

>> Creating delighted customers who generate positive word-of-mouth referrals

>> Capturing and owning markets long-term as a result of solid product strategy which drives overall company efforts

These are just a few of the benefits. No other group in the company understands all aspects of the business the way that product managers do, and thus they become the central point of responsibility for product success or failure.

YOU'RE IN GOOD COMPANY

Many CEOs started in product management as their training ground. Some notable examples include Marissa Mayer (who started at Google, moved into product management, and became CEO of Yahoo!), Steve Ballmer (who started as a product manager at Proctor & Gamble and became CEO of Microsoft), and Scott Cook (who started as a product and brand manager at Proctor & Gamble and later founded Intuit, the maker of Quicken, Mint, QuickBooks, and Turbo Tax). In fact, the last seven CEOs at Proctor & Gamble started as product managers or brand managers, as they are known in the packaged goods industry.

Recognizing the Critical Role of Project Management

Companies with great product management have a much higher degree of success. But what is product management? The following sections shed some light on what a product manager actually does.

Defining product management

You can think of *product management* as the function in a company that is ultimately responsible for making sure that every product the company offers to the market is as successful as possible both short-term tactically and long-term strategically. In other words, the buck stops here. You, as a product manager, must own everything about product success. Product managers rarely, if ever, have any formal authority or people reporting to them, so they must lead and influence in subtle yet effective ways.

Serving as a strategic driver for business

In a company each functional group has expertise and strives to be the best it can possibly be at what it's responsible for. Engineers, also known as developers, build great solutions for customers. Marketing maximizes awareness and interest in products and services. The marketing folks ensure that the market knows the product differentiation and is enticed to consider purchasing. Sales is responsible for closing the sale with customers that are already enticed. Operations makes sure that the solution is delivered efficiently and at a low cost and that the company is operating as cost effectively as possible. Technical and customer support ensure the customer's problems, if any, are resolved.

The role of product management

So how does product management fit in? One way to think about it is that product management is in the center of all company departments, as shown in Figure 1-1, as well as external entities such as customers, press, analysts, and partners. Although each of the other groups understands its role in making the company successful, product management is the only group that has a holistic point of view and understands how all the pieces fit together.

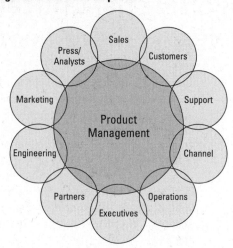

Product Management: The Buck Stops Here

Sales · Press/Analysts · Customers · Marketing · Support · **Product Management** · Engineering · Channel · Partners · Operations · Executives

© 2017, 280 Group LLC. All Rights Reserved.

- Responsible for overall product success
- Central point for all aspects of the product
- Vision and strategy
- Whole product
- Road map/requirements
- Leading the team

FIGURE 1-1: The role of product management.

Without great product management, no one can take responsibility for all aspects of customer success. After all, someone has to make sure that the short-term tactical work gets done to make the product successful. Someone also has to set out and drive the product strategy so that success is ensured longer-term. This is the role of product management (see Chapter 2 for more on what the product manager role covers).

Owning the whole product

When customers think about your product, they have a mental pro and con list that includes items that have nothing to do with product and feature benefits. Does it meet industry standards? Who will install it? Do I trust them? Who do I call if I have a problem with it after I buy it? Will they pick up the phone? Can I purchase it in a way that is convenient and familiar to me? Can I finance it? If the product lasts many years, who is going to support it for all that time? These additional aspects of your product are called the *augmented product*. You can see how the core product, actual product and augmented product are related to each other in Figure 1-2.

The augmented product is the additional parts of your overall solution that support the customer's experience with your product, such as warranty, support, purchase process, and many other factors beyond just the product and its features. A *product promise* is the implied guarantee of what kind of experience you're offering to customers through your marketing, sales, brand, and other activities. This concept is covered further in Chapter 10.

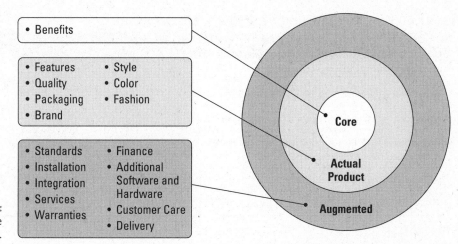

FIGURE 1-2:
The whole
product offer.

TECHNICAL
STUFF

If you've ever purchased a product that seemed to have great features and everything else you needed, yet you were disappointed with support or some other aspect of the experience, then you've experienced a *broken product promise.*

To further grasp the concept of product promise, check out this example: Say your product is a car and your company doesn't have adequate infrastructure in place to ensure that customers can have it repaired locally. The market may love your car, but few potential customers may buy; they're too worried that if the car breaks they'll have to go hundreds of miles away to get it repaired. Do you as a product manager have full control over the company's strategy and execution for making sure local repair centers are readily available? No. But you do have the ability to influence the people in your company who are responsible for this strategy and to hold them accountable for delivering this part of the solution. You also have the ability to tell the company not to proceed with making the car available if any part of the whole product offering will stop it from succeeding. Head for Chapter 18 to learn more about influencing without authority.

Keeping the product promise

As a product manager, you need to be aware of your product promise and how the augmented product delivers in a way that customers expect. Your responsibility is to try to do whatever you can to influence the other parts of the company to resolve any disconnects between customer experience and the product promise. Table 1-1 can help you to clarify how your product delivers (or doesn't) what is promised.

TABLE 1-1   Delivering on Product Promise

Question	Answer
What are the product's core benefits?	
What are key features that support the benefits?	
What does my brand represent to my customer?	
Outside of the intrinsic properties of my product, what else is involved in a customer's decision to choose my product?	
How do these augmented product elements add to or detract from my product?	
How can I influence this augmented product offering to better fit my product?	

Product Management in a Nutshell: Checking Out Your Day-to-Day Life

A product manager's job is varied and interesting; just look at Figure 1-1! In fact, there's much too much of it to do. The question really becomes, "What is important to do right now?" The following sections offer a glimpse into the daily duties of a product manager.

Managing a product during every phase of its life

In Chapter 3, we discuss the *Optimal Product Process,* which is a seven-phase model that describes everything that happens in product management, from coming up with a great idea to officially retiring the product. As your product goes through its life cycle, you can expect to do the following as a product manager:

>> Generate and prioritize great new ideas for products or features by collaborating with a team, researching the customer, and analyzing the market (Chapters 4, 5, 6, and 7).

>> After an idea is chosen, perform in-depth planning around concepts such as the market strategy (see Chapter 10), customer needs (Chapters 5 and 11), business case (Chapter 9), and other areas to ensure the plans are well thought out and support the strategic and financial goals of the company.

>> Communicate market needs to the engineering team and ensure that the product it's producing delivers in a way that solves the problems of your customers (Chapter 11).

» Negotiate with engineering to ensure that changes made to the plans keep the product on track (Chapters 12 and 18).

» Work with external customers to validate whether the product is ready to officially launch in the marketplace (see Chapter 13).

» Plan and execute highly effective product launches that ensure the company can meet the revenue, profitability, and strategic objectives of the company (Chapter 14).

» Maximize revenues and profitability after the product is available (Chapter 15).

» Determine whether and when to retire or replace the product and plan and execute a successful end-of-life campaign (Chapter 16).

Don't worry; you'll have plenty to do.

Reaching in to your bag of tricks

As you perform all your daily tasks, you need to draw upon a range of skills. You have to get executives and other key team members to buy in and support your plans. You've got to learn to say no to feature and schedule requests that don't support your strategy and plans. You need to become perceived as the de facto leader of the team — the expert on the market and the voice of the customer. And you need to execute all of that with passion, persistence, and a drive to do everything possible to make sure your product succeeds.

Product managers succeed because they have skills in the following areas:

» **Communication:** Product managers communicate when times are good and handle the tough situations as they come up.

» **Influence:** Product managers use their communications skills and more to influence and negotiate with the many stakeholders they meet in their work.

» **Analysis:** Product managers request, create, and absorb quantitative and qualitative data and communicate what it means effectively.

» **Empathy:** Product managers have great empathy for their customers and all their stakeholders. They are interested in what makes people tick and how they can help others succeed.

» **Forward driving and thinking:** Product managers can see into an ideal future and create almost tangible visions of what the world should look like once the rest of the world catches up to them. They want to bring others along with them in this amazing journey as they create valuable products and experiences.

NEVER STOP LEARNING

Although this book offers a boatload of information, you may want to consider some outside sources to further your skills and knowledge about product management. Consider attending an in-depth course that covers the entire product life cycle and allows you to practice what you've learned. Check out 280group.com for a schedule of our classes, such as Optimal Product Management and Product Marketing. If available, join your local product management association; you can find a nearby one online. Join the online Association of International Product Marketing and Management (www.aipmm.com), and attend and volunteer in a local product management meetup. Work to build your product management network.

Chapter **2**

Getting in Character: Discovering Your Role as a Product Manager

Getting started as a product manager is a question of how to wrap your arms around a very complex role, as quickly as possible. Your co-workers and boss will expect you to hit the ground running. The best approach to being a successful product manager is keeping a level head. In this chapter, we break it down so you can approach your role with outward calm and set the stage for long-term success.

Orientation Day: Examining Your Role as Product Manager

The product manager is responsible for delivering a product to market that addresses a market need and represents a viable business opportunity. A key component of the product manager's job includes ensuring that the product supports the company's overall strategy and goals. Although the product manager is ultimately responsible for managing the product throughout its life cycle (conception through end-of-life), he receives assistance throughout this process from specialists such as designers, developers, quality assurance engineers, supply chain and operations experts, manufacturing engineers, product marketers, program managers, sales engineers, professional services engineers, and more.

REMEMBER

The terms *engineer* and *engineering* are typically used for hardware products. In the software world, the terms used are typically *developer* and *development*. In this book, both terms are used interchangeably except when it relates specifically to a particular product type.

Whereas engineering is responsible for building the tangible product, product management is responsible for the whole product. The *whole product* is what the customer buys, and it includes everything that augments the product, from warranties, support, and training to peripherals, third-party applications, and value added partner services. The whole product encompasses the entire customer experience.

In most cases, the description of product manager covers an incredibly wide range of skills. However, most product manager roles have several key components:

>> **Domain expertise:** Very often, this market is why your company hired you. The fact that you know the customers and the business is the main reason you're now a product manager.

>> **Business expertise:** People say that the product manager is the CEO of the product. Though that may or may not be true, making sure the company is generating a profit is usually involved. You need to have a suite of business skills to keep your product profitable.

>> **Leadership skills:** Many people within your company are looking to you for guidance. If you don't have leadership skills under your belt, you need to develop them quickly. Chapters 17 and 18 give you more details on developing leadership skills.

>> **Operational ability:** Product managers need to dive deep into the many nitty-gritty details needed to manage a product: for example, creating part numbers or updating a spreadsheet. Sometimes you can get someone else to do these tasks, but many times you have to be responsible for them.

REMEMBER

Keep in mind that the amount of time you spend on a particular part of your job varies depending on whether you sell to businesses or consumers. The terminology used here is business to business (B2B) and business to consumer (B2C). The type of product you manage also determines how much time you spend on different tasks. A software product manager is often very focused on customer journeys and user experience. A hardware product manager may spend a lot more time on supply chain issues and forecasting. As you change from one product to another, be mindful of the critical success factors that face you in this position.

Checking out the job description

Why refer you to the job description? It's where your boss has put in all her hopes and expectations of what you'll bring to the role. And companies often define product management differently. You may see items that are usually part of project management, sales, or user experience that are included.

WARNING

Because you're providing product direction, expect to see a reference to product strategy in your role. If it isn't there, you may actually be in a junior role or managing a very customized B2B product where your customers are more likely to dictate your every move. If neither of these is the case, your company may not understand the benefits of strong product management. You aren't alone. According to the 280 Group's 2013 LinkedIn survey of product management professionals, 75 percent of executives didn't understand product management. And Actuation's team performance survey confirmed that about half of companies had a poorly defined product management role.

If this is your situation, talk to your manager about the lack of responsibility for strategy as discussed in this chapter. In some rare instances, strategy isn't part of the product management role.

Primary responsibilities of a product manager

Here are some bullet points you may find in your job description:

>> Defines the product vision, strategy, and road map.

>> Gathers, manages, and prioritizes market/customer requirements.

>> Acts as the customer advocate articulating the user's/buyer's needs.

>> Works closely with engineering, sales, marketing, and support to ensure business case and customer satisfaction goals are met.

>> Has technical product knowledge or specific domain expertise.

>> Defines what to solve in the *market needs document,* where you articulate the valuable market problem you're solving along with priorities and justification for each part of the solution.

>> Runs beta and pilot programs during the qualify phase with early-stage products and samples (see Chapter 13 for a detailed discussion of this phase).

>> Is a market expert. Market expertise includes understanding the reasons customers purchase products. This means a deep understanding of the competition and how customers think of and buy your product

>> Acts as the product's leader within the company.

>> Develops the business case for new products, improvements to existing products, and business ventures.

>> Develops positioning for the product.

>> Recommends or contributes information in setting product pricing. This point isn't true in all industries, especially insurance; however, an awareness of competitive pricing is part of what companies expect you to provide as part of the pricing decision.

Other common responsibilities

Depending on your product line, you can also be asked to do the following tasks.

>> Work with external third parties to assess partnerships and licensing opportunities

>> Identify the market opportunities

>> Manage profit and loss

>> Research products that complement your product

>> Review product requirements and specification documents

>> Make feature versus cost versus schedule trade-offs

>> Ensure sales and service product training occurs

>> Develop product demos or decide on product demo content

>> Be the central point of contact for the product inside the company

>> Partner closely with product marketing

Common deliverables

Product managers drive action throughout the company mainly through written documents supported by presentations. Here is a list of the most common documents that you may be asked to create — be aware that each company has their own specific list and terminology:

>> Business case

>> Market needs document

>> Product road maps

>> White papers, case studies, product comparisons, competitor analysis, and user stories

Required experience and knowledge

Product managers call on a wide range of skills and have a broad set of business and product experiences to call on. Here is a list of what managers look for in hiring product managers:

>> Demonstrated success in defining and launching products that meet and exceed business objectives

>> Excellent written and verbal communication skills

>> Subject matter expertise in the particular product or market — this should include specific industry or technical knowledge

>> Excellent teamwork skills

>> Proven ability to influence cross-functional teams without formal authority

Pinpointing product management on the organizational chart

Product management can report into various parts of the organization. In tech-heavy roles, it sometimes reports into engineering. In more consumer-oriented companies, it sometimes reports into marketing. More and more, companies recognize that a synthesis of what the customer wants and what the business can provide is best placed at the highest level of an organization. So VPs of product management now often report into the CEO or the executive manager for a division. See Figure 2-1 for an organization chart example.

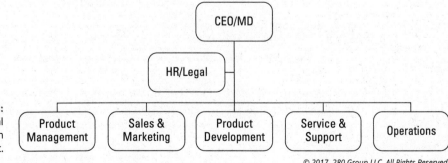

FIGURE 2-1:
A typical organization chart.

If you're part of an organization that doesn't understand product management well, it may not be able to operate as effectively. This isn't a theoretical difference. A study by Aegis Resources Inc. found that when a company empowers product managers, products get to market 50 percent faster. That's a lot of profit left on the table.

TIP

You may need to start educating your co-workers as to the best way to take advantage of product management. There are resources available on the 280 Group website (www.280group.com) that help you in transforming how your company can best take advantage of product managers to grow their business.

Drafting your product management manifesto

Someone once compared product management to refrigerator function. You don't notice when it's running well, but when it's broken, things start to stink. Remember that when you do your job well, the company hums much better — even if it doesn't know you're the source of the humming. There is less confusion and more direction. Getting to function this well comes from really knowing how you fit in and how you drive your vision forward. With this idea in mind, try to draft your own product management manifesto. This document is your guiding philosophy on how you do your job and provide direction.

Here are a few guidelines:

>> **The Is have it.** This manifesto guides your actions. Start each sentence with "I": "I am committed to...," "I have a plan...," "I will do...," and so on.

>> **It's a 360-degree view.** List all your stakeholders and determine what your stance is for each of them.

>> **Balance is key.** The one constant in being a product manager is that it involves a lot of trade-offs. Make sure you have a plan for communicating how you will decide between two courses of action. For example, "When in doubt, I will focus on validating my opinion using customer feedback."

>> **Know your decision-making plan.** In fact, the entire decision-making process underpins your success. How will you make a decision? For example, write "I will be open to many opinions before I make a final decision."

The manifesto should be no longer than one page and, because you're giving direction to other people, provide the philosophical support for how you approach your job. See Figure 2-2 for a sample of a product manager's manifesto.

I am a product management professional.

I am dedicated to bringing great products to market — products that delight my customers, are massively profitable for my company, and help change the way people work and live.

In the course of managing my products, I choose to own the responsibility for the thousands of small decisions that must be made and tasks that must be accomplished. The sum of these items can add up to a phenomenal product.

I am an expert in all areas regarding my products: customers, the market, technology, competition, channels, press, analysts, trends, and anything else that must be taken into account in order to win.

I have a strong vision for my products and develop winning strategies that align with my company's goals and ensure that our investments of time, money, and energy are well spent.

I am committed to using the best methodologies, tools, templates, and techniques available to be more efficient and effective at my job.

I have a plan for my career, and I will further my professional status by attending training courses; becoming certified; and reading books, blogs, and newsletters to learn best practices.

I am the voice of my customers and represent them in every critical decision made.

I am a leader. I develop strong alliances with everyone I need to in order to ensure the success of my product, including salespeople, engineers, support, customers, channel and business partners, management, the board of directors, and anyone else necessary. Some of these people will be very difficult to work with, but I will find a way to make everyone successful as a team.

I refuse to settle for mediocrity, and I will be tenacious and professional in my approach to getting the best possible results.

I believe that product management is one of the toughest yet most rewarding jobs in the world. Though I will face great odds and challenges, I refuse to become jaded or negative.

Though I have all the responsibility, I likely have little or no formal authority. Therefore, I will do whatever it takes to persuade others to do what is right for customers and my company.

Comparing Product Management to Other Related Roles

One of the oddest parts of being a product manager is how busy you are and yet how often what you actually do feels transient. In other words, as you work through a product's life cycle, at certain times you may just be producing a short Word document or a simple tracking spreadsheet while many other people are off writing pages and pages of code or creating tons of marketing material. However, without your direction, these folks wouldn't be able to be nearly as productive.

In this section, we cover some of the roles you work with closely. Sometimes you're checking in with each other hourly and sometimes you're in contact less frequently because you're in a different phase of the product life cycle, working with different departments or working with different development methodologies. However, knowing how the roles fit together is integral to producing a successful product.

Checking out product marketing

Creating or updating a product is always such a great feeling. One small problem: Your customers need to learn about it, too. That's where product marketing managers come in. Their primary goal is to create demand for the product through effective messaging and programs. If these people do their jobs well, your product has a shorter sales cycle and higher revenue.

The product marketing manager role is broken down into four parts:

>> **Market strategy expert:** Market strategy lays the foundation for market success. It is the high-level thinking, planning, and research that happens before a product goes to market. The product marketing manager has an in-depth knowledge of the market and how the product should enter that specific market. In practice, this idea means knowing which customer segment to target, how to reach it, and what combination of messages will drive these customers to buy (see Figure 2-3). Note that in the figure, the messages aren't the taglines, and the benefits are stated in the language of the customer. Then the strategy is executed through the launch and eventually marketing plan.

FIGURE 2-3:
Examples of a marketing message and corresponding tagline.

Old Spice Message: Real men aren't afraid to be noticed.
Tagline: Smell like a man, man.
iPod Message: You have an amazing number of songs available to you in a small form.
Tagline: 1000 songs in your pocket.

>> **Marketing expert:** After the product marketing manager analyzes market opportunities for your product, he then creates key messages that guide marketing efforts. In conjunction with marketing communications (also known as *marcom*), the product marketing manager's goal is to generate customers that demand or *pull* your product through to sale. This comprehensive market understanding is one reason that the product marketing manager participates in or decides on pricing.

In many companies, pricing is part of finance or is a specialty function. But it can also be in the hands of product management. Wherever it is, product marketing should at the very least participate in the decision making so that any market forces are understood before a final decision is made. Involve your product marketing manager in any pricing decision that takes place.

Product marketing managers ensure that all the messages are consistent. Consistency builds awareness, layer by layer, in the customer's mind. And she works with marcom to make sure that what product managers decide to say about a product translates correctly into web, mobile, or printed materials.

>> **Marketing program guidance:** This piece is the traditional core of the product marketing role. It's here where a product marketing manager, in conjunction with the product manager, outlines the product positioning which articulates the value proposition. On the basis of the positioning, he works out the messaging and links each feature to a customer-oriented benefit. Chapter 10 has more information about creating compelling marketing messages.

Value proposition is a clear statement of what problem your product solves and why customers should choose your product over someone else's.

>> **Supporting sales:** Product marketing managers can create a library of marketing collateral, which should generate market pull. However, your salespeople may need to work harder for a sale. They're the ones who generate market *push* by convincing customers to buy your product. To do so effectively, sales needs great sales tools. For example, they often need good product training, a solid product presentation, and a compelling demonstration. A product marketing person knows what salespeople need for them to get their jobs done and what points to emphasize so that the sales pitch is more successful.

Some companies expect you to do both product management and product marketing plus the entire marketing role all by yourself. If that's your situation, read *Marketing For Dummies* by Alexander Hiam (Wiley) to see how the responsibilities of product management, product marketing, and marketing all fit together.

Looking into program management

Program management is typically a department dedicated to managing the critical internal processes of an organization so that it meets internal targets. For example, program managers might work across the company to develop a new way of delivering a product to market. Or they may track how much is being spent to deliver a new product platform. In companies that are regulated or in which precision is very important, program management ensures that the important processes are reviewed and complied with. In some instances, project managers report into program management, but this isn't universally the case.

AGILE-SPECIFIC ROLES

Agile is a flexible way of developing products that mostly applies to software development. Refer to Chapter 12 for more details. Agile has two very specific roles that you don't see in other development environments: the product owner and the scrum master. The scrum master is typically only used in a specific version of Agile called *scrum*. The following figure illustrates which responsibilities lie exclusively with the product manager (PM), which are shared according to preference and skill between the product owner (PO) and product manager, and which are specifically allocated to a product owner. Use this figure and the later sections on RACI and DACI to have a discussion within your own organization to clarify roles and responsibilities.

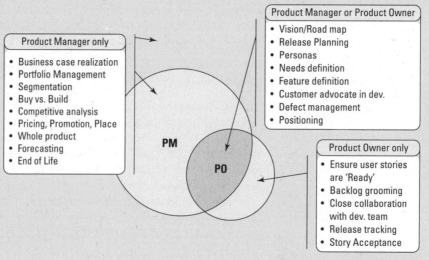

© 2017, 280 Group LLC. All Rights Reserved.

Here are definitions of the specific roles:

- **Product owner:** The mission of the product owner is to represent the customer to the development team. A key activity is to manage and make visible the *product backlog,* or the prioritized list of requirements for future development. In fact, the product owner is the only person who can change the order of items in the product backlog. One unusual aspect of product owner responsibilities is that she must be available to the development team at all times to answer any questions team members have regarding the customer's view of how they're implementing a product feature.

A product owner shouldn't be a scrum master. In many teams the product manager is also the product owner. This situation leads to a crushing workload and difficult-to-manage expectations because product managers should be spending a fair amount of time understanding customers' needs by being outside of the office. The need to be in the office as a product owner— and yet still have a deep understanding of customers — is a conflict that continues to create great difficulty for product managers and product owners in Agile development organizations.

- **Scrum master:** The scrum master role is to keep the development team working at the highest level of productivity. This person facilitates scrum rituals that drive the iterations with the scrum team and the product owner. She ensures that scrum processes and scrum-specified meetings are being followed and checks progress against expectations. Critically, she acts as a coach or facilitator for the team, helping team members solve problems and remove impediments to their progress.

  The scrum master can be a part time role or shared among multiple scrum teams, but under no circumstances should scrum master be a product owner.

Because the term *program management* is used inconsistently, get clarity with your program manager about what program management folks are specifically supposed to do. In your interactions with them, they'll continually be looking at process and control issues. You may need to explain that the strategic and integrative parts of the product management role aren't quantifiable in the way that those people like to look at work, but the output from product management is generally very beneficial to the company. Use the promise of the key product management deliverables (market strategy, market needs, and business case) as a measure of items to be checked off their list of tasks that need to be completed as part of the process of deciding which products to invest in. Then you only need to worry about making sure what you've written makes sense and will create great products.

Exploring project management

Project managers are a product manager's alter ego. Product managers keep the customer and the big picture in mind under all circumstances. *Project managers* make sure that all team members are doing what they promised to do to keep the project on track and that each detail is completed on time. There are two models of project management. One is the project manager reports into engineering and helps with keeping the product on track until it is completed and available to the market. A second, if you're very lucky, is your company has adopted a more complete view of the role of project management and makes sure that every aspect of the product is completed. This includes marketing, sales, operations, and support teams, which are all ready to deliver the product to market successfully. Ask which model your company uses so that you can set your expectations of what the project manager is willing to do for and with you. Often they know what even the most obscure tasks are that are necessary to bring a product to market, and their information can be worth its weight in gold.

Both product management and project management functions are necessary to effectively get a product out the door and into customers' hands.

WARNING

In smaller or growing companies, the role of project manager can be assigned to the product manager. If this is your situation, as product manager, you find that you are spending all your time filling in spreadsheets of tasks that have been done or need to be done. You have little or no time for strategic work or reaching out to hear the voice of the customer. As project and product manager combines, you may be perceived much more as a doer than a thinker and generally have less influence within the organization to develop new concepts and markets.

Companies have project managers to manage risk. By communicating often, project participants can voice their opinions and concerns. The project manager must consider not only the technical skills of each person but also the critical roles and chemistry between workers.

Key duties include the following:

>> Assembling a complete list of tasks required to complete the project, including those from other departments, and incorporating these items into a project schedule

>> Creating and managing the project schedule (as part of the overall master schedule)

>> Monitoring and tracking progress against the schedule and reporting progress, slippage, and changes in the schedule to the company

>> Identifying and managing potential risks in the schedule, ensuring there are contingency plans if something doesn't go to plan

>> Managing the project documentation, especially the latest versions of plans and schedules

>> Defining project milestones: entrance, intermediate and integration stages, alpha, beta, and final product release

>> Being the expert in the product development and delivery processes

>> Leading project team meetings

>> Coordinating sign-off at the completion of each stage

>> Analyzing development progress, including defect resolution

>> Managing resource allocation and load balancing

MAKING A LIST, CHECKING IT TWICE

Because the role of product manager interacts with various people in a company, start by interviewing people in different roles and making a list of the responsibilities mentioned. Ask each person what he does and what he expects of you. You may be surprised by what people say and what tasks have ended up as your responsibility. Of course, check with your manager to see whether the tasks people are flagging as being your job are really places where you add value and are things no one else could do effectively.

WARNING

If you work in an Agile development environment, the role of project manager either disappears or is elevated to oversee schedules and plans for several development teams. If the role disappears, it's because Agile environments have less need for project tracking. A core definition of Agile is that the teams organize themselves. The development team and the scrum master split what is left. And the software that tracks product backlog items allows anyone to easily see the project status. If any issues are identified during the regular planning and review meetings that Agile prescribes, the product manager (or product owner), the scrum master, and the development team have to bring a project back on track.

For larger development efforts where there are many scrum teams, there are different organizing methodologies. Under a commonly used one, named SAFe (Scaled Agile Framework), the role is renamed as a *release train engineer*. For more information, look at the "Agile-specific roles" sidebar earlier in the chapter.

Knowing what other roles you interact with

As product manager, you touch almost every part of an organization and may not even realize it. Only many years after you've left a product management role and find someone in an obscure part of the company who recognizes you do you realize the extent of your reach. It's a humbling thought.

TIP

One excellent practice is to swing through the building once or twice a day checking in with key functions. If certain functions are remote, check in with them via email, a meeting, or a phone call at least once a week. You can address any issues and concerns while they're small.

The following sections emphasize how your relationship with various roles in the company works. Working with this many different people requires excellent people skills. Look to Chapters 17 and 18 for tips on dealing with varied personalities on a day-to-day basis.

Sales

The overall goal of a sales function is to facilitate the sales process. A *sales process* is one in which customers come to the conclusion that they should purchase your product and then do so. However, sales isn't a monolithic function. Breaking down the sales department into its various roles shows how important they are to a product manager:

>> **Sales representative**: These are the people who actively talk to customers and convince them that they should buy a product. Sales representatives are usually paid at least partly on commission. If they can't figure out how to sell your product, they'll sell something else so that they can "make their sales number."

   Your job as a product manager is to make sure that they have a deep understanding of your product and become successful at selling it. Along with your product marketing manager, your job is to make sure that sales representatives have the right information to make the case for your product. Sales presentations, competitive selling sheets, and benefit/feature and pricing comparison charts are a good place to start.

>> **Sales engineer or technical sales**: For technical products, often someone has to have a highly technical conversation with a customer about creating an elegant solution to a complicated customer problem. This person is typically called a sales engineer, although this title can vary wildly.

   Just like the sales representative, the sales engineer explains your product story to the customer. The one big difference is that he might actually using your product at the time running a demonstration. You want to give your sales engineers a much more in-depth briefing about the technical aspects of the product than you give to your sales representatives.

   These folks have another important role to play in the life of a product manager: They talk to customers — in many cases, unhappy ones. If you can't get out and talk to customers directly because they are too far away or you simply don't have the time to see each unhappy customer, the sales engineer is great source of unsolved customer problems. And unresolved problems are a great source of new product ideas.

>> **Sales operations**: Sales operations staffers make sure that the back office work is done to make the sale. Part of the nitty-gritty work you do as a product manager is to make sure that sales operations have done a great job of setting up any necessary business systems so that products can easily be sold. These people know what that job entails — in detail. Visit them often in case issues arise. They know how to create workarounds quickly and fix problems in the long term.

Marketing

In the sequence of getting product into customer's hands, marketing is the next function over from product management and product marketing (see Figure 2-4). Though over time you communicate with the entire company, marketing translates what you do into the overall context of the company messaging for all products and brands.

FIGURE 2-4: The information sequence from product management to sales.

The marketing role includes generating customer demand, helping product marketing and sales respond to competitive moves, taking care of public relations, planning events, and creating material that supports the sales force and channel. You'll spend many productive and thought-provoking hours with marketing.

Legal

Your involvement with the legal department depends on the type of industry you serve. If you're in the insurance or medical fields, legal is highly involved with your product specifications. For many product managers, legal only gets involved whenever the company is making a contract with an outside party. For most products, your legal department needs to vet any kind of binding or implied promise made to a customer, partner, contractor, or third-party vendor.

Product development

Product development or, as it is sometimes called, engineering, is the organization that creates your product. Many specialties fall under this one title, including (but certainly not limited to) the following categories:

>> User experience or interface designers

>> Software developers

>> Hardware engineers

>> Quality assurance

Your relationship with product development is key to your success as a product manager. The product development people translate the customer problems that you define into real products that address those needs. How well they do depends on your ability to clearly explain what customers have told you into something that product development can act on. The quality of your communication and influencing skills is critical in making sure that you're heard well.

One issue that arises is how much direction you provide them. Engineers like to solve problems quickly. In many instances, you want to thoroughly discuss what the customer's problems and needs are while the engineers want to quickly get to a solution. Your job is to keep them in the problem space long enough so that they really flesh out the ins and outs of the customer problem. Once you believe that everyone on the team has fully understood the customer problem, you can use mind maps and other tools to work through possible solutions. Engineers take the lead once the search for a solution is underway.

Finance

Finance is really focused on keeping the numbers straight and making sure the company is making more than it spends. You work with this department on the following topics:

>> **Expenses:** How much did your product cost to develop, and how much is the actual cost of the product to product or deliver to customers?

>> **Revenue and profits:** What is expected revenue, and how much of that can accurately be allocated to profit?

>> **Pricing:** This area is a combination of the two previous bullets. During a pricing discussion, you need to keep a clear head on the real value of a product to a customer given all the other alternatives. Avoid turning it into a discussion about the amount of money that the company will make per unit. If no one buys the product because the price is too high, the price is wrong no matter how profitable. Chapter 10 has a more detailed discussion on pricing.

Operations

Operations ensures that your product actually reaches your customer with as few hurdles to overcome as possible. You want the process to be friction-free because each hurdle is another opportunity for the sale to stop. The operations department is in charge of mapping out each step, and you need to convince them to implement as simple a process as possible so that your customers can easily buy your product. You may also need to bring in product development to make sure your customer's journey is mapped out into as few steps as possible.

Here are a couple of examples of ways in which having operations working with development improved customer experiences:

>> Amazon wanted to decrease the required number of steps when purchasing a product from its website. The company eventually developed 1-Click ordering by engaging all aspects of its operations team to speed purchases.

>> When Starbucks began offering Wi-Fi in its coffee shops, logging into the service took two clicks. Today, Starbucks has combined both steps so patrons can accept and connect with one click.

Working with operations is detailed work. You must be prepared to sort out any of the following:

>> Settings in the data tracking systems such as SAP that drive the company.

>> How a part number is constructed to give internal audiences information.

>> The actual process for requesting a part number. Who do you ask? Is there a particular form or way to make this request?

>> Transportation flows of physical product as it moves from manufacturing through a distributor and eventually to a customer.

Each company has its own way of setting up internal systems and processes so that the company runs properly. You need to understand the details of how these systems intersect with your goal of getting products in the hands of customers. In the end, it's rewarding work to get right, and your operations people will love you for spending the time to get all the details done correctly.

Service and support

Service and support are the unsung heroes of your success. Much like sales engineers, service and support people hear directly from customers — and mostly from unhappy customers (it is rare that customers contact support to tell them how pleased they are.) They provide the after-sales support that keeps your customers satisfied as they use your product. As a product management your interactions with service and support happen for three main reasons:

>> You want to know what problems customers are having with today's products so you can improve the situation in the next revision or maybe even develop something entirely new, if the problem is big enough.

>> If a lot of customers are calling to complain about a particular issue or bug, service and support are great at collecting data on the problem and letting you know (in no uncertain terms, at times) that the bug needs to be fixed.

Be clear with them on any constraints that you have in fixing a product issue. Whatever you do, take their comments seriously.

>> As part of the product launch process, plan training sessions with anyone who supports customers so that they are ready to take calls and answer customer questions on day 1 of product availability.

When your service and support agents are great, they can keep your customers loyal for many years. Take time to visit them, train them, and respect them.

Service and support are part of the whole product offering. The service and support department is often seen as outside the control of the product manager. However, if the department impacts your customer's happiness and willingness to buy the product, you should speak up and ask for support and service department changes if necessary.

Conducting a Self-Assessment: Traits of a Great Product Manager

Becoming a great product manager is the work of a lifetime. The work is complicated. The skills and talents that you have to bring to the role are many. And just when you think you've mastered them all, you realize you haven't used one in a while and need more practice. Having the characteristics and skills of an amazing product manager make the job a great one if you like variety and challenges. The following sections detail the eight most important traits of great product managers. You can use Table 2-1 in the section "Scoring your product manager traits" later in this chapter to rank yourself.

Business acumen

You know that product managers need to focus on getting the product right and listening to customers. However, your company needs to make money to survive. This hard-core business acumen is what it takes to make profitable products. Business acumen includes careful consideration of the following topics:

>> **Pricing a product at the level that leads to a safe profit margin.** You need to know the complete cost structure of your product and offering, including corporate overhead.

>> **Double-checking all contractual business terms to make sure you haven't given too much away to your channel, your partners, or your customers.**

>> **Being aware when a business negotiation with an internal and, especially external person or organization isn't proceeding with your interests in mind.** You need to balance both sets of needs.

You don't pick up business skills in a vacuum. You get them from more experienced people in your company. Luckily, most of your negotiations focus on internal exchange of resources like people and money. Prior to any serious negotiation, get as complete a list as possible from your manager as to what is allowed to be part of the discussion and what is outside of the discussion. Then walk in with a list of the boundaries that you can operate in. Don't lead with those boundaries. If you're uncertain, stop and double-check to make sure that you haven't given up something that your department shouldn't commit to. Safe is better than sorry.

Industry knowledge and expertise

Many product managers come from the industry that they serve. They're industry specialists first and product managers second. In general, this attribute is great because you're already familiar with your industry and the key business drivers.

What happens when an industry is in transition? As you use your industry knowledge and expertise in a product management role, keep an eye over your shoulder for industry disruptors. Imagine you were a product manager for the taxicab industry. Would you predict that a service like Uber would transform the taxi industry? You then need to shift your energy to convincing your company that it's time to move — or possibly watch your company die.

Technical knowledge

One of the fun parts of the product manager role is having a technical conversation with someone even more technical than you are. Yes, you need to know the core technology that supports your product. So ask a technical person to give you an in-depth briefing on all the ins and outs of your product. As the briefing continues, add your own notes as to the difference this information makes to the customer. Your goal is to know the technical terms and translate that into the value that the technology delivers to your customer.

REMEMBER

The "Why is this important?" part is where you add critical value as a product manager. The world is filled with products that have a great deal of technical coolness but don't deliver real value, such as the self-stirring coffee cup that ensures the mocha or sugar in your coffee stays thoroughly mixed. On the surface, this technological innovation is wonderful, but from a customer's point of view, the additional value may not warrant spending $10 more to buy each cup.

People skills

Look at the many business books on the shelf at a bookstore. Now calculate how many are about the ins and outs of business dealings and how many are about working in the best possible way with other people. The ratio is strongly tilted toward books on people skills versus books on spreadsheets or business plans.

Good people skills underpin much of your success as a product manager. The earlier sections in this chapter present a long list of different departments and functions that you need to bring into alignment with your job description. As much as you spend time analyzing and planning your next product, you need to analyze and plan your strategies in working with your co-workers.

The basics are simple: Listen carefully, ask open-ended questions, and make sure you communicate requests and delegate clearly and succinctly. Chapters 17 and 18 go more in depth on strengthening your people skills.

Decision-making skills

The reason product managers have such a large impact on their companies is that they're one of the key functions that is asked to make forward-looking decisions on a regular basis. This is great if the decisions you are asked to make are ones where you have expertise. For example, which target markets and customer groups to pursue with your product are topics that should be your call.

The problems product managers face can have many possible right answers. The question you have to answer is, "Which is the best answer with the amount of data I have available right now?" You're trading off an early decision that creates forward movement with a more certain decision you could make at a later date. Some useful questions to ask yourself include these:

>> When is the last responsible moment to make a decision?

>> Can I make progress and leave some flexibility down the road?

>> What happens if I don't make the decision now?

>> What are my risks?

>> What are possible rewards of moving sooner or waiting longer?

In Part 2, you become familiar with tools that help you make decisions with more confidence.

Problem-solving aptitude

Product managers are known for adopting a can-do attitude. Actually, it's probably a bit more than that. Obstacles that are placed in your way are just opportunities to succeed regardless of the odds. Keep in mind that obstacles are boundaries. Give yourself permission to expand your area of control past the boundaries that seem to be in your way.

When you're faced with a difficult situation, whether it be a holdup in the life cycle of a product, a misunderstanding with another department, or any number of issues that can arise, start by gaining a good understanding of the problem. Write down all the parameters and invite other people to help you figure out where the obstacles are slightly lower (see Figure 2-5). Keep working on them until you can see a way through the problem. Many barriers are put there by organizations because they had a purpose at one time or another. If they no longer serve their original purpose, dig deeper to understand all aspects of the problem and you can find your way through.

FIGURE 2-5:
Expand your area
of control.

This mental toughness of not stopping until a problem is solved is an important attribute of a product manager. It's related to another critical attribute: optimism. No matter how bad the situation is, your ability to believe that you can solve problems gives you the opportunity at getting the best possible outcome.

A cool head

Product managers spend a lot of time under the kind of pressure that breaks many people. Product management is now considered the fourth most important job in corporate America, according to a 2013 CBS News poll. That just means that what you're doing is highly visible and very hard to do well.

Many roadblocks can crop up as you prepare a product to go to market; how you deal with the problems is a measure of your character. Every person finds a way to cope with the stress. The ones who do it best are like ducks, outwardly calm, but paddling like crazy under the water. Here are a few hints for keeping your cool:

>> When you get bad news, it's okay to leave and take a short walk — outside if possible.

>> A deep breath (or two or ten) makes a big difference in your ability to respond calmly.

>> Meditating regularly in whatever way you find productive is very helpful. So are gardening and long walks.

The main idea is to look for the gap between your surprise and your reaction. In that gap, you can choose to be calm and cool, taking the mental space to call on all the other skills that we cover in earlier sections. You're going to need them all — and a smile to go with them.

Leadership chops

A product manager needs to have leadership skills. When you're asking others to go above and beyond their comfort level, you need them to trust you.

You can read about leadership for the rest of your life, but learning to actually be a leader takes time and practice. Leadership is a practice of kicking all the traits in the preceding sections up a notch.

>> **Business acumen:** Do you know everything your decision will mean as it rolls out into the real world?

>> **Industry expertise:** How confident are you that what you know to be true today will be true as your market evolves?

>> **People skills:** Are you really listening?

>> **Decision-making skills:** Once you listen deeply to people, can you integrate all the information to come up with a truly creative decision?

>> **Technical skills:** Is the technology really going to evolve in the way you believe it will?

>> **Problem-solving aptitude:** Can you find a solution no matter how dark the situation seems to be?

When all else fails, rely on the following four qualities as part of your leadership chops:

>> Can people trust you?

>> Do you instill hope?

>> Do you have compassion for your people and your customers?

>> Do you make people feel safe?

Scoring your product manager traits

Check out Table 2-1 to see how you rank you as a product manager. For each product manager attribute, choose the box which you feel most represents your skill level. For example, for business acumen, you could score yourself as "I'm Wonderful in This Area," "Most of the Time I'm OK in This Area," or "I Really Need Some Work in This Area." Set personal goals in the areas that you want to improve in. And give yourself a pat on the back where you are wonderful. These skills are not ones that you develop overnight, so creating a development plan with a coach, your boss, or even on your own will take you far in your career.

TABLE 2-1 **Ranking Your Product Manager Traits**

Product Manager Attribute	I'm Wonderful in This Area	Most of the Time I'm Okay in This Area	I Really Need Some Work in This Area
Business acumen			
Industry knowledge and expertise			
Technical knowledge			
People skills			
Decision-making skills			
Problem-solving aptitude			
Leadership chops			
A cool head			

RACI and DACI: Understanding Responsibilities

As organizations grow, the complexity of who is responsible for doing what becomes greater. Product managers have a long list of responsibilities, and making sure that everyone is clear on what they need to be involved in and what they can safely pass onto other roles is important to document.

There are two management tools that are useful for making sure that everyone knows who participates in finishing an activity and who makes a decision about a particular topic:

>> **RACI:** Who is responsible for completing certain tasks?

>> **DACI:** Who decides on a course of action for a particular task or function?

Depending the whether the issue is one for responsibility or decision making will guide the product manager in which tool to use.

Going the RACI route

A key concept that solves the responsibility part of the puzzle is called RACI. The acronym stands for the following:

>> **Responsible:** Who is responsible for participating in completing an action?

>> **Accountable:** Who is accountable for making sure an action is complete?

>> **Consulted:** Who is consulted during the process of completing an action?

>> **Informed:** Who is informed about the state of an action?

An example is planning a company potluck beach party. Preparing for an event means that anyone responsible for bringing food or other materials as part of the event is listed as *responsible*. Volunteers for food, blankets, and so on are *accountable* for making sure that commitments are met. Executives are *consulted* on key matters as the event is rolled out. And anyone who isn't a volunteer is simply *informed* as to the state of affairs.

Table 2-2 shows a completed RACI chart for an Agile development group that uses scrum methodologies. Creating this chart as a group will allow the product manager or product owner to clarify who is responsible for which tasks and decrease confusion among group members.

TABLE 2-2

Agile Group RACI Chart

Agile Group RACI Chart	Product Manager	Product Owner	Scrum Master	Engineer	User Experience	Quality Assurance	Mgmt
Develop QA tests	I	I	I	C	I	R	I
Attend daily standups	C	R	R	R	R	R	I
Create product vision	R	C	I	I	I	I	C
Estimate story points	I	C	C	R	R	C	I

Taking a DACI direction

For many organizations, creating a RACI chart like the one in the preceding section works well. Product managers face further complications. They're trying to move forward on various fronts. Without clear decision making, entire projects can stall while everyone gets to the point of saying yes. This situation is why many product managers turn to a DACI chart. It's just one letter different, but the organizational impact is dramatic when all levels in the company adopt it.

DACI stands for

>> **Driver:** Who drives a decision to a conclusion?

>> **Approver:** Who approves a particular decision? For best results, keep the number of approvers low.

>> **Contributor:** Who contributes to a decision?

>> **Informed:** Who is simply informed about the final decision?

The DACI model is great for clearing up decision confusion. For the picnic example in the preceding section, the vice president of human resources is the *driver.* She wanted a team building event for the company. The CEO is the *approver* for the plan to have a picnic, and the *contributors* are the employee activity council who helped the vice president of human resources with decisions like inviting employee family members or not. The rest of the company employees are *informed* about the event.

It's the same event, but there's a world of difference between who drives and who is responsible. Multiple people can be responsible, but only one driver is allocated in the DACI model. Who is in charge is crystal clear. Who is allowed to approve, who can contribute a point of view, and who can stop the project is also very clear, as shown in Table 2-3.

TABLE 2-3   **Agile Group DACI Chart**

Agile Group DACI Chart	Product Manager	Product Owner	Scrum Master	Engineer	User Experience	Quality Assurance	Mgmt
Decide on product vision	D	C	I	I	I	I	A
Decide when product is ready for release	A	C	C	C	C	D	I
Get a user story ready for the team to review	C	D	C	I	I	I	I
Agree that user story is ready to be made part of the sprint	I	C	C	D	C	C	I

Using RACI and DACI effectively

The best time to create a RACI and DACI chart is at the beginning of a project. Program management would be called in to assist in working through the details since this is a company process If you wait to create this agreement after conflict arises about who does what and who can decide what, agreement is harder to reach. Depending on which issues you expect in your project, plan a working meeting to detail every task that needs to be finished and then clearly allocate responsibility. If your team is having difficulty making and sticking to decisions, hold a DACI meeting and hash the issues out. You may need a facilitator. Human resource personnel or trainers often have training in facilitation. Ask them to run the meeting for you so that you get impartial results. And a key decision maker is always welcome at the meetings to provide weight in a tie-breaking situation.

Once you have agreed on a DACI or RACI configuration, you can reuse it from project to project. If you find yourself in disagreement again or there's a large turnover in the team, it might be worth hashing out a new one.

One last benefit: If you're drastically overworked, a RACI chart makes this imbalance obvious to everyone. Then you can negotiate taking certain tasks off your plate.

IN THIS CHAPTER

» Understanding the product life cycle
and how it integrates with various
development methods

» Spelling out the seven-phase product
life cycle

» Digging into the Optimal Product
Process and its nine core documents

Chapter **3**

Checking Out the Product Life Cycle

Every product or service goes through seven distinct phases in what's called the *product life cycle.* Understanding the life cycle and knowing what phase your products are in allows you to know what the right next step is in order to ensure success. This chapter guides you through all seven phases. Different information is needed during each phase. Nine core documents are used at specific phases to store and pass on what you have learned, record a decision that has been taken and signed off, track what needs to be completed, and crystalize the thinking behind each key activity.

Defining the Product Life Cycle: What It Is and Isn't

A product begins life as a small thought: a "what-if" spark that captures the imagination. But before a product sees the light of day or reaches the customer's hands, it must go through a series of phases that involves all the departments within a company.

These seven phases capture everything that happens with a product throughout its entire life and all critical decisions that must be made. Following the product life cycle gives product managers a road map on what to do for their product as it gets closer to being released. Here are the benefits of using this process:

>> **Clear decision making.** The appropriate information needed to make a decision is available at the right time and presented to the people who have authority to make that decision.

>> **Information delivery is consistent and complete.** Everyone knows what to expect and where to look for it, and the information available is sufficient for the next phase to start off well.

>> **Each phase is accounted for and completed correctly.** Creating products is stressful. In the rush to get a product out the door, it's tempting to skip a phase. A good process ensures that you don't miss doing something and make a mistake that will be hard to recover from later on.

>> **Product management and product marketing know their role in each phase.** These roles participate fully and appropriately during each phase. They know what they need to complete to ensure a great product. Both roles support delivering a complete product using the whole product concept as defined in Chapter 1.

Phases and gates

The seven-phase model uses a *phase-gate* approach. Each *phase* consists of standard tasks that must be accomplished. Different departments and functions are aware of their work during the phase and the deliverable they bring to the party when the decision is made at the end of that phase.

To complete a phase and move on to the next one, the product must be scrutinized at a gate. The *gate* is a decision based on the work in the phase. Figure 3-1 shows the phases and gates of the product life cycle. At the gate meeting or approval session, the company can decide to move forward with the concept or product, put it to one side, cancel it, or ask for more information. Critically, the information for a gate decision ensures management can correctly evaluate the risk and opportunity of investing significant money or resources.

FIGURE 3-1:
Seven phases of
the product life
cycle with phases
and gates.

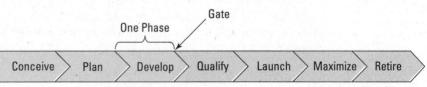

Conceive to retire from AIPMM Product Management Body of Knowledge (ProdBOK) Version 1

HOW DO YOU KNOW YOUR PROCESS ISN'T WORKING?

Finding what doesn't work is sometimes easier that knowing what is working well. If you see the following symptoms, most likely your process isn't very effective.

- **Decision making is extended.** Every decision is hard fought and can be arbitrarily reversed at any time. And once you are allowed to start the next phase, you're often in a rush to complete your product.

- **No one really says yes.** If you're not sure that your project is funded or can't find someone in authority to agree to proceed with a product idea, then your company may not actually have a product life cycle process at all.

- **Different departments deliver information in different ways.** In this situation, management can't consistently make decisions on the same basis and in the same way. Or they have to keep asking for different kinds of information which one department doesn't routinely provide.

- **Some phases are ignored or shortchanged regardless of the negative impact on overall product success.** You can tell that this is your failure point if you have just completed a product and your sales people don't know who to sell it to, and the first customers who look at it can't tell why they'd want to buy it.

- **Product management doesn't routinely participate in parts of the product life cycle.** Product management and product marketing are restricted to just a few of the phases and participate in developing and defining only part of the whole product. Chapter 1 discusses the whole-product concept in more detail.

Mapping phase-gate to Agile methodologies

A phase-gate process is well known and commonly used in the development methodology called *waterfall.* In waterfall development, product management describes a product and then hands it off for product development to create. When the development folks are finished, they hand it off to quality assurance. There's no explicit review loop during the develop or qualify phase that allows teams to catch mistakes or misinterpretation. In reality, there are continuous reviews during each phase between project team members to make sure that the product is still on track and to deal with out-of-bounds issues as they arise.

Phase-gate processes are great for making sure that the right thinking is done at the right time with the result that products are more successful. In software development, many companies have shifted to Agile development processes. There are different versions called scrum, Lean, and kanban. They are described in more detail in Chapter 12. And Figure 3-2 compares what product managers and product development are doing when under both waterfall and Agile.

Here's how to use Agile with a phase-gate process. Agile is great at managing the uncertainty and risks of software development. It isn't great at keeping track of the long-term direction your product is headed during development. The strategic context provided by the conceive and plan phases keep projects on track as the focus is on a longer time horizon.

The big difference between Agile and waterfall development methods is in the level of product detail defined in the plan phase. Under waterfall, every detail is supposed to be defined before the engineers start. In Agile, the high-level market needs and the problem that the product should solve are defined during the plan phase. The actual implementation details are left for product development and the product manager or product owner to flesh out as the work proceeds. Figure 3-2 shows that under Agile in the develop phase, the product manager is still refining requirements. They then work with product development to plan the next small chunk of work (called a sprint). And then the development team proceeds to design, code, and test before coming back to define the next sprint.

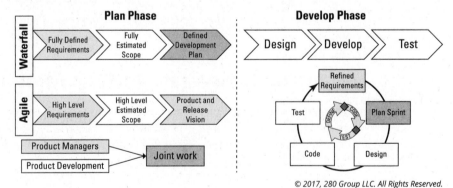

FIGURE 3-2:
Agile versus waterfall work in the plan and develop phases.

WORKING WITH A FOUR-PHASE PRODUCT LIFE CYCLE

You may also know of another commonly used product life cycle. This one starts from the premise that a product is in the market. It has four phases:

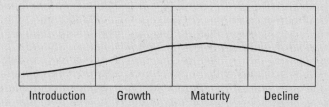

Introduction   Growth   Maturity   Decline

- **Introduction:** The goal in this phase is to build market awareness for the product. The job here is to educate customers as to the value of the product.

- **Growth:** During the growth phase, the company is guiding market share and creating brand preference in the eyes of the customer.

- **Maturity:** Strong growth slows, and the product may encounter much more competition. If your product has good market share, you need to defend it. If your product is new in this market, your chances of success are diminished unless your product is vastly better. Even then, the cost of marketing a new product from a new provider in a mature market is expensive. Products can remain in the mature phase for a long time. Arguably, lightbulbs have been in a mature market for over 100 years. As new technology arrives, customers need to understand only the difference in technology and pricing to buy the new products; they already understand why they need lightbulbs in general. The actual companies that play in this market are remarkably stable.

- **Decline:** As sales decline, companies have a limited set of choices. One is to maintain the existing product and sell what they can. Another alternative is to reduce costs and focus sales to a loyal niche segment. And another option is that the company decides to discontinue the product or sell it to another company who is interested in remaining in the market. Review Chapter 16 for a detailed discussion of your options.

The four-phase cycle is a useful tool for understanding what works best in gaining ground for your product at particular points in time. In fact, another name for this life cycle is the industry life cycle or market life cycle. The four-phase life cycle doesn't have decision points between each phase. Instead, you emphasize different aspects of marketing and sales activities at each phase.

It's Just a Phase: Breaking Down the Product Life Cycle

The deliberate execution of the appropriate tasks during each step in the seven-phase product life cycle maximizes your company's chances at delighting its customers and increasing company profits.

Phase I: Conceive

During the *conceive* phase a company or team generates new ideas and evaluates and prioritizes them to determine whether to move forward with them and spend time and resources. Anyone can come up with new ideas: executives, engineers, product managers, salespeople — even customers may propose new ideas.

TIP

One key difference between companies that do the conceive process well and ones where success is more hit and miss is whether the work of observing customers and identifying currently unmet (*latent*) needs is intentional or accidental. The best companies spend a lot of time and effort on researching and observing customers to make sure what's created has value.

The key role of the product manager in this phase is to articulate the customers' needs and the solvable problems in such a way that the potential solution to the problem can be accurately validated with customers. By applying ideation exercises and using prioritization techniques discussed in Chapter 4, product managers can lead the company to identify and focus on new and innovative ideas that can become the engine for future company growth and success.

Keep the following in mind:

>> **Key tasks:** Discover product opportunities, validate product-market fit, develop preliminary strategic documents listed in key deliverables.

>> **Key deliverables:** Preliminary versions of the business plan, market needs, and market strategy documents.

>> **Decision at the gate:** Will the company agree to provide the funding and resources to proceed to the plan phase and gain a deeper understanding of the key parameters of proceeding with the project?

Phase II: Plan

After a new idea seems to have some potential, you can spend more time to actually decide whether the investment of time and energy is worth the estimated financial gain. During the plan phase, product managers conduct more detailed and specific market research and competitive analysis to determine whether the opportunity is large and profitable enough to be viable. They determine the market need (what problems customers have) at a deeper level. (Many companies use the term *market requirements*, but we prefer the term *market needs* because it more accurately states the information being captured.) And they finalize the business case to justify spending the money to develop the product. Once the market needs are delivered to engineering, they then create a *product description document* that shows what they would build in order to meet the customer needs and solve the problems the customer is having.

It's not enough to just determine that you have a market need and that your company can put the product in place in the market. Taking a product into market successfully requires additional information — and a different document: the *market strategy document.* This piece, completed by the product marketing manager, describes exactly how, strategically, the company can take the product to market. It identifies any issues that may get in the way of a successful introduction. Additionally, a road map showing the future of the product is often created to give an idea of the longer-term strategy and viability as the product develops over time. Road maps are driven by product management with input primarily from product development, executives, operations, and sales.

Key tasks: Create market and product strategy and corresponding road map. Product manager completes the business plan and market needs documents. Product marketing completes the market strategy document. Engineering completes the product description document.

Key deliverables: Business plan, market needs document, product description document, market strategy document, and road maps. Chapters 9, 10, and 11 have more detail on all these deliverables.

Decision at the gate: The company agrees to fund actual product development.

Phase III: Develop

Once the key deliverables from the plan phase are approved, the product moves into the develop phase. In the final stages of planning, feature and schedule trade-offs are made so that at approval, the actual work can begin. The team moves forward with creating a product that is above the bar in terms of what it must deliver to customers. Most of the development money is spent during the develop phase. The role of the product manager during develop is to make sure that the customer problem is solved by what the engineers actually create. Chapter 12 has more detail about the develop phase.

Key tasks: Solidify any development plans that remain uncertain. Develop a final feature list, finish the beta testing plan, and adjust plan as issues arise in development to make sure that a valuable, customer-oriented product is the outcome.

Key deliverables: Product manager: beta plan. Engineering, quality assurance, support, service, operations, marketing, and other departments have a long list of deliverables that are provided to the rest of the company so that everyone is ready to support and sell the product at launch.

Decision at the gate: Agree that the product is ready for beta testing with real customers.

Phase IV: Qualify

As the end of development nears, the team decides whether the product is ready to go into its official final qualification phase before it is released to the general public. Engineering will generally decide whether the product is ready for this, but product management and quality assurance can be gatekeepers to make sure that a product is good enough to undergo field testing in the qualify phase. Don't confuse this stage with making sure that the product is perfect and is fully ready to ship to customers. At this point, the product needs to be good enough so that you can confirm with a select group of customers that the product functionality actually meets customer needs. Does it have the required level of quality and features to fulfill the overall product objectives? Chapter 13 goes into the details of the goals and execution of the qualify phase through running a beta program.

WARNING

Unfortunately, many companies either minimize or rush this phase. In a rush to ship, they don't really try the product in real-world scenarios. This move can cause a major catastrophe for the product and/or company if the quality level turns out to be subpar for its brand image. Imagine spending significant amounts of money launching and marketing a product without ever having verified that the quality and customer satisfaction levels are adequate to drive sales.

For example, consider the Microsoft Kin phone. After shelling out hundreds of millions of dollars (perhaps billions including acquisitions) developing the Kin phone, Microsoft then spent a huge amount to launch the product and even had a launch party at its campus — before canceling the product after less than six weeks because sales were so anemic. Had Microsoft tested with real users in addition to internal quality testing, it could've avoided serious embarrassment.

Key tasks: Run the beta program, complete the beta report, finish the launch plan, and begin preparing launch deliverables. Test marketing messages and position the beta program participants.

Key deliverables: Launch plan, completed beta plan with customer feedback that the customers find the product to be valuable.

Decision at the gate: Does the decision-making team agree that the product is ready to launch?

Phase V: Launch

Great news! You qualified the product with your customers to make sure they feel it's a worthwhile product and an investment they're willing to make to resolve a current problem. For a revision to an existing product, your customers are likely already primed to embrace and accept this new offering. For a brand new market offering, you have confirmation that the product has its first customers interested, and you have a plan to get more of them interested during the launch phase. Fantastic! Your company is ready to officially launch your product. What you've been working on for a long time is now going to become visible in the marketplace.

Once again, this process has many pitfalls. First, recognize that at launch the company can generate interest in the new product — provided the product is actually available. If a product isn't ready to ship or look at, it rapidly becomes old news, and no one is interested in reviewing it or seeks it out. Your work during and even before the launch phase is to prepare your channel and other partners (the people that actually sell your products to customers) to successfully introduce, sell, and support the product. Your company has the opportunity to set the competitive argument against other companies and products.

During the launch phase, your task is to communicate, communicate, communicate. You brief every internal and external audience that you can think of. Your marketing department rolls out electronic and physical communications to a long list of people who will go on to sell the product to potential customers. Launches are an amazing amount of work and if done successfully generate excitement and initial sales. Chapter 14 has more details on the inner workings of a launch.

Key tasks: Release product, gather feedback, finish the on-going marketing plan for your product as part of overall company activities, and perform launch review.

Key deliverables: Ongoing marketing plan, launch review document.

Decision at the gate: Is the company ready to begin the maximize phase and spend additional dollars and resources to achieve the revenue, profit and strategic goals for the product? What worked and didn't during the launch? Were projected sales results achieved? If not, why? What changes need to be made to the marketing plan? What product changes should be fed back to the product development team?

Phase VI: Maximize

Launch is such an exciting phase. Product managers are able to talk to anyone about their new shiny toy of a product. To support ongoing sales, however, the product requires ongoing marketing. And the marketing department typically takes over at this point. The marketing activities and plans they define include a vast array of activities that encompass demand generation, public relations, and enabling sales to do their job. This all links tightly in execution, messaging, and timing. Product managers don't stop, though. They track how successful the marketing is. They look at competitive responses and continue gathering customer feedback to ensure the voice of the customer is included in the next revision of the product. If appropriate, they participate critical support for the sales force and channel as sales becomes better and better at selling the product. Chapter 15 has more details on ongoing marketing that maximizes sales.

Some companies have dedicated product marketers who ensure the product gets what it needs to keep sales going and achieve revenue goals. In other companies, the product manager may have this task in addition to full-time responsibilities of planning and working on new products.

Key tasks: Product managers: Continue support of sales on an exception basis and look for product adjustments or additional product opportunities. When sales drop, plan end-of-life activities. Marketing: Develop marketing plan and integrate new product into ongoing marketing activities. Measure, review, and adjust activities to maximize sales.

Key deliverables: End-of-life plan.

Decision at the gate: Is the product ready to be retired from the market?

Phase VII: Retire

Product managers and salespeople really want a product to continue to be sold forever. For that to happen, they may revise the product, meaning a new version comes to market. A company may also sell a product on an ongoing basis without putting much effort into it, simply retiring it at some point. For some products, this process isn't much of an issue: The company sells off the inventory or removes the product from a website or price list. For other products, sales decrease to the point that the company may intentionally discontinue it.

For some types of products, such as enterprise software or products being sold in the financial, government, or medical fields, planning for the end of life is a critical operation with many specific and public steps along the way. Even in the consumer space, the retire phase can be critical to the value of the brand and the company.

Consider what would happen to a large consumer oriented company if it didn't carefully plan the retirement of a product when coming out with a new version. It could end up with millions or billions of dollars of useless inventory and corresponding financial losses. Making the wrong step during the retire phase has been known to kill off companies. One all-too-common example is companies that pre-announce the new product too early and then create a situation where the old product won't sell. That's why the retire phase is a carefully considered necessity for product success. And at this stage, the product manager typically drives this process to conclusion by delicately balancing the competing needs to the entire company in achieving a graceful end of life for a product.

Key tasks: Product manager: Investigate fully the impact of retiring a product on all parts of the business; sales, operations, and service are primary departments to check with.

Key deliverables: An executed end-of-life plan.

Decision at the gate: There is often no gate at the end of retire. If you are diligent, review and document what went well and what didn't go so well.

Detailing the Optimal Product Process

Building on the seven-phase model from AIPMM, the 280 Group team created the Optimal Product Process (OPP). This process is a comprehensive method covering everything a company or team needs to manage products successfully — from start to finish — without skipping any important steps.

The OPP further defines the same seven phases we discuss in the earlier section "It's Just a Phase: Breaking Down the Product Life Cycle" to include corresponding activities for each particular phase. The gates are key decision points to ensure that moving to the next phase is worthwhile. The OPP also includes nine core documents to help guide team members in their activities as their product proceeds through the life cycle.

Taking a look at how the process works

To set the process in motion, clear and crisp product management and product marketing roles and responsibilities are identified and agreed upon. Product management focuses primarily on the internal planning of great new products.

Product marketing focuses primarily on outbound marketing, ensuring the messaging, positioning, pricing, launch, and marketing motivate customers to purchase. To make sure that all tasks are completed, companies rely on project managers or program managers to ensure that each critical task is assigned and clear records are kept of what each participant must do and at what phase.

The Optimal Product Process expands on the AIPMM model to capture the following:

>> Roles and responsibilities

>> Decision-making criteria for each phase and gate

>> Common activities for product managers and product marketers

>> Tools to work through the challenges of each phase successfully

The result is a more precise view of the realities of bringing successful products to market. See Figure 3-3 for a complete look at the OPP.

Optimal Product Process™ (OPP)

	STRATEGY		EXECUTION				
Product Management	Business Case Document		The OPP framework is completely customizable and flexible, making it easily adopted by any company regardless of size, maturity, or development methodology. Development – Agile, Hybrid, Waterfall Documentation – None, Lightweight, Formal Maturity – Startup, Small/Medium, Enterprise				
	Market Needs Document						
	Product Description Document						
	Roadmap Document		Beta Plan				
Product Marketing	Market Strategy Document			Launch Plan	Marketing Plan	End of Life Plan	
Exit Criteria	Approval to fund business planning	Approval to fund development	Product ready for field testing	Product and organization ready	On-going marketing ready	New version or retire completely	
Phases and Activities	Conceive	Plan	Develop	Qualify	Launch	Maximize	Retire
	Discover opportunities	Create roadmap and strategy	Solidify develop plans	Run Beta/Pilot program	Release product, gather feedback	Run/monitor marketing	Communicate EOL
	Validate product/ market fit	Finish business plans	Finish beta plan	Finish launch plan	Finish marketing plan	Support sales	Plan sunset or replacement
	Develop preliminary documents	Deliver final documents	Final feature list	Test messaging and positioning	Perform post mortem	Plan EOL and next release	Perform post mortem
		PM + Engineering (Agile, Hybrid, Waterfall)					

FIGURE 3-3: Optimal Product Process.

The OPP shown in Figure 3-3 has the seven phases across the bottom and shows the major activities that are performed most often by product managers or product marketing managers during each phase. For example, during the conceive phase, product managers discover opportunities, validate the product and market fit, and develop preliminary documents.

The exit criteria (gates) shown in the figure show what decision needs to be made in order to move to the next phase. For example, in order to move from conceive to plan you have to obtain approval to fund the business planning.

Shown above the exit criteria are the nine core documents used in the OPP to keep the product idea moving forward. Each document has an assigned role and is either strategic or tactical. Product marketing is generally responsible for writing the market strategy document, launch plan, and end-of-life plan as well as writing or contributing to the marketing plan. Product management is responsible for the business case, market needs, product description, road map, and beta plan.

The documents listed under "Strategy" are strategic documents that represent the critical thinking and decision making that should happen up front. The documents listed under "Execution" are tactical and outline the goals and specific tasks and steps that must happen in order to successfully move your product through the corresponding phase.

Understanding the nine core documents

The Optimal Product Process identifies nine key documents associated with the seven phases of a product life cycle. Templates for these documents are included in the 280 Group Product Management LifeCycle Toolkit (included as a free download with this book; see the Introduction, page 4, for details). Each of these documents (see Figure 3-4) includes the critical questions, issues, decisions, and considerations you must address in order to ensure a product's success. They represent a comprehensive way of ensuring that nothing falls through the cracks and that everything is thought through thoroughly and effectively.

The list of nine key documents provides enough information to guide the core work of a project while you bring the product to market. Though you may generate many other documents along the way, think of these core nine as the guardrails of the project to make sure that it stays on track.

TIP

The nine documents are intended to be guidelines. In some cases, filling them out, writing comprehensive documents in every phase, and getting sign-off from the appropriate parties in your company makes sense so that everyone is on the same page. In other cases, such as a start-up that's moving fast, you can simply use the templates and documents as a checklist to make sure the team has thought out all the critical success factors as early as possible. The level and formality of documentation is up to you based on what your company requires for success.

Document	Purpose
Business Case	Evaluate opportunity
Market Needs	Describe the customer needs and problems
Product Description	Describe what to build
Market Strategy	Determine how to take the product to market
Road map	Determine long-term goals and strategy
Beta Plan	Ensure product is ready
Launch Plan	Create initial awareness and leads
Marketing Plan	Create demand and meet revenue goals
End-of-Life Plan	Minimize customer and profitability disruptions

FIGURE 3-4: Nine key documents from the Optimal Product Process.

In Parts 2 and 3 of this book, there are detailed instructions on how to generate content for the documents and the overall outline. The 280 Group Product Management LifeCycle Toolkit (included as a free download with this book; see the Introduction, page 4, for details) also includes completed sample versions of the templates for you to look at to get an idea of what a good document looks like.

2

Discovering, Evaluating, and Planning for Great Products and Services

Discover a process for coming up with great product ideas and then evaluating and prioritizing them.

Develop an approach to understanding customers that gives you the best handle on grasping their real needs.

Reduce the risk of product failure by effectively conducting market research and competitive analysis.

Figure out how to best select among the many product options that may be successful.

Work through the five key documents for your product so you can sell the ideas throughout your organization.

Chapter **4**

Coming Up with Great Product Ideas

A major component in product management is coming up with innovative new products and ideas for new features for existing products. Producing product ideas is the first step in the conceive phase of the product life cycle (see Chapter 3). Unfortunately, no app lets you easily select a perfect product idea that precisely fits your requirements. So where do these ideas come from, and how can you come up with a *compelling* list that you can later prioritize to determine which to pursue? This chapter gives you some useful tips and techniques for doing just that.

Getting a Handle on the Creative Process

Entire books have been written on how to generate ideas. To help narrow the creative process, in this section we present some of the most common methods and places to find ideas. These techniques are by no means exhaustive, but they should be more than enough to help you develop a healthy list of ideas to choose from.

LETTING YOUR SUBCONSCIOUS WORK FOR YOU

An important part of generating ideas is getting into a creative state of mind by engaging all parts of your brain. Because most of your brain is working at a subconscious level, you want to let your conscious brain kick off the problem and then leave your subconscious mind some time to mull it over. When engaging in finding new ideas, plan for several rounds of one or more techniques with time in between to let your subconscious do its work. Then you should be well on your way to some really creative insights.

Exploring sources for new ideas

New ideas are the fuel that keep an organization from stagnating. Luckily, many sources can help generate new ideas. Looking both inside and outside the organization can help you discover a plethora of possibilities. Consider the following:

>> **Existing customers:** Observe your customers and see what types of problems they're having. Talk with current customers to have them open up on the problems that they are experiencing. This information may uncover *latent needs,* which are needs that have not yet been identified. And they are a great source of ideas for a potential new product or procedure.

>> **Existing products:** Try to make something old new again. Look at an existing product and think about ways to improve it, innovate the current business model, and/or compete with the present processes, such as developing more effective distribution, using low-cost strategies, or launching a higher- or lower-end brand.

>> **Demographic changes:** Large-scale changes in society or groups may create new, untapped opportunities. For example, aging populations in many countries create opportunities for products that address the needs of older people and their desire to *age in place* (continue to live comfortably and independently in their own homes and communities).

>> **Unexpected occurrences:** Any time something new, out of the ordinary, or surprising happens, you may be able to capitalize. For example, Avon found that male customers were buying Skin So Soft body oil to use as insect repellent. As a result, Avon now has a line of Skin So Soft insect repellant in packaging that makes it easier to apply quickly and completely.

>> **Technology shifts:** As new technologies emerge, they make existing solutions obsolete. The introduction of the smartphone integrated several electronic devices. The digital camera, portable MP3 player, and personal digital assistant markets either disappeared or shrank considerably.

>> **Process or other inefficiencies:** Look for difficult, time-consuming things you can do in a significantly more effective way. If you've ever seen a container being pulled off a transport ship and placed directly onto a truck, you can appreciate just how efficient modern shipping has become. The days of taking out individual pallets of product from each container are long gone, and the prices of many products decreased as shipping costs dropped.

>> **Large-scale trends:** Find an existing larger wave of activity and change that you can tap into and benefit from. One huge trend has been the Internet and all the services that can now be accomplished at much lower cost.

Letting your team play

Many times product managers, entrepreneurs, and other businesspeople are tempted to come up with great ideas completely on their own. Most people want to think that they're the next Steve Jobs and that their unique, brilliant insights make them the only person who could possibly predict the next one-in-a-million idea.

The reality is that you aren't Steve Jobs. And even Steve Jobs was known to surround himself with incredibly brilliant people and occasionally "borrow" an idea or two. The most effective strategy for coming up with killer product ideas or new features is to include your team. Team members have unique insights and often come up with ideas that you never would've dreamed of on your own. When you explore new ideas, your role as product manager is to facilitate the process of product discovery and then carefully evaluate and prioritize what has been discovered.

LEVERAGING AND SERVICING TRENDS

Companies can choose to *leverage a trend* or two as a new way of doing business emerges. Uber leveraged three trends: smart phones, geo location, and a sharing economy to create a new type of taxi business. Small companies and startups leverage technologies like the cloud-based services such as Amazon web services (AWS) to dramatically decrease their costs as they explore business opportunities. Before AWS, cheap open-source software and storage like GitHub, a small software development company, would have to spend a lot of time and effort on creating and managing their own information. Now that AWS and other resources are available it eliminates the costly and time-consuming overhead of creating it themselves, so companies can move more quickly to create products. And large companies aren't standing still. They, too, are taking advantage of the same services to dramatically decrease IT costs and produce innovative new products rapidly.

Consider your team for the product discovery and evaluation exercise to include your engineers, salespeople, executives, customer and technical support folks, and anyone else who spends time working on the product or interacting with customers. On occasion, you may want to consider bringing in customers, but since they are company outsiders, their understanding of internal constraints is limited.

Why get so many people involved? Each of these roles provides a unique perspective on the customer's problem. While your potential team may be large, specific team members have particularly important and ongoing roles to play. Customer and technical support will have heard about what doesn't work well directly from the customer. If they've heard about it many times, it's a good indication that the problem is worth solving.

Engineers are wonderful because they understand the technical structure of the product, and they can bring a sense of how to best approach solving the customer's problem. When you have the team members talking together, good ideas take flight. Each area adds another perspective. You can watch a complete solution appear as you dissect the problem and develop a potential solution. The other roles typically don't participate on an on-going basis. They come in to validate and expand on what the core team has developed. Sales often doesn't like to spend time hashing ideas out in detail, so get their feedback separately. And executive participation can be a double-edged sword. They may have a non-validated opinion that others are afraid to contradict. Get their opinion offline.

See Chapter 2 for a complete view of roles when you choose the team you want to work with. Chapters 17 and 18 give you more ideas on how to bring the group together and focus them on the same goal.

Having team members feel included in the process helps you get buy-in when you do decide to move forward with prioritizing and evaluating the top ideas.

WARNING

One of the biggest mistakes product managers can make is to brainstorm and plan completely on their own without involving other functions. This is particularly true of excluding their engineering teams in the process. Delivering a plan to your engineers about what product to build and what the customer needs are without their understanding the process you went through and providing input along the way is a recipe for resentment and poor team dynamics. Don't be afraid of their input and ideas; embrace them. That way, when you do finish planning and they start to build the product, they're on board and working together with you as a team.

Generating Creative Ideas: Techniques and Tips

Generating creative ideas is a numbers game. Research shows that the more ideas you create, the better your chances of coming up with one that makes it to market successfully. This section offers some great ways to successfully unleash the creativity of your team. And you'll almost always have loads of fun in the process.

TIP

After you've generated a list of potential ideas by using the techniques in this section, the next step is to prioritize them to determine which ones are a good strategic fit for your company to pursue and are viable candidates to do more in-depth planning.

Brainstorming

Brainstorming sessions can be a fun and productive way to generate ideas. *Brainstorming* is a way for groups to generate ideas quickly by gathering a team of people together and letting them all work on the same idea at the same time. The keys to success are careful planning ahead of time and managing the initial and final parts of the exercise appropriately so that you achieve your brainstorming goals. Read on to find out just how.

Planning for a brainstorming session

Walking into a brainstorming session with no plan is a recipe for failure. Answer these key questions before setting up the session:

>> **Who will participate in the meeting?**

>> **What is your end goal?** Do you want to simply generate a list of ideas, or do you want to group and/or prioritize them with the team's help?

>> **Will you ask for people to submit ideas prior to the meeting via email, a web form, or some other method?** This approach is a great way to include a much larger group of people in the process while keeping the brainstorming session manageable.

>> **Where will you hold the meeting?**

>> **What supplies do you need in order to brainstorm (white boards, sticky notes, markers, flip chart, laptop, projector, and so on)?**

>> **How long will the session be?** Will it be broken into more than one meeting?

RULE NUMBER 1: NO IDEA IS A BAD IDEA

The most important rule to remember is that during the brainstorming and idea generating activities, the group should capture but not eliminate ideas. No idea is too silly, stupid, outrageous, impossible, or daunting. The goal is to get people rapidly generating both ideas that are known and obvious and ideas that are completely out of the box. Research has shown that by lightly challenging ideas and then expanding and adding to them during a brainstorming session, the resulting pool of ideas at the time is better. In the exercise in the section "Part 1: Using sticky notes to get the ideas on the table," look for opportunities to gently challenge and expand particular ideas especially during the grouping part.

That said, don't allow anyone to scoff at other people's ideas. When you run a brainstorming session, you need to make sure that everyone agrees to these ground rules before you get started.

» **Will you forbid participants from using their cellphones or laptops so that they devote 100 percent of their attention to the activity at hand?**

» **Who will capture the ideas, keep meeting notes, and distribute them to the team?**

One excellent practice is to send out a description of what you're trying to do and ground rules for the session. Setting expectations is a key skill of a product manager, and this approach is a great way to practice this skill.

TIP

Wonder how you're going to gently expand on someone's idea without stepping on it? One great communication skill to adopt for brainstorming and, in fact for most situations, is to start using the phrase "Yes, and. . .." When people comment on someone else's idea, the common phrase they use is "Yes, but. . .." This has the effect of negating what the other person said. Using "Yes, and. . ." is a supportive statement and indicates that you are adding to the idea. Plan to use this phrase in the next hour and you'll see how powerful it is.

Part 1: Using sticky notes to get ideas on the table

Though very simple in concept, this technique can deliver some of the best results. Each member receives a pad of large (3-x-5-inch) sticky notes and a large marker. Each person quickly writes as many product or feature ideas as possible in a set period of time — usually five to seven minutes — using just a few words. The idea here is for ideas to flow freely. You're looking for quantity over quality at this point.

Have someone time the exercise and let the team members know when two minutes are left, thirty seconds are left, and then finally when to put down their markers.

One at a time, the team members then place their ideas on the wall and explain each idea. You may find that the other team members have questions about an idea as it's put on the wall. Whoever is posting the idea should clarify what it's about at the time. If more ideas come up, document them immediately. This synthesis of many people's point of view is one huge benefit of brainstorming.

TIP

One way to get more — and more synthesized — ideas is to run a second round of brainstorming. In round two, all team members have put up their ideas and explained them. You then repeat the entire exercise but with a three-minute time limit for writing new ideas. Have everyone then post and explain any additional ideas. At this point, you should have a comprehensive list of possible product and/or feature ideas that you can use for grouping and prioritization purposes.

Part 2: Grouping ideas

Grouping ideas is a very useful technique to use at this point. Have the team do this job together. Ask members to move the sticky notes around and arrange them in logical groups such "next steps." If you use the lens of the topic you are brainstorming, logical groups arise very naturally. This strategy helps identify and eliminate duplicate ideas and spot themes for possible products and features.

Consulting customer councils

Creating a customer council is a very useful technique for getting product feedback. Forming a group of 10 to 15 representative customers for your products and having them meet once a quarter helps generate new and innovative ideas. Because they use the product day in and day out, customers often have great ideas that you and your team wouldn't have thought of. You can do the sticky note exercise (see the earlier section "Part 1: Using sticky notes to get ideas on the table") with your customer council to add to the list of ideas your team created.

REMEMBER

You want to invite people who actually use the product on a day-to-day basis; they can provide detailed feedback. Other types of customer councils involve managers and executives, but these audiences are better suited to reviews of strategic direction.

TIME LIMITED BRAINSTORMING: 3-12-3 BRAINSTORM

One approach in generating ideas is to reduce the amount of time people have to work on the idea. Doing so focuses everyone on the task at hand. One possibility is using the 3-12-3 brainstorm from the gamestorming.com website. In this version, you use time to keep ideas coming in a very focused way.

1. **Define the topic or problem and distill it to two words, such as "more fun."**

2. **Distribute index cards and markers to each person.**

3. **Give each person three minutes to generate a pool of characteristics of the topic.**

   Focus on nouns and verbs. Don't filter ideas.

4. **Break the group up into teams of two or three for 12 minutes with the instruction to draw three cards from the pile and develop a concept using descriptions, sketches, and prototypes.**

5. **Have the small groups present these ideas to the rest of the group for the last three minutes.**

What other ways can you think of to use time and space to get people to collaborate quickly and with low conflict? You may be amazed at how much laughter comes as a side effect of these simple exercises.

Tapping the power of mind mapping

Another common and powerful technique is mind mapping. *Mind mapping* uses a visual framework for generating related ideas; for many people, it fits in well with how they think and learn. Physically, each member of the team is next to each other member. This arrangement decreases conflict because the problem is literally on the wall to be worked on together.

Mind mapping works by starting with one central concept and then branching out. You can create mind maps by using special software, or you can simply use a white board or flip chart with one person (or everyone in the team) capturing the ideas as the team works together to come up with them.

To create a mind map, use the following process (see Figure 4-1):

1. **Draw a rectangle in the center of the white board or flip chart.**

2. **In the center, state the problem you're trying to solve and draw several branches extending from the center.**

   For example, in Figure 4-1, the problem is energy waste caused by leaving the lights on.

3. **For each branch, write a possible solution to solve the problem.**

   If you run out of branches before you run out of ideas, add more branches.

4. **Draw smaller branches for each main branch and write possible variations or more detailed implementations for each solution.**

   Continue until you've come up with a wide variety of possible solutions. Include as much or as little detail as seems appropriate. In Figure 4-1, the idea of rewarding kids for turning off lights triggered thoughts of more specific actions, so the team added those ideas. Team members may expand on the notion of using energy efficient bulbs at a different time or implement it as an entire project by using a different tool.

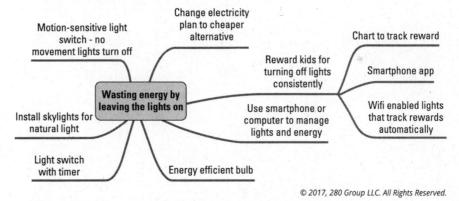

FIGURE 4-1:
A sample mind map.

Trying a more structured approach: The four actions framework

Another approach for coming up with ideas is to take an existing product (yours or one currently in the marketplace) and apply the four actions framework from Blue Ocean Strategy.

To apply the *four actions framework,* draw a four-quadrant matrix with an oval or rectangle in the center. Write the product name in the oval. In each quadrant, write ideas for removing, reducing, improving, or creating new features or aspects of the product as shown in Figure 4-2. This approach can lead to product ideas that provide differentiated products and that may meet customer needs better. For example, the framework in Figure 4-2 shows the creation of the flip camcorder, an innovative handheld video recorder before smartphones had video cameras. It was created to compete with more complex and expensive products and make it simple to create and post videos. Instead of focusing on adding features, the flip took away features, made things much simpler for the user, and allowed for a lower price point.

Four Actions Framework

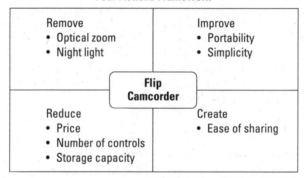

FIGURE 4-2:
An example of the four actions framework.

Chapter **5**

Working to Understand Who Your Customer Is

C ustomers are the lifeblood of a product manager. They give you the information you need to create and market products. However, product managers make decisions on the best kind of customers to target depending on all the attributes of their product including, but not limited to the benefits, the features that support those benefits and the price. In this section, the focus is on defining a customer segment and then sharing that information in an effective way within the company. Key terms that you use are *target markets, segmentation,* and *personas.* The goal is to develop a shortcut in communicating both within your teams and outside the company. Accomplishing this work usually involves direct contact with customers, so in addition to the market research section in Chapter 6, there is additional material here on how to get the most out of each customer visit.

Moving from Markets to Segments

Before diving into a discussion of segments, you need to understand some very basic marketing terminology that drives the rest of this chapter and is useful throughout this book. The basic premise is that there is an entire world of potential customers. However, to communicate with and understand customers more effectively, you need to divide them up first into customers that want or need your product and second, of these, into ones that may actually buy your product. This is the core of all market analysis and marketing activity.

Defining markets and segments

REMEMBER

Markets are defined simply as customer groupings. Adding more detail to this simple statement, from the perspective of your product, different customers fall into different choice groups. Each choice group decides to interact with and purchase products based on a different set of criteria. The official term for each customer grouping is a *market*. In a simple example, large households tend to buy milk in larger quantities than smaller households. From the perspective of the milk supplier, these are two different *market segments*: large and small households. In reality, developing market segments involves much larger set of variables. And your job as a product manager is to determine which market segments exist for your product and which variables are important to distinguish one segment from another.

The markets that you determine are the most interesting for your product are your *target markets*. In the milk example, if you produce gallons of milk, then larger households are your target market. Smaller households are not your target market.

Deciding on which target markets are valuable is the process of *segmentation*. To segment your market, you divide your customers into groups depending on the *attributes* they collectively share. These attributes are common needs, interests, and priorities.

Determining market segments

To begin the process of segmenting your market, the first decision is typically whether the product is oriented toward consumers (B2C) or businesses (B2B).

>> **Consumers:** If your product is sold primarily to consumers, market segments are divided by the following initial attributes

- Demographics: Age, sex, and income.

- Psychographics: Different personality traits (such as outgoing, competitive, or homebody); values (such as family-oriented or live for today); and attitudes, interests, and lifestyles (such as urban, suburban, or rural).

- Verticals: Interests such as hobbies, expertise, and education.

>> **Business:** If your product is sold primarily to business, market segments are divided by the following attributes

- Firmagraphics: You can subdivide companies by their industry, location, size, structure (such as LLC, corporation, or nonprofit), and performance.

- Verticals: B2B segmenting commonly focuses on the vertical attribute because it's the core business a company conducts (for example, telecommunication, construction, software development, or insurance).

Additional factors that you want to take into account include the following:

>> **Geographical segmentation:** Where are your customers? What town, state, and even country?

>> **Cultural segmentation:** Specific cultural and religious behaviors can help you distinguish the actions of one group from another.

Whenever you can distinguish between two groups of customers such that you need to change the way you market and communicate with them, you have different segments.

To bring segmentation to life, fill in the segmentation worksheet provided in Figure 5-1 for a product that you're familiar with.

Target Segment (Name or Description)		
Needs		
Goals and Motivation		
Buying Behaviors (Esp. Buying Triggers)		
Values and Attitudes		
Lifestyle		

FIGURE 5-1: Segmentation worksheet.

Harnessing the Creativity of Personas

Using segments to group customers who act alike is useful. Creating more of a personality around the segment is helpful because a segment definition can be awfully dry and impersonal. To add more flavor and depth to the segment, you can create *personas*. Personas are best defined as an archetype or stand-in for a segment.

Each persona is typically given a name so that they stand in for a group of customers in a more compelling and real way. As your personas become more lifelike, your product and marketing team members develop better offerings for the persona.

If you define two personas, Aneesh and Susan, you start to hear team members talk about how "Aneesh wouldn't buy the product in that way" and "Susan could find the user interface confusing." With names, the team can develop real empathy for the customer and better understand the design and marketing goals. Importantly, personas help the team avoid imposing its own view of the world over that of the customer.

What is included in a persona description

Persona descriptions include the following information. Use Figure 5-2 to follow along with an example.

» **Goal:** What is the persona trying to accomplish? Frame the goal in the language of the customer, not the product: "Aneesh wants to buy the product as quickly as possible."

» **Role:** What's the persona's role as part of the process of selecting a particular product? Flip to the section on persona roles for more details about this topic. For example, "Michael's role is as a buyer of this product."

» **Background:** Age, education, salary, and family status all may make a difference in how someone perceives products. *Remember:* Here you're looking only at the aspects of a persona's background that matter for your product. For example, the fact that a persona likes having credit cards that accumulate cash back may matter when she buys gas, but her marital status probably doesn't.

» **Attitude:** What attitude does your persona have? Does she consider herself smart? Well read? Clumsy? The attitude should relate to the product in question. For example, clumsy would be an important attitude to track if you are the product manager for roller skates.

» **Behavior:** Faced with new technology, is your persona adventurous and able to figure out things on his own, or is he cautious and insistent on reading manuals?

» **Insights:** Insights covers the "anything else that matters" category. What other insights about this persona should your team be aware of? For example, if your product deals with sensitive personal information, has your persona had her identity stolen? Is she naïve about passwords, using "Password123" everywhere?

Goals	
	Quick and painless input of his sales data to satisfy management
	Access to customer account information with minimum disruption to his job
Role	
	Salesperson
Background	
	30-45 years old, male, lives in California, college graduate, $97,000/year in enterprise software sales
	Used Salesforce.com at previous employer
	Understands and uses Windows at work, prefers his Mac at home
	MacBook, Firefox, Mac Office 2011, Wi-Fi at work and home, iPhone
Attitudes	
	Doesn't trust most websites with personal information of any kind
	Doesn't see a personal benefit of CRM (customer relationship management software) but management requires it as part of his job
	Values style and elegance
Behavior	
	Often uses the iPhone to browse the web while mobile
	Often buys latest gadgets and software
	Loves to brag about his technical competency
Insights	
	Used to being in control at all times
	Enjoys the influencing part of the sales role, always on the go – will never be a 9 to 5 desk worker

FIGURE 5-2: Sample persona: Steven.

Developing personas

While useful, the process of developing great personas may take an extensive amount of time. That doesn't mean that it isn't a worthwhile effort. Here is a useful process for getting you going.

Proto personas

If you don't have a lot of time, your team can use the knowledge that you and your team know of your customer base to develop a persona. A *proto persona* isn't validated or supported by actual customer data. It represents your beliefs and assumptions, which may be biased or incomplete. For a short-term, low-value project, it may be sufficient to keep your team focused what a typical customer needs.

Developing and validating personas

For more important projects, spend the time and energy to develop a validated persona.

>> Decide what the primary purpose of developing a persona is. In particular, decide which roles are important for you to develop and whether the primary use is for marketing or product development.

>> Conduct user research into actual customers. Table 5-1 has a list of good categories of questions to start with as you begin your research. Providing you a complete list is impossible given the different uses of personas. Do not limit yourself to these categories if it doesn't address the qualities that you need described in your persona. Notice that the questions used to define personas are an in-depth variation on the attributes you define for segments.

>> Condense and synthesize the data. Look for groupings under each attribute such as age or salary. The questions you ask of your customers naturally filter the groupings.

>> Refine your personas and add appropriate details to make them more real. These small touches bring a persona to life.

Initially, product managers develop many personas for each product. Over time, and with experience and as your team uses them, the number of personas usually decreases to three to six.

TABLE 5-1   **Potential market research questions to define personas**

Overview questions

Where do you live? Would you define this as urban, suburban, or rural?

Which age group are you in?

What are your interests? (List interests that will highlight and distinguish customer differences.)

How do you behave when. . .?

Do you prefer x or y activity?

What is your job?

How long have you . . .? (worked, had a hobby, lived somewhere; the rest of the question depends on your product)

Domain knowledge questions

What skills do you need to. . .?

How do you approach x task or situation?

Goals

What do you want to accomplish with your life, your work. . .?

What does success mean to you?

What does progress mean to you?

Attitudes and motivation

What do you like doing?

What motivates you to. . .?

What do you value?

Process

Describe your typical (day, week, month, visit to the doctor. . .).

How do you. . .?

How do you change what you do?

Environment

Describe your (work, home, school. . .) environment.

Does it have any of the following items in it? (List appropriate items for your product.)

Is there anything else that is key to your (work, home, school. . .) environment?

(continued)

TABLE 5-1 *(continued)*

Mental Model
What kind of (people, actions, activities) do well in x environment?

Pain Point
What is challenging in x environment? (You can ask this question over for different environments that you need to know about.)

Tools and technology
What tools/technology do you use to accomplish (work, home, school. . .) tasks?
What doesn't work well with these tools/technology?

Relationships and organizational structure
Who do you work with/report to?
Who works for you?

Future vision
If you could wave a magic wand, what would you change about. . .?

REMEMBER

When you define a persona, you're looking for similar characteristics only as they're important for your product. Here is a potential persona, Tom. Through research you discover that among his many attributes and characteristics, he is a college-educated, middle-aged married man who has two teenage children, drives a Subaru wagon, earns $120,000 per year, and uses Macs and PCs. A very simplified persona based on the data in this paragraph would be described as follows:

» College educated, 40, earns $120,000/year

» Uses Macs and PCs

If your product involves determining car gas usage, you would use the following attributes:

» College-educated, married, earns $120,000/year

» Two teenage children

» Drives a Subaru wagon

Cherry-pick the attributes that make a difference to your product.

Making Sure You Cover All Persona Roles

It's tempting to think that the main focus of personas is on the user. Instead, you need to develop different kinds of personas depending on what kind of roles are involved in the process of making a purchasing decision. Consider the case of buying a family car. The parents could each have a different role to play; perhaps one will be the primary driver, while the other is there to weigh in on cost matters but will drive the car less. And how about children? Think about their roles as influencers if the parents bring them along to buy a car. Some of the most common roles that you define are as follows:

>> **User:** A *user* persona is the person who will actually use the product. In complex B2B sales, you may have two user personas: one persona for the person who does work with the product and the other for the user who monitors the work. Both are considered user personas.

Product managers can spend too much time focused on user personas and forget or pay too little attention to the other personas. Remember that unless you cater to all personas, a sale is much less likely.

>> **Buyer:** The buyer persona represents the entire class of buyers. Remember to break down the different parts of the buying process. For example, you may have a chief technical officer (CTO) as a buyer along with the manager of a department. You need to take both personas into account, especially if they have different concerns in the buying process.

>> **Purchaser:** The purchasing persona may have an entirely different set of criteria when deciding between products and offerings. For example, purchasing departments may get bonuses based on the discounts they get from suppliers or insist that the payment terms be longer than the usual 30 days. You need to document this information correctly and prepare your salespeople for the reality of their purchaser persona. Remember too that this persona impacts how you prepare pricing and finance options. Work with your salespeople to develop this persona.

In both the B2B and B2C context, the purchaser can also be a channel partner. A *channel partner* is an organization that sells your product on your behalf. They are the distribution channel for your product. For electronic products, the Best Buy chain is a channel partner for many different manufacturers. If you sell through a particular distribution channel, you have a purchaser at the distributor level and at the retail level. Define each of these purchasers carefully to make sure your product finds its way easily to the end user.

>> **Influencer:** The role of the influencer is to provide another point of view on large-ticket purchases. People typically buy smaller items without too much concern over the cost; if you buy a ream of paper and it doesn't meet your

needs because it is too flimsy, the cost of making a mistake is minimal. However, many people are more careful about purchasing a high-tech printer without a trusted second opinion, so for this purchase they may ask influencers they know for an opinion. Common influencers are analysts, bloggers who focus on a particular market and even review websites like Trip Advisor.

Visiting Customers

Visiting customers is a great way of internalizing a deep understanding of your customer. In many cases you're asked to explain what a customer would do in a particular situation. Having a mental image of a customer site and what actually takes place there is very valuable for product managers. Product managers visit customers early on in the product development process to check and see if the product is meeting their needs during development and meet once a product is installed. Sometimes visits are needed because a product isn't performing as planned. Make visiting customers a regular part of your product management schedule of events.

Product managers are usually welcome at customers' sites because they're seen as the people who can really change the direction of a product. However, the sales department is often in charge of the relationship with a customer with B2B products. Always ask permission from your salespeople before visiting a customer, and keep the account relationship owner informed about every interaction with the customer.

Observing customer visit courtesies

REMEMBER

Visiting customers means being on your best business behavior. Here are a few simple guidelines to create a good impression for your customer during your visit:

>> **Arrive on time.** Plan to get there a few minutes early so you can park, find the right building, and, if necessary, be moved to another building for the actual meeting.

>> **Dress appropriately.** Depending where you work, casual dress may be typical. Even if your customer is wearing shorts, no shoes, and a ripped t-shirt, you should dress up. If the environment is casual, that means a jacket and dressed-down pants are appropriate. In more buttoned-up environments, suits work well. In typical business environments, women often dress one level up from whatever the men on the team are wearing.

>> **Be personable.** Ask about your contacts as individuals before tackling the subject at hand. Starting with small talk convinces them that you care about them as people as well as customers. The people you're visiting relax and share more details if you start with pleasantries.

>> **Be timely.** If you asked for 30 minutes, leave when your time is up.

>> **Say thank you.** Send an email or a card as soon as possible. (The latter is more memorable.) Outline what you discussed and follow up promptly on any actions you took after the meeting.

Interviewing customers

It's a good idea to bring others from your team with you on customer visits, such as your user experience designer or engineers. If you bring engineers, make sure you choose ones who know enough not to talk about future product designs (the customer might assume these are commitments being made about what will be delivered) and who really want to listen to customer feedback.

TIP

Use customer visits as a perk for developers who do a great job. It allows them to travel with funding from the company and it gives them a chance to get a break from their routine and get out of the building once in a while.

Visiting customers is a great way to get feedback. Doing it well builds long-term benefits for both the customer and you. Follow these guidelines to get the most out of your interview:

>> **Keep a consistent process.**

Include these steps:

- **Goal:** What's your goal in conducting the visit? What are you looking to discover? Remember that as your discussion proceeds with a customer, new information may be uncovered. At that point, follow the customer's lead and explore the new information without being tied to a rigid line of questions. You are effectively conducting market research. Read Chapter 6 for more details about market research guidelines.

- **Preparation:** Prepare a list of guideline questions ahead of time and make sure to bring them with you. (Check out the nearby sidebar "Great customer interview questions" for a few suggestions.) If, during the interview, certain questions don't make sense, don't ask them.

>> Utilize two roles during the interview.

No, we don't mean good cop/bad cop. Know going in which team member is the interviewer and which is the observer. If you are unable to source an observer to join you in a customer interview, go anyway.

- **Interviewer:** This person asks the questions. Her job is to keep the conversation going as naturally as possible.

- **Observer:** This person takes notes as she listens to the conversation. On occasion, she may notice that the interview has gotten off track and is missing a key question. The observer can then either bring the question up casually or pass a note to the interviewer. In general, bringing the question up as an "Oh, by the way. . ." comment helps the interview go more smoothly and naturally. After the point is made, the observer must return to his listening role.

TIP

You want interviews to be as close to a natural conversation as possible, albeit with a goal in mind. Of course, unlike most casual conversations, you also want to have some tangible record of what you discussed. To best achieve a balance between these two desires, take notebooks and, with the permission of the interviewee, possibly record the conversation. Most customers agree to have the conversation recorded as long as they know that it is only to share with your team members.

Try not to use a laptop to take notes though: The physical barrier of a screen, not to mention the sounds of a keyboard or mouse, can be very distracting and get in the way of the interview process.

TIP

GREAT CUSTOMER INTERVIEW QUESTIONS

Trying to get to a customer's underlying needs is a challenge of digging deep into understanding both what customers say and what they mean to say. Here's a list of some great questions. Some of them are suitable no matter the circumstances, some are more useful when you're investigating completely new product opportunities and some make more sense when you're exploring opportunities to expand and extend an existing product.

When a customer answers your question, follow up with "Why?" at least once or twice to get a more complete answer. "Why?" is a great go-to question under virtually all circumstances. Just be sure to follow the five-why rule: Asking "Why?" more than five times puts you at risk for sounding like a 2-year-old.

Other good words to start questions with to more deeply explore issues are "What" as in "What would having . . . do for you?" or "How." Many questions below start with "What" and "How."

- How do you do that today?

- How would your job be different if you had x [our company's capability, feature, product, service, or solution]?

- How much money would you save or how much more money would you earn with/because of x?

- Tell us what kind of problems you face in your day to day work.

- What's your favorite thing about using x? What's your least favorite thing about using x?

- What's the most frustrating thing about [doing a certain task, using our product, solving a problem, or whatever]?

- Give me an example of _____ .

  This is a great question for clarifying what people actually do. The more you can have very specific instructions on how a task is completed, the better off you are. Observing people simply doing their work is also a powerful technique. Take notes and, when you're finished, ask the people why they did what they did.

- If x were available today would you buy it? How much would you pay for it?

- How do you measure whether it's been a successful day/month/year?

- Of the problems that we've discussed today, how would you prioritize solving them?

- If you could wave a magic wand and change one thing about x or how you're solving problems, what would it be?

These questions are wonderful in everyday life as well. Make a habit of asking versions of these questions at least once a day. You'll be surprised at how much more you learn about issues at work and at home. And you'll then be more comfortable using them when you need to in a customer interview situation.

Chapter **6**

Doing Your Homework: Evaluating Your Ideas

For every idea that makes it to market, many others aren't as worthy of pursuit as the one or two that you finally focus on. This chapter covers market research as it applies to product managers. For example, understanding what your competitors are doing — and not doing as well as they could — is important research as you find an opening for your product to be successful. Validating ideas is critical to avoiding the many possible pitfalls of customers not accepting your product. And some simple calculations can help you sell your idea into the company by showing that the product can be profitable. In fact, you'll reuse these tools and techniques throughout your product's life cycle as you need to make further validated decisions about product next steps.

Understanding the Importance of Market Research and Competitive Intelligence

Market research is the way in which product managers gather information about customer needs and market drivers. If you want to gather information from actual customers to make a decision, then you need to understand and use market research. *Competitive intelligence* is a subset of market research. When you investigate your competition, you use market research techniques and concepts to understand what your competition is doing today and gain insight into its plans for tomorrow.

Market research helps avoid the *four-walls problem* that stems from using only the collective wisdom of the people in the meeting room to make a decision. The solution is to step outside the confines of the company to get another vantage point.

TIP

Here are some good opportunities to gather information and create solutions:

>> Identifying market needs and customer problems

>> Prioritizing possible features

>> Deciding on new target markets

>> Segmenting a market

>> Determining your market share

>> Measuring customer satisfaction

>> Learning about the competition

>> Deciding on final pricing

>> Defining or testing new product concepts

>> Creating and testing messaging

The value of market research is almost infinite. And the reason that you should actively seek information is because in every decision you make there is an implied hypothesis. As you may know from science class, a hypothesis needs to be tested. In the terminology of product management, an idea requires *validation.*

The investigative loop shown in Figure 6-1 is a common concept used in product management. Usually you start with a discovery; you then form a hypothesis, which is a set of assumptions about your product, and then validate and test it. From there you experience some learning and apply it to adjust your plans.

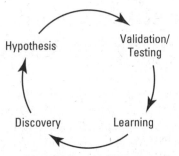

FIGURE 6-1:
Investigative loop.

Chapter 3 discusses different phases of the product life cycle. To make decisions in every one of those phases, plan on gaining real market insight and information to make the most informed decision that you can.

Subdividing kinds of market research

In product management, the core of any solution begins with an in-depth understanding of the needs and problems that your customers are facing that you think you can solve with a product offering from your company. Initial understandings of any problem can be very vague; in fact, if you're emphatic early on that you know exactly what the problem is, you should look again.

Qualitative and quantitative market research

Because the problem definition is so hard to create and is critical to success, the best way to get a handle on all aspects of the problem is to talk to people who are experiencing it. Yup. That's it. Talk to them. Ask questions about how they do things now and what their biggest challenges are and listen. Focus at least initially on a conversation as opposed to a questionnaire or survey. Chapter 5 discusses how to hold these conversations with your customers.

In market research terms, the conversation is called gathering *qualitative data.* Once you have gathered qualitative information about your customer's problem, you can use *quantitative data*, such as a survey, to gather more concrete information.

Primary and secondary research

Another consideration when conducting research is whether you're able to buy research done by specialist companies, use research provided by the government, or create your own research study. Research that you pay for and therefore own is called *primary research*; it's known only to you. Research that you don't do yourself or purchase is called *secondary research.* Check out Table 6-1 for examples of secondary and primary research sources.

TABLE 6-1   ## List of Research Data Sources

Secondary Research Sources	Primary Research Sources
Government sources of demographics and economic statistics; trade associations	Customer interviews
Specialist reports: The Economist, Harvard Business Review, Forbes Magazine, Articles about the industry or competitors	Customer relationship management (CRM) data, including the most common requests of customers that sales receives and the problems that support captures

(continued)

TABLE 6-1 *(continued)*

Secondary Research Sources	Primary Research Sources
Websites of competitors; annual reports; press releases	Support database
Industry analysts and research organizations	Customer surveys and focus groups
Internet searches for industry and market data and trends	Research done in other parts of your company that may apply

Looking for the right place to start

When starting in on a market research project, know that you'll be reading a lot of material both quantitative and qualitative in nature in printed material and on the web just to get a few nuggets that are of real interest. Think of it as panning for gold. Finding a few flakes of valuable gold is a cold and wet business, but without the flakes, you can't continue your work, and no one will join you on your journey to find even more gold.

Qualitative secondary research

The typical starting point in conducting research is to read any and all secondary research that you can get your hands on. You're looking to understand the lay of the land. What do people who experience this problem understand the issues to be? Where do they believe upcoming technology and business solutions are coming from? Larger companies often subscribe to secondary research from specialist industry analysts. If you're short on market research funds, search the Internet and look to sites that share presentations, such as slideshare.

Quantitative secondary research

Fantastic! You've identified a promising market or problem to solve. Do enough people have this problem? Is this problem growing or shrinking? Using secondary research often starts with qualitative analysis and then follows it up with quantitative market sizing numbers of all kinds:

>> How many companies or customers have this problem?

>> Where are they located and what are their demographics?

>> What common characteristics do they have (company size, revenue, business profiles, industry)?

>> Are any companies currently solving the problem you have identified. If so, which ones?

>> Is this market growing or shrinking?

To find quantitative secondary research use the list in Table 6-1 to locate any research sources that might be available. There may be some available from industry analyst firms such as Gartner, IDC, or Forrester. These reports are often somewhat costly, but they can contain very useful data. Check with your market research and competitive analysis department (if you have one) to see what they might have on hand or have access to. Sometimes they pay for subscriptions to the analyst reports. You may find after an extensive search that there is nothing available, but at least you know that no one else who might be investigating the opportunity has any more data than you do.

Qualitative primary research

To perform qualitative primary research, you'll need to talk to customers. You may not be able to visit each customer in person, but your focus is to get answers to the questions that you can't find in publicly available (also known as secondary) research. By conducting in-person interviews, focus groups (which require a lot of expertise to do right — you'll want to hire an expert to do this for you), or customer council meetings, you can ask more specific questions about your hypothesis and get a deeper level of understanding about the customer problem you're trying to solve.

When you believe that you've identified your target customer, you're ready to develop a research plan including the list of questions (such as the following) that you want to ask the target in a conversation. Review Chapter 5 to determine which persona types you should target your questions to.

>> Can you tell me a bit about yourself? What is your job title? What education did it take to get this position? What is your age range?

>> Do you experience the following problem(s)? Which other problems do you also experience?

>> If you do, how do you overcome it?

>> Can you show me the steps you take to overcome it?

>> Do you have any ideas or suggestions for a product that might help you with this?

Undertaking the Market Research Process

Doing more formal market research right means going through a series of steps designed to get you the information you need. The following sections help you do just that, leading you through the kinds of questions you should ask and the research methods product managers everywhere use.

Spelling out the market research process

Whenever you have a question and decide that conducting market research is the right solution, keep in mind that following an established process will lead you to better results:

1. **Decide on your research objective.**

   What are you trying to achieve with the research — assess whether the company should develop a specific product line? Change the direction of an existing product in development? Simply validate that a new feature will meet customer requirements? Your objectives also determine the scope and cost of the investigation. Deciding on whether to enter a $300 million market opportunity justifies more effort and spending than prioritizing a few features for a $99 product.

2. **Determine what questions you need to answer to satisfy your research objective.**

   Write down an initial set of questions and discuss them with your colleagues and peers to get input. They may point out that the questions are very broad, or they are too specific and won't allow for you to potentially uncover any additional valuable information.

   Here's an example:

   - Too broad: What kinds of exercise equipment do you use to stay healthy?

   - Too narrow: Do you use legs weights to stay healthy?

3. **Choose the best research technique(s).**

   As a rule of thumb, you move from secondary qualitative research through to primary quantitative research as shown in Figure 6-2. In reality, you may go through one of these categories pretty quickly and then spend a lot of time getting your primary qualitative research right. (See Table 6-2 later in the chapter for a list of the most commonly used market research methods.)

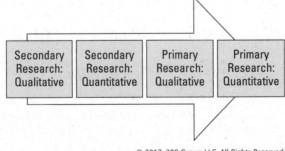

FIGURE 6-2:
Sequence of
market research.

4. **Design your research study.**

   Designing a good research study requires a lot of expertise. Use the options in Table 6-2 to determine what type of research you need to conduct. If possible work with someone who has done it before, such as a peer in your company, your internal market research department, or an outside vendor. It is easy to accidentally design a study that has a lot of bias, so be careful to scrutinize your design accordingly. If you can't find anyone to help you design your study or to critique it for you and provide feedback, we recommend you find a book on the topic that covers it in an in-depth fashion.

   Asking the right questions is a critical part of getting good answers. The following section has more specifics on this topic.

5. **Conduct research.**

   Conducting research may take you as far as across the world or as close as a car ride to a nearby town. It is highly dependent on what type of research you have decided to conduct. Customer interviews may be held in person or on the phone. Focus groups may be held in multiple cities or conducted virtually. Customer councils often involve having customers fly in to your location.

6. **Collect and analyze data.**

   Qualitative data is basically listening to people answer your questions with few boundaries. Decide how you want to record this information. In person, avoid taking notes on a computer; the presence of a screen creates a barrier between you and the customer. If the customer agrees, recording the conversation is always an option. A good technique for taking notes while recording is to make a note of the recording time when the customer says something interesting.

7. **Present findings to take advantage of new knowledge.**

   Going through all the trouble of getting data to support a point of view isn't going to do you any good if other parts of your organization don't understand it. Use the tips in Chapter 17 to make sure your message is heard. A convincing presentation and/or written report should be short with lots of clear graphics. For presentations aim for 10 slides and no more than 20. Have someone with good graphic skills review your materials, and you should practice before any presentation.

Asking the right questions

Asking questions. It seems like such a simple thing to do, and then you ask a question and get a response that isn't at all what you asked for. Now imagine trying to get answers to specific questions that will guide product development. Yes, it's hard.

Here are some things to keep in mind as you formulate your questions:

>> **Consider how specific you should be.** A good gauge is knowing how specific you need the answer to be. At the beginning of the process, the questions are generally qualitative and very broad. Open-ended questions that start with *why, what, how, where,* and *when* are a great way to go. Then shift to quantitative questions. Quantitative questions have more specifics than qualitative questions, as you are seeking to get hard data to use.

>> **Ask how important something is, not just whether a customer desires it.** If you ask a customer whether she wants a feature, the answer is almost always yes. For example, if you're evaluating two specific features, you may want to ask the following questions and place the responses in a table such as the one in Figure 6-3.

- On a scale of one to five, how much do you like features one and two?

- On a scale of one to five, how would you rate feature one's and feature two's importance?

FIGURE 6-3:
Charting customer answers.

	Like	Importance	Total = Like × Importance
Feature 1	5	1	5
Feature 2	3	5	15

In this case, you'd develop feature two before feature one because 15 is greater than 5.

>> **Ask follow-up questions.** In qualitative research, continue the conversation that the customer has started. The topics raised may not be on your list of questions, but this is the time to find every nook and cranny of opportunity.

>> **Avoid bias.** If you ask questions with enthusiasm for your preferences, you are more likely to get biased answers. If you can't avoid asking a question with bias, get someone else to ask the questions while you take notes with a poker face. This applies to both the question content as well as the inflection with which it is delivered.

TIP

No matter how great a product manager you are, always have someone look over your questions. What seems crystal clear to you often won't always make sense to someone else.

Examining market research methods

Table 6-2 covers most of the popular methods of market research. When you start a larger project, work with a market research specialist, either inside or outside your company, who can advise you on which type of research method will work best to achieve your research objective. If you contact an outside organization, make sure that it doesn't specialize in only one type of market research. Those companies will inevitably want you to use only their method.

TABLE 6-2   **Market Research Methods**

Type of Market Research	Details	When to Use	Relative Cost
Ethnographic	Anthropological-based observation and questioning. Usually conducted one-on-one or in small groups.	Great for the conceive stage when the concept is still unformed and a lot of unknowns exist.	High
Customer panels	Ongoing dialogue with a static group of key customers who provide real-time market intelligence. They're an early alert system to identify upcoming opportunities.	Can be gathered in a series of meetings and fed into early product development or, more typically, ongoing product evolution.	Low
Usability testing	Evaluation of customers using a product and providing input. Can be done at the customer site, in a lab, or virtually. Services exist to conduct this research for you.	During development and the testing and validation phase of product development.	Low
In-person interviews	Qualitative input from a few (3–20) people. It works well when defining positioning of key features.	Any time in product development. More commonly used earlier in the product development cycle.	Medium
Focus groups	Small group discussions facilitated by third-party specialists on a focused topic such as obtaining rich qualitative data; issues that exist with the product as currently developed; or refining positioning, names, and packaging.	Primarily used for fine tuning a product and in the market launch stages.	Medium

(continued)

TABLE 6-2 *(continued)*

Type of Market Research	Details	When to Use	Relative Cost
Telephone interviews/surveys	Quantitative information to support or reject a hypothesis. Also can be used to get qualitative input from a small group of people.	Interviews: At any time in the product process. Surveys: Primarily in full production and market launch stages.	Medium
Web or print surveys	Quantitative input to fine tune and prioritize possible product options. Beware that how you ask questions can tilt the responses.	Primarily in full production or market launch stages.	Low to Medium

Figure 6-4 gives an overview of market research methods. On the left are *high-context methods*, meaning that you need to conduct them in person and often onsite. High-context methods give you a broader understanding of the world that your potential customer lives and works in. You use these methods mostly in early stages of decisions to provide a background to further research. On the right are *low-context methods*, which are very arm's length and impersonal without much background information. Low-context methods are great for getting quantitative results — the numbers.

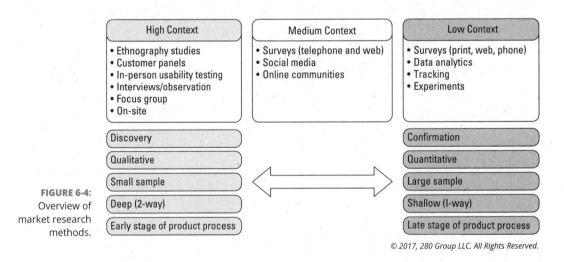

FIGURE 6-4: Overview of market research methods.

© 2017, 280 Group LLC. All Rights Reserved.

Studying Competitive Intelligence

Competitive intelligence is also known as *competitive analysis.* It's the intelligence acquired about your competition that allows you to compete more effectively. Competitive intelligence uses a lot of the techniques from market research. Check out the techniques in Chapter 5.

Identifying competitors

Here are some common ways to discover your competition:

>> Reading product reviews and comparisons gives you an idea of who your customers and industry pundits believe your competition to be.

>> Your own salespeople are a great early warning on newcomers or changes in what your existing competitors offer. Offer a (small) reward when sales comes up with a new competitor or feature that you should know about.

>> Industry analysts create periodic reports that compare your company to other companies.

REMEMBER

In stable markets, focus only on the top two or three competitors. If you can beat these competitors, you should be able to easily beat the smaller ones. In emerging markets where what customers really value is less clear, you want to keep track of a few more competitors until the customer value picture becomes clearer.

Collecting all the competitive intelligence possible

For a true 360-degree view of your competition, your research will encompass the areas in the following sections.

All this information creates a map of potential competitive moves. You need to synthesize the key indicators. If you find this synthesis challenging, explain what you've found to a few colleagues to uncover the likely next moves of your competition. Present any significant issues to your manager and decide what the next steps will be.

Basics

Consider these bigger-picture issues:

>> **External performance:** Are your competitor's sales increasing or decreasing? How about their profits? How many people work there, and what is the revenue per person? The trick is to look for changes in numbers from last year to this year — and even the years before that. If the company you're tracking isn't public, search press releases for whatever information you can find. Check the company's annual report if it's public, funding announcements if it's private, and press releases (all available online).

>> **Funding and spending:** Are competitors spending more or less money on sales, marketing, and research than they did before? You can compare their spending to your company spending. Beware that your competitor's company could be structured differently from yours, so investigate large differences between companies. For private companies, you can sometimes find more data on the website of the venture capitalists about this. For public companies, the notes in the annual report as well as some analysis of the profit and loss statements can give you clues (particularly if a company breaks its profits and expenses down for each type of business it's in).

>> **Management:** What is the range of skills found in competitors' management? Do the managers lack certain expertise? How diverse is their membership? How well are they connected to key influencers in their industry? You can often find this information on the "About the company management" page on their website, in the LinkedIn profiles of their executives, and in interviews that may have conducted with their management team by magazines and online news sources.

>> **Attitude:** Are competitors aggressive? Complacent? Do they like risk or profoundly avoid risk? Which quadrant are they in on the performance and organizational health scale shown in Figure 6-5? Gathering this information can be done by having conversations with your salespeople about what they have seen the competitor do, from former employees of the competitor and from articles written about it.

Product comparison

TIP

Most competitive analysis that product managers do is typically a side-by-side product comparison chart that compares only features. Remember to add in aspects of service, warranties, finance, service, and reliability that may add more strength to the competitive argument. Figure 6-6 is a great way to organize your thoughts in a way that educates your customers and internal audiences at the same time.

High External Performance

Troubled	Successful
Crisis	Complacent

Low Organizational Health (left axis)
High Organizational Health (right axis)

Low External Performance

FIGURE 6-5: Performance and organizational health quadrant.

Feature	Benefit	Customer Value	Your Product	Product 1	Product 2
Camera sensor resolution	Large prints and closer cropping	Medium	8 megapixels	5 megapixels	2 megapixels
SIM card	User information can be transferred to another device	High	Yes	Yes	No
Battery capacity	Use time between charges	High	10 hours	6 hours	4 hours
Available applications	Greater utility	Medium	150+	200+	500
2-year warranty	Sure that your product will work no matter what	Medium	Yes	No	No

FIGURE 6-6: Product comparison table.

Marketing and distribution

Marketing and distribution are other important areas of competitive analysis. Think about the following:

>> **Marketing:** What does your competitor's brand stand for? How well does the market believe in that positioning? What is the competitor's positioning at the product level? What are it's marketing programs? Which trade shows does it attend or avoid? How sophisticated are its digital marketing efforts? Which keywords (terms that, when typed into Google, result in ads related to them) does it target for AdWords and online advertising? Search for some likely

terms and see if their ads show up. Is the company's marketing more sales, product, or technology focused?

>> **Distribution channels:** What are the competitor's distribution channels? Does it go direct, use distributors, or have special relationships with certain channel partners? Most importantly, what advantage or disadvantage its distribution model provide?

>> **Market share:** What is your market share? What is your competitors' share? In mature markets, the market leader usually has at least twice the market share as the next biggest competitor. Market share can lead to market dominance and possibly complacency.

Porter's five forces

In 1979, Michael Porter wrote "How Competitive Forces Shape Strategy" in the *Harvard Business Review.* His concepts, shown in Figure 6-7, are as valid today as they've been throughout history. Consider each of these aspects when evaluating your competitors and your market overall. To use Porter's five forces, answer the following questions for your product or market:

>> What is the bargaining power of your suppliers when they negotiate with you?

>> What is the bargaining power of your buyers when they negotiate with you?

   The fewer or more specialized your suppliers and buyers, the more power they have in controlling negotiations and determining pricing that is less favorable to you.

>> What about potential new companies and services coming into your market? Can these entrants compete easily, or is it difficult for them to compete with you?

>> What about substitute products? What kind of products could replace your products in solving a customer need?

>> How strong is rivalry in your industry? Are your competitors aggressive in taking business from you?

A couple of handy acronyms

PESTEL and SWOT. No, we haven't forgotten to use spell-check. These concepts are two pieces of the competitive analysis puzzle.

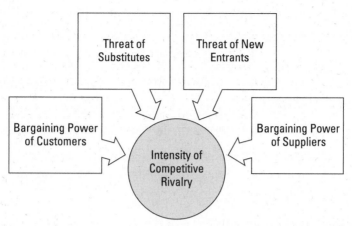

FIGURE 6-7: Porter's five forces.

PESTEL stands for political, economic, social, technological, environmental, and legal. PESTEL analysis is used to understand the overall context within which you do business and within which your product is evaluated. To complete a PESTEL analysis, answer the following questions. What is the overall social and business environment that you operate in? What is changing? What are key trends in each of these areas? How these stresses impact your competition isn't always the same as the way they impact you. List each factor and examine your situation closely to see where opportunities and threats lie.

SWOT is an acronym for strengths, weaknesses, opportunities, and threats. The first two terms, strengths and weaknesses, refer to the state of the competitive company that you are conducting a SWOT analysis for. The second two terms, opportunities and threats, refer to external impacts on your competition, their markets, and their products. By doing a SWOT analysis for each main competitor you can get a more accurate view of who you are actually competing with and where they are strong and weak. This forms the basis of your own strategy for beating them in the marketplace. Use Figure 6-8 to understand how the different information in each quadrant interacts to give you a synthesis of

>> Strategies the company can exploit to take advantage of opportunities

>> Strategies the company must deal with to take advantage of opportunities

>> Strategies the company can use to defend itself from threats

>> Strategies the company must deal with to defend itself from threats

	Strengths	Weaknesses
Opportunities	Strategies the company can exploit to take advantage of opportunities	Strategies the company must deal with to take advantage of opportunities
Threats	Strategies the company can use to defend itself from threats	Strategies the company must deal with to defend itself from threats

External

Internal

FIGURE 6-8: SWOT analysis.

Keeping track of the competition

Competitors aren't standing still. To make sure you keep on top of their moves, allocate regular time to competitive evaluation — monthly or quarterly, depending on the industry. Consider these suggestions:

- Create a weekly Google Alert for whenever the competition is mentioned (search Google for the term "Google Alert" to learn how to create alerts). For example, if your company sells smoke detectors, create an alert for the phrase *smoke detector.* Then every time this phrase is mentioned in the news or on a website, Google will send you an alert letting you know where and when it appeared.
- Check your competitor's website monthly for any announcements or updates to its product. This time frame should be enough that you pick up significant changes. Make written notes about your findings that you can refer to later if needed.
- For publicly traded companies, listen in on the analyst call quarterly. Download and read through the latest financial report. What has changed? What issues has the company listed as risks?
- Call channel partners monthly or quarterly for a chat on how business is going, whether you've lost or gained competitive ground, and, if so, to whom and why.
- Plan a full-blown annual review to present to your management. Preparation for the review will force you to pick up any details that you've missed along the way with your weekly, monthly, and quarterly work.

REMEMBER

One fantastic benefit of all this tracking work is that doing it in small pieces takes less effort than having to whip it up suddenly on an annual basis. And your organization will have full confidence in your thinking in other areas if you're current on your competitive analysis.

Reality-Checking Your Ideas and Hypotheses

Chapter 4 provides some tools and ideas for coming up with new product ideas, and the market research and competitive analysis section of this chapter shows techniques for exploring potential markets further. One other technique that you may want to use for a market or product that is brand new is doing some additional reality checking.

For newer markets, finding a really good winning idea often means direct validation with actual potential customers. The goal in doing this is to present enough of an impression of a product (whether it is a description, data sheet, or working demo) that customers can imagine themselves buying it and then tell you what they think.

Using a simple validation process

You have a product idea that you think may work for certain customers. That's wonderful. You now have two choices:

>> Spend a lot of money developing it before you talk to a customer at all.

>> Spend virtually nothing by creating a product concept and then asking target customers what they think about it.

Remember that you may want to test out quite a few potential products and the associated hypothesis. The wise course of action is to take the second option and see what customers say first.

Here's a simple and relatively fast validation process:

1. **Create a hypothesis about a potential product.**

   For example, "Customers who use digital forms want to fill them out online and have them automatically routed from one person on to another for signature."

2. **Create a list of target customers.**

   In this example, the target customers might be multinational companies that sign forms across the country and possibly across the world; small digital media houses that need sign off on final artwork for various projects; and small companies that need forms signed as part of their workflow inside and outside the company.

3. **Create certain artifacts to prove to customers that this product is real.**

   The artifacts are a datasheet, a price list, a short presentation on the features and benefits of the product, and a demo done in Microsoft PowerPoint or Word. Note that you create no actual product, but you create enough of the product concept to present it to customers so they get a realistic idea of what would be offered.

4. **Hold individual meetings with several people from each target customer group and see what they say.**

   Is the target group interested in the product? Which features does each group deem critical? How are they solving the problem today?

When you have a list of each of the target groups that is interested in the product, you can go back and research how big that target market is and then create a rough, back-of-the-envelope estimate of how much potential revenue and profit you could generate. With actual customer feedback, you can proceed to more in-depth planning with more confidence.

An example of product validation

Zappos, the online shoe distribution company, tested its concept by making arrangements with actual shoe stores. Rather than building out a warehouse and distribution system first, Zappos tested the concept by putting pictures and prices of shoes online and then filled orders from a physical shoe store. In this way, it avoided upfront costs of a warehouse until it had validated its concept.

Crunching the Numbers with Financial Forecasting

At some point, the decision about which, if any, products to move forward with will come down to profitability. And at this stage of product development (or non-product development), you don't want to get bogged down in enormous reams of financial data and overly complex forecasts. However, you really do need to support your hypothesis with some simple financial analysis and a list of assumptions that went into creating them. To do this, you want to create a draft profit and loss statement, do a break-even analysis, and calculate the return on investment (ROI). Chapter 9 has more detail about how to create these financials.

Chapter **7**

Prioritizing and Selecting Your Ideas

This chapter shows you how to prioritize all the great ideas you have generated so far so that your company can determine where to invest its money and resources. Through the use of simple yet powerful prioritization techniques, you'll be able to determine which ideas to proceed with.

Prioritizing Your Ideas

You have a long list of product ideas. They all are possible opportunities. However, your development budget often restricts you to just one choice. What's the best way to make this choice?

Your job as the product manager is to make sure the idea you choose to recommend investing in is a good fit that will work for your company. Use Table 7-1 to find an opportunity that your company will welcome.

TABLE 7-1

Finding Ideas That Fit with Your Company

	Company	Product	Match: Yes or No?
Vision	Put the company's vision statement here.	Put the product's vision statement here.	
Brand	What's the company's brand?	What do you want the product's brand to be?	
Positioning	How is the company positioned in the marketplace?	How might the product be positioned in the marketplace?	
Competency	What are the company's existing core competences? What other competencies can it acquire?	Does the product take advantage of the company's core competencies?	
Distribution	What distribution channels does the company currently have?	What distribution channel does the product need?	
Unique Selling Proposition (USP)	What's the company's USP?	What are the product's USPs?	
Value	What value does the company provide?	What value does the product provide?	

Finding the right fit with the product-market fit triad

Getting a profitable product to market successfully isn't for the faint of heart. Figure 7-1 shows the product–market fit triad, which is a way of looking at the three major components that you must balance in order to bring a successful product to market. You're balancing these three areas at all times as you build your solution:

» **Problem:** Address the correct and valuable customer needs.

» **Product:** Meet those needs well.

» **Business model:** Have the product available through the correct channel (where the customer can find it) and at an attractive price (where the customer will purchase the product and sustain the business).

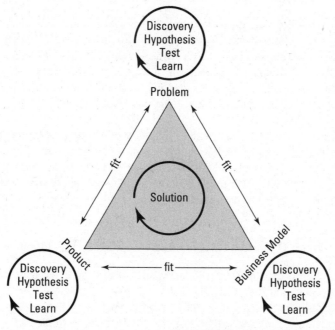

FIGURE 7-1: Product-market fit triad.

Chapters 1 and 4 discuss solving customer problems and define what exactly a product consists of. A *business model* is how you sell the product to the customer and make money, including the entire product offering, support, and service and other expense and revenue items. For example, a popular business model is called the *razors and blades* model, which many razor manufacturers use. Rather than trying to make a lot of money selling you a fancy razor up-front, with the razors and blades model the company sells you an inexpensive razor knowing that it will make a profit many times in the future when you purchase replacement blades that you can only get from that company.

Using the product-market fit model is like juggling with 3 hands and 12 balls. When something changes with one hand, the other two need to know whether it impacts them — and how. You use a process of *discovery loops* to proactively manage learning about how to optimize for each vertex of the product-market fit triad: the product, the problem, and the business model.

Each discovery loop has four phases: discover, hypothesis, test, and learn. Typically, you start with discover as your first step. Using the market research methods in Chapter 5, you gain insight into one of the three parts of the product-market fit triad. On that basis, you develop a hypothesis. Try a simple example: earphones for smartphones. On the product side, you discover or observe that customers like to talk but not have the phone to their ears. Maybe wired earphones could provide a solution to this customer problem. You then hypothesize: "I believe that a wired earphone with a small speaker would resolve the problems of customers having to use the phone on speaker because they want to use their hands to do something else at the same time." The next step is to create a test. You could have someone solder together rudimentary earphones and have a few friends try it out. You'd learn that though the hypothesis is true. However, you would then discover that the headphone wires get tangled up. So you'd write another hypothesis, test the hypothesis, and modify the product accordingly.

Remember that three-handed juggle? While you're changing the product, you keep refining your view of the problem it solves and researching the market to ensure enough potential customers exist to merit the investment in manufacturing or otherwise bringing a product to market. Each of these discoveries leads to its own loop of interconnected learning.

Putting business canvases to use

A business canvas is a simple template for writing down your assumptions about a product and then tracking how they change over time. Three types of business canvases include the problem canvas, the product solution canvas, and the business model solution canvas. Figure 7-2 gives an example of the problem canvas. The sections on this canvas help you define the *customer* and the *problem* (you create a product to solve the customer's problem). In the *scenario* section, you have room to dig deeper into the customer's problem. Think of a customer who's a father working in a home office with a paper shredder in the corner. His problem is that he is concerned his children may be hurt if the shredder turns on easily while they're playing in his office. This scenario is your opportunity to give more context to his situation by describing aspects of his problem that will help your engineers create potential solutions.

Under *alternatives* on this canvas you would write down what else the father could do to protect his children. He may decide to put the shredder high up on a shelf or cover it with a heavy box when he isn't using it. And then under *success*, write down how customers define success. In this example, it could be that the solution involves being able to shred a document within one second and knowing that, regardless of whether he turns it off, the shredder can't injure his children. In this example, the *evidence to pay* may include assumptions about how much disposable income the expected customer has. If he has a lot of disposable income, then the cost versus the benefit of keeping his children safe may be an obvious trade-off that means he'll invest the money in your shredder solution.

The product solution canvas in Figure 7-3 includes the most important aspects that you need to consider with respect to all parts of the product solution as you evolve and advance your ideas.

In Figure 7-4, the business canvas helps you know what to consider in terms of all the parts of building a workable and profitable business model around your product idea.

Problem Canvas

Title:

Owner:	Date	Version

Problem Clarity (place mark at level of understanding of problem)

Defined [_____] Undefined

User has an explicit need and can describe it fully

User has little awareness of need or ability to articulate problem

Customer — List the customers, considering Users, Buyers, Influencers, and Approvers (note each one with U, B, I, A). In thinking about the early solution, which customers are most valuable (one), who will you optimize the solution for (two), who will the solution support (yellow), and who solution initially exclude (three). Work vertically down the rest of the canvas.

Problem State problems for each customer and rank them for that customer

Scenario Describe scenario where the problem is encountered

Alternatives In considering the top ranked customer/problem pairs, explore the product alternatives (Including do nothing) and pros and cons of alternatives. Rank customer satisfaction with alternatives (H, M, L).

Success Describe how customers define success

Evidence to Pay Describe evidence that customers will pay to solve this problem

In considering the top ranked customer/problem pairs, rate confidence in the scenario statements made on users, problem, and definition of success (green, yellow, red)

FIGURE 7-2:
Problem canvas.

Product Solution Canvas

Title:

Owner: | Date | Version

Product Solution Clarity (place mark at level of understanding of product solution)

Defined [████████████████████████████] Undefined

The product solution is well understood, in a good fit with the problem, users understand how to use the product, and it is feasible with current technology.

The team has a general product solution to the problem is understood but specific features and usage is not well understood.

Key Customer/Problem Pairs

List the top ranked customer/problem pairs from the Problem Canvas that the product will seek to address.

Market Entry Strategy

Identify market entry strategy for the product solution and comment as needed.

Create a new market	Existing market with optimized product	Create a new segment with simpler/less expensive product	Create new segment with niche product

Product solution

Sketch the product solution: what will it look like, how many configurations will be supported, what functions will it perform, how do we want the customer to feel when using the product, how will customer learn to use product?

Risks/Legal/Regulatory

What are the solution/development risks or legal/regulatory considerations?

Alternatives List top 3	Differentiation State differentiation. Rate differentiation as incremental, major, discontinuous.
1.	
2.	
3.	

Competitors List top 3	Response What are competitors' likely responses and timeframe?
1.	
2.	
3.	

In considering the top ranked customer/problem pairs, rate confidence in the scenario statements made on the product solution.

FIGURE 7-3: Product solution canvas.

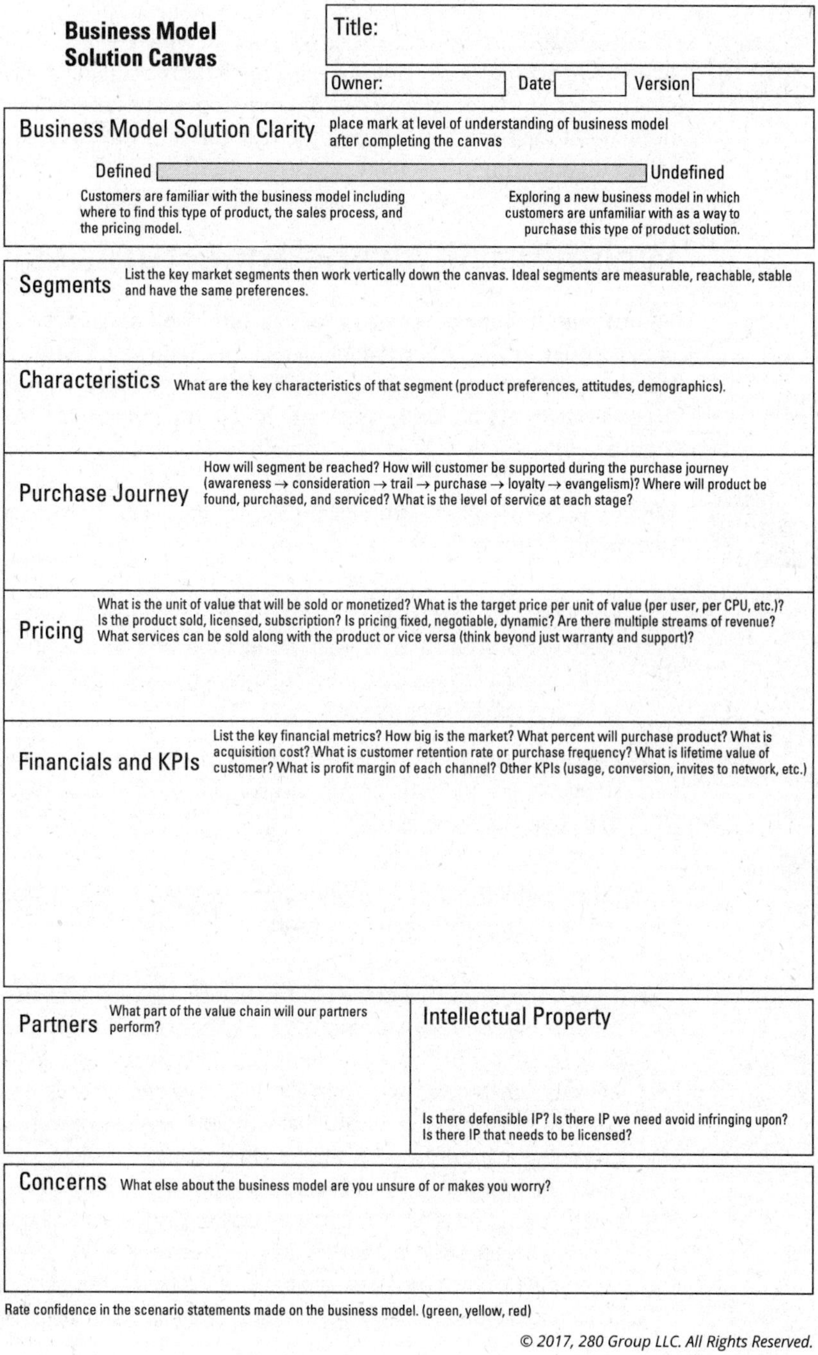
Business Model Solution Canvas

Title:

Owner: | Date | Version

Business Model Solution Clarity
place mark at level of understanding of business model after completing the canvas

Defined — Undefined

Customers are familiar with the business model including where to find this type of product, the sales process, and the pricing model.

Exploring a new business model in which customers are unfamiliar with as a way to purchase this type of product solution.

Segments List the key market segments then work vertically down the canvas. Ideal segments are measurable, reachable, stable and have the same preferences.

Characteristics What are the key characteristics of that segment (product preferences, attitudes, demographics).

Purchase Journey How will segment be reached? How will customer be supported during the purchase journey (awareness → consideration → trail → purchase → loyalty → evangelism)? Where will product be found, purchased, and serviced? What is the level of service at each stage?

Pricing What is the unit of value that will be sold or monetized? What is the target price per unit of value (per user, per CPU, etc.)? Is the product sold, licensed, subscription? Is pricing fixed, negotiable, dynamic? Are there multiple streams of revenue? What services can be sold along with the product or vice versa (think beyond just warranty and support)?

Financials and KPIs List the key financial metrics? How big is the market? What percent will purchase product? What is acquisition cost? What is customer retention rate or purchase frequency? What is lifetime value of customer? What is profit margin of each channel? Other KPIs (usage, conversion, invites to network, etc.)

Partners What part of the value chain will our partners perform?

Intellectual Property Is there defensible IP? Is there IP we need avoid infringing upon? Is there IP that needs to be licensed?

Concerns What else about the business model are you unsure of or makes you worry?

Rate confidence in the scenario statements made on the business model. (green, yellow, red)

FIGURE 7-4: Business model solution canvas.

These canvases are meant to be large. They're typically 3-x-5-foot (1-x-1.5-meter, or about A1 size) posters. You can also create them by using a couple of sheets of flip chart paper taped to the wall or even drawing a free hand chart with colored non-permanent tape and then writing the title for each on a large sticky note. Get creative and have fun.

Weighing different opportunities

Identifying the type of opportunity you think you may have is important to make sure you're working on a product idea in the right way. There are some opportunities that may be very straightforward, while others may be much less well-defined. A good way to get a handle on this is to use the *product and problem quadrant* (see Figure 7-5).

REMEMBER

When you first look at a potential product idea, you need to understand it from two points of view:

>> **Problem:** Do I truly understand the problem that I'm trying to solve? How much of the problem is defined/understood, and how much isn't well understood at any level? A problem that is not well understood is considered to be an undefined problem.

>> **Product solution:** How much definition do I have around a possible product solution? How much of the product solution is defined, and how much is yet to be defined/understood?

Using the product and problem quadrant in Figure 7-5, the following are definitions and examples for each quadrant:

>> **Type I:** The problem and the product solution are both defined. If you're the product manager for word processing software at version 10 and looking to develop version 10.1, the problems your customers have are likely to be very obvious. Customers for the last 20 years have decided that they need to create written documents and that word processing software is much easier to use than typewriters. As you search for more features to add or ways to make the product easier to use, you can be sure that whatever product solution you find is on the right track as long as it tests well with customers. Luckily, most product managers find themselves managing the relatively less complicated Type I products and never think twice about how difficult it is solving for solutions where the product or the problem are not defined.

>> **Type II:** The problem is defined, but the product solution is undefined. As with the example from Type I, customers need to create written documents. Rather than proposing a well-understood solution like a computer with word processing software, perhaps you want to explore products that write documents

without a keyboard. How else can customers achieve this goal? What if they make gestures in the air? Talk? Solving this problem has become undefined. Any possible solution in this quadrant usually needs extensive validation before you can really believe that the solution will work for customers. A classic example of this was the iPad. The problem was how to consume content like books and movies where you could hold the product easily and not need a battery for long periods of time. The iPad represented an undefined product solution that solved the problem in a new way and created a new market.

>> **Type III:** Here, the cart has come before the horse, so to speak. You have a defined solution; you just aren't actually sure you have a defined problem for it to solve. One of your engineers might have come up with a great solution based around emerging technologies. The proposed product or product idea does something. Your job now as a product manager is to make sure that whatever it does has value to customers. This area is a graveyard for lovely techie products that no one really needs but that engineers built because they seemed "cool". If your idea is in this space, validate with customers over and over again to make sure that you have defined the problem that you're solving.

>> **Type IV:** The problem and product solution are both not clear, or at least only vaguely defined. You may never have to deal with a product in this quadrant. One example of Type IV product is Twitter before it launched. What problem does 140 characters solve? How does the product solution best match up to the customer problem? Did anyone know that many people are interested in publicly sharing minute moments and thoughts of the day? If they did, did they imagine that the product would need pictures, messaging, and followers? Establishing a product like Twitter isn't a juggling act; it's more like spinning four plates on sticks while riding a unicycle over bumpy ground. One misstep, and it all fails spectacularly. Type IV products require an extreme level of flexibility and a willingness to adjust both the problem definition and the product solution simultaneously.

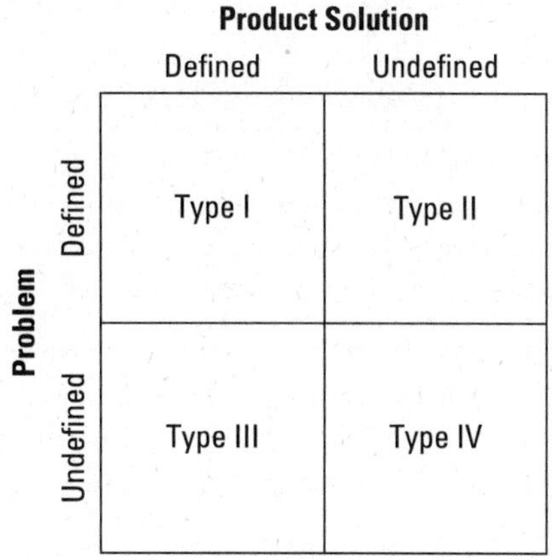

Product Solution

	Defined	Undefined
Problem — Defined	Type I	Type II
Problem — Undefined	Type III	Type IV

FIGURE 7-5: Product and problem quadrant.

© 2017, 280 Group LLC. All Rights Reserved.

Applying Scoring Models

Scoring models are flexible tools used to establish where customer value lies and in what order you should solve customer problems. They help you to determine where your engineers should focus their efforts both short and long-term.

The following sections cover various scoring models; try out different ones and see which works best to tell your product's story most effectively.

Scoring for differentiation: The Kano model

You can win in the marketplace of products in basically two ways: Make it cheap or make it different. Your company should already know which space its products play in. At IKEA, for example, each development project starts with a final cost. The company knows its customers are looking for a low-cost solution and develops products accordingly. A luxury handbag, on the other hand, starts with a concept of how different it can be from other handbags on the market, and the designers spare no effort or expense to make something unique.

REMEMBER

Most products are somewhere between these two extremes. The key idea here is that customers select one product rather than another. The Kano model is a way to categorize features of your product to get a better handle on how your product fits one of the extremes. In the Kano model shown in Figure 7-6, any product feature or benefit fits into one of three categories: must haves, performance, and delighters.

>> **Must haves:** A feature in the *must have* category constitutes the bare minimum. When you buy a car, you expect it to have a heater and brakes. You wouldn't buy a car without those features. Delivering a well-done must have feature doesn't leave customers thrilled with your product. Deliver a poorly done must have feature and customers are unhappy.

>> **Performance:** A *performance* feature is one where more is considered better. More engine horsepower in a car is, generally, perceived to be more valuable. For a different customer, great gas mileage would be a performance feature. The better the gas mileage, the happier the customer.

>> **Delighters:** *Delighters* are the features and benefits that cause customers to go "Wow!" In today's cars, delighters may be a rear-facing camera and self-parking features. These bells and whistles are the ones that give customers a reason to choose one product rather than another.

How would you define features and benefits of your product with the Kano model? Beware if you have no delighter features; when that's the case, you're competing on the strength of your brand or maybe only on price.

REMEMBER

Here's the real kicker about the Kano model: Any feature that's a delighter today will become a must have in the future. At one time, heaters in cars were a delighter, but that day is far in the past. It's a never-ending search for the next delighter feature.

In the Kano model, having delighters that meet more and more needs increases the overall customer satisfaction. On the other hand, must haves are mandatory to ensure customers are not dissatisfied. And performance is in between — delivering performance features can increase satisfaction but not as much as delighters.

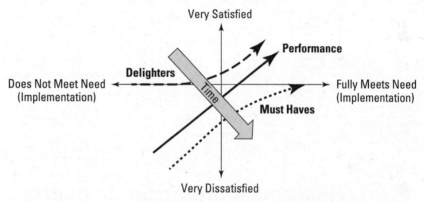

FIGURE 7-6:
Kano model.

Scoring for efficient use of development resources: Value versus effort analysis

In many instances, you're prioritizing many opportunities and have a sense of how much effort each of these activities requires. In order to choose the opportunity that provides the most bang for the buck, you'll often want to choose the one that takes the least amount of development time and money while providing the highest value to customers. Four-quadrant value to customer analysis (shortened to value versus effort analysis) allows you to quickly and easily do this.

TIP

When you use value versus effort analysis (see Figure 7-7), it quickly focuses your mind on how much value an activity or feature provides and how much time, cost, risk, or effort it takes to get the result. The value versus effort analysis takes advantage of the fact that humans are great at comparing alternatives and not so good at accurately evaluating one item on its own.

When all the options are placed in the correct quadrant, you can then focus your attention on which opportunity to choose:

1. Quadrant IV: High value, lower cost or risk

2. Quadrant II: High value, higher cost or risk

3. Quadrant III: Low value, lower cost or risk

4. Quadrant I: Low value, higher cost or risk

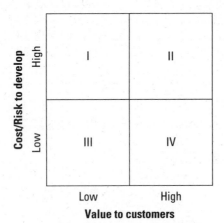

FIGURE 7-7:
Four-quadrant analysis.

Filling out a prioritization matrix

The four-quadrant analysis is wonderful if you can simplify the decision to two different axes. (Head to the preceding section for more on the four-quadrant analysis.) However, if you're weighing more than two factors, the prioritization matrix in Figure 7-8 is a more useful tool. Instead of two ways of evaluating options, you have up to six different criteria. With six criteria to choose from, at least one or two can focus on the strategic value of a particular option and give a stronger voice to more long-term aspects of an option. Each criteria can have a different weight as long as the total of all weights is 100 percent.

On the left side, you list all the possible ideas; the next two columns have space for more detailed information about the particular idea in question. Each idea is then judged using each criteria on a scale of zero to five, where five is the top score. On the right-hand side, the spreadsheet keeps score. In this example, the top score is 60; your company should work on priorities with or closest to this score first.

Using the prioritization matrix is great when you have a group that can't decide on anything. Because the pieces are broken down into such small decisions, the final decision pulls out the group consensus and knowledge.

The prioritization matrix is part of the Product LifeCycle Toolkit (included as a free download with this book; see the Introduction, page 4, for details). The criteria that are already in the matrix are pain for user, percentage of customers impacted, upsell revenue for existing customers, revenue from new customers, key product differentiator, and competitive necessity. Change them to better suit your needs.

Prioritization Matrix

0=low
5=high

Criteria for judging ideas

	Application/Major Feature/Service	Overview	Requestor	Pain for User[2] (0 - 5)	% of customers impacted[3] (0 - 5)	Upsell revenue from existing customers[4] (0 - 5)	Revenue from new customers (0 - 5)	Key product differentiator (0 - 5)	Competitive necessity (0 - 5)	TOTAL SCORE
Weight[1]				25	20	15	15	15	10	Total points 100
1	Performance	Reduce screen rendering to <2 second	Customers, Tech support	5	5	0	0	0	5	55
2	Single Sign-on	allow our apps to no longer require multiple authentications	Customers	3	5	2	1	0	4	52
3	Integration with SF.com	Full data synch with SF.com	Sales, Customers	4	2	0	2	4	0	46
4	IE 8.0 support	Full compatibility with IE 8 plus support for new security features	Customers, Management	4	3	2	4	0	5	60
5										0
6										0

Ideas

[1] weights should total 100
[2] consider how difficult a feature is to use and how frequently that feature is used in assessing pain
[3] must take into account the % of customers impacted and their importance
[4] You should count retaining customer who would otherwise leave as $

Score 0 - 5

FIGURE 7-8: Prioritization matrix.

Collecting ballots: Dot voting

Dot voting is another simple way to prioritize opportunities (as well as options such as ideas, features, time, or next steps.) Give each person one to three dots. In general, more dots are needed if there are more options to choose from. Have all parties place their dots to make their priorities known; people strongly invested in one priority can place all their dots next to that option. For example, in Figure 7-9, a group is prioritizing the top two choices for dinner. Each person has two dots and places them next to whatever option they prefer.

Hamburgers
Lasagna
Vegetarian Stir Fry

FIGURE 7-9: An example of dot voting.

At the end review the selections made with the group to ensure no one is crucially unrepresented. For example, in this selection of dinner options, going with either of the top two choices leaves a lone vegetarian to starve. In this case, the group may reach a compromise for lasagna and vegetarian stir fry.

TIP

If you don't have physical dots, give people colored markers and ask them to draw their own circles.

Buying features

If you need to understand how valuable a particular feature is, having your customers spend cold hard cash (or some facsimile) on them is a great way for them to make trade-offs.

Give each customer a fixed amount of play money to allocate to the features that are available. If a feature is worth a lot to people, they spend more money on it. Less valuable features receive less money. Try it out on Table 7-2, pretending you have $100 to spend on smartphone features. How much is each feature and the associated benefit worth to you? Do you know someone who would have a dramatically different answer?

TABLE 7-2   **Buying Features Worksheet**

Smartphone Feature	Amount You'd Pay for This Feature
Fingerprint access without having to type in a passcode	
Smudge-free screen	
Wireless headphone access: No need to physically plug headphones into your phone	
Ability to pay for items by holding your phone to a reader	
Total (not to exceed $100)	

Chapter **8**

Planning to Plan: Choosing a Suitable Approach

I n this chapter, we discuss all the variables that affect how you decide to plan a new product or new addition to a product. This chapter ensures you understand the lay of the land in your specific situation and shows you why changing the way you plan to achieve better outcomes can be valuable.

Adopting Planning Best Practices

The key benefit that a well-functioning product management organization can bring to a company's success is making sure that the products developed actually deliver valuable solutions to customers and that the product is profitable for the company. The planning phase is where you do the detailed work to make sure that you are focusing the organization on a valid problem to solve and that solving this problem will actually translate into company revenue, profits, and any other goals that you've set for the product. Planning to plan may sound odd, but the planning process has so many variables to look at that the safe and sane way to proceed is to plan carefully.

Starting early

In our experience with client after client, the most common problem with the way many companies create products is that they view the process as serial rather than parallel. In reality, as Figure 8-1 shows, product development often starts early and continues at the same time as the ongoing work of understanding how the product will best be brought to market, positioned for a market, and sold.

FIGURE 8-1:
Product and marketing activities taking place at the same time.

© 2017, 280 Group LLC. All Rights Reserved.

The most important thing about planning is to make sure that you start early. In fact, you should always start much earlier than you think you need to in order to determine both the product and the marketing parts of the product delivery equation. As you investigate an idea in the conceive phase, plan ahead to what it will take to actually get funding for a project.

TIP

While you're in the conceive phase — as you examine and then quickly reject or accept many options — completing the product, problem and business model canvases helps creates an outline of what you will need in the plan phase. Head to Chapters 4 and 7 for details on the conceive phase.

Including your team

Here's an interesting phrase: "PM as a GM." It means that a product manager should think about his work much as a general manager does. No, most product managers don't have the scope of full financial responsibility that a real general manager does. However, the concept of a product manager acting as an executive overseeing all aspects of the plan and execution is very valid.

Products are best brought to market by an integrated team, including members from all parts of the organization. In our consulting work, where we find organizations that are struggling to reach their potential, we often hear of *siloed* functions that aren't working together or communicating. Siloed functions happen when information isn't shared between departments or where each department only looks after its own interests or charter without adjusting to other departments. The result is disjointed and inefficient transitions between internal groups who don't see themselves as part of a cross-company team. As you get started, bring your integrated team together and share your vision. Have each member contribute to the vision so that everyone has a stake in it. This is one secret to great products: great teamwork.

Treating your plan as a living document

Remember: Information changes. Each document you create for your project needs to have version controls so that you're clear on what the latest version is and you can keep adapting the document. Arrange for some time each week or month to update the document that you're developing. At some point, you may not be the product manager for this product anymore, so make sure others who follow in your footsteps can understand the changes you made and why. Table 8-1 shows a simple addition and revision history of a change. Changing the version number can also help readers easily identify whether they have the latest copy. Online documentation such as shared wikis often include planning information using change logs and allowing readers to subscribe to a document so that they receive alerts when a document is changed.

TABLE 8-1   **Change-Tracking in a Living Document**

Marketing Strategy Plan	Date	Description of Change	Change Made By
V 1.2	Mar 2017	Added "shipping" as additional target market with associated positioning statements	Julie Harris

Deciding on the Right Amount of Planning

Different products require different amounts of planning. For one project, imagine that you're developing an app to help customers keep track of gas mileage. For a second project, imagine that you need to track all the different kinds of propulsion types and their current statuses on a manned rocket headed for Mars. In both instances, you're checking to see how much farther you can travel. The differences in the projects — who the client is, the risks involved with the project, the overall cost of the investment — contribute to how much planning needs to happen.

Here is a list of items that would indicate that you're going to have to do a lot more planning:

>> Your industry and line of products are highly regulated.

>> Development times are very long.

>> Development costs or the cost of change during a project very high.

>> The team working in the project is very large.

>> What you're working on is only part of a much larger solution, and you need to be closely integrated with the other parts of the solution.

>> Your company or organization is very risk averse and needs many levels of approval in order to proceed.

After you know what your planning scope will be, you can align your time and effort accordingly. In general, the more clearly written your material is with a compelling story driving the narrative, the less work bringing the rest of the company along will be.

Comparing Lean versus in-depth planning

The two popular methods of planning are Lean and in-depth. We further discuss both later in this chapter, but here we give a brief comparison of the two types. The term *Lean* has become very popular in the world of product, product management, product development, and even plain old management. At its core, the Lean method of planning is built on two core concepts:

>> **Respect for people:** Focus on the customer and empowering the individuals doing the work.

>> **Continuous Improvement:** Focus on repeated changes to the product based on a consistent method of dealing with uncertainty. One great Lean tool is the Discovery, Hypothesis, Test, Learn loop (shown in Figure 8-2). Using this learning loop, the team working to solve problems starts by discovering new information, developing a hypothesis to test against, and then learning from the tests. Once new information is acquired, the team feeds it into the next round of learning. The best teams don't adopt any new idea until it has been tested and proven to be better.

Unlike in-depth planning methodology, where you develop extensive plans upfront and don't expect them to change much, Lean methodologies build in learning and change as you go.

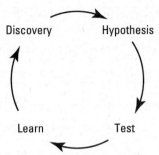

Discovery → Hypothesis

Learn → Test

FIGURE 8-2:
Discovery,
Hypothesis, Test
and Learn loop.

REMEMBER

In-depth planning is predicated on getting to the right answer. There are versions of the answer, but after everyone agrees on it, backtracking or adding in new learning is really hard. The process isn't fast enough to accommodate new learning and adjust the plan. That's why many teams file their completed annual plans and don't look at them again. When the planning cycle comes around again, they dust off the previous year's plan, and everyone may read it and adjust it with the learning that has happened in between. But a year is a long time. Given the fast-changing nature of many markets, industries, and products, incorporating aspects of Lean thought processes and planning typically improve business results.

Completing the types of new products and services grid

In Chapter 7, we introduce the product-market fit quadrant to determine what kind of product and problem space — defined or undefined — you're working with during the conceive phase. In this chapter on planning, your focus is adding an additional dimension of business viability. You need to know that you have a business model that generates profits given the problem that you are solving and the product that you develop to solve the problem.

Take a close look at Figure 8-3. If you're investigating a Type I product, where you know both what product solution you have and what problem it solves, then you have a lot less work to do in determining financial viability. The example shown is for Microsoft Word 10. If you have sold Word successfully for many years, then there is not much financial uncertainty. Recently Microsoft has moved some of its products to a subscription model, which increased financial uncertainty. The focus of the Word product manager is then to discover what impact a change in the pricing model would have on overall revenue. The product and the problem it solved remained unchanged as they had already been successfully defined.

Type		Optimize (Type I)		Market Driven (Type II)		Tech Driven (Type III)		Visionary (Type IV)	
Problem		Defined	Defined	Defined	Defined	Undefined	Undefined	Undefined	Undefined
Solution	Product	Defined	Defined	Undefined	Undefined	Defined	Defined	Undefined	Undefined
	Business Model	Defined	Undefined	Defined	Undefined	Defined	Undefined	Defined	Undefined
Example		MS Word 10 Samsung Galaxy	Dell	Flip	YouSendIt (Hightail)	Gore Assoc. Vocera	Salesforce Redbox	Post-it® Notes	Xerox Twitter

FIGURE 8-3: Combining problem, product, and business models.

If, on the contrary, you identify that you're working on a Type IV product, where you're simultaneously working on defining what the customer problem is while defining which product may solve that problem, your planning should be much more cautious and use a disciplined empirical process like the learning loop discussed earlier in the chapter. *Empirical process* means one that is driven by evidence.

Start with undefined factors, the product management equivalent of the medieval map label "there be dragons" for unknown territory. Tread carefully. Examine every assumption. Validate constantly, and be ready to accept that throwing it all out and starting over or switching directions (*pivoting*, in the Lean start-up terminology) is the right thing to do. For those factors that are defined, make sure to document them very carefully in customer-oriented language.

Finding the right level of planning for your company's culture

Only you know your company's culture well enough to decide what level of planning is expected and necessary. Here your focus is on balance and balance can be lost as one or another department takes over the planning process. Organizations are typically driven more in one of the following directions than another as shown in Figure 8-4:

>> **Financially:** Every decision is run through a strict financial lens. This approach can work for the next version of an existing product. For cutting-edge products or products that deliver softer benefits like happier customers or long-term strategic position in the market, driving decisions on a financial basis can be challenging. And with your finance department in the driver's seat, understanding real customer value buried under the numbers becomes a challenge. The planning process is drawn out, detailed, and complicated.

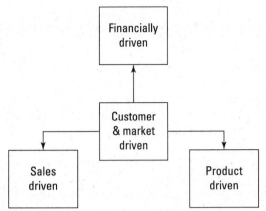

FIGURE 8-4: How are you being pulled out of being a customer- and market-driven (modifies organization)

>> **Sales:** In this environment, the focus is on making the customer (perhaps several customers or just one demanding customer) happy at all costs in the short-term to complete the sale. You have to be careful here because there are a few common traps of sales-driven planning:

- **Different versions:** Doing different versions of a product for each customer produces multiple custom versions of your product. This may cripple the product delivery and support organization as they struggle to support many flavors of one product.

- **Understanding customer wants:** Sales may not have really understood what the customer asked for. If you are unable to validate the request because sales rushes the product change through, you could easily develop the wrong product. Make sure you validate and clarify the needs and requests before committing resources to build anything.

  One big caveat applies in sales-driven planning. Some companies serve very few customers. Virtually every product that they produce is custom. In this scenario it is best to create an underlying product platform that suits most of what customers want and proactively create a boundary above which the product is customized.

>> **Product:** This method is also known as the bright, shiny object scenario. Someone, typically high in management or in the product organization, thinks that this cool new product idea or feature is just what the market needs. An organization like this one may feel no need to do detailed market and customer analysis. It instead is driven by someone's gut feel and hopes everything will work out fine. This approach is very common in the founders of start-ups. Planning can be short circuited or revised often as the next shiny object to be developed is pushed to the top of the development list.

ANALYTICS AND THE FEAR OF RISK

Making sure you base all decisions on hard facts and clear analysis is tempting because having the numbers support every decision you make can be comforting. The underlying assumption is that each decision you make can have an absolutely correct answer that clearly excludes other options. The only solution to the problem 2 + 2 is 4. This kind of thinking and problem space is often called *well defined.*

Unfortunately, the product management problem space is one in which the problem being worked on (customer, product, and so on) and therefore the solution may be *ill defined.* You simply have too many variables you can't define and put numbers around with an exceptional level of accuracy. Overanalyzing may lead to paralysis by analysis. By recognizing which problem space you're in, you may be able to determine key guideposts and then use Lean methods to pivot or shift the project in a different direction as you explore the problem further.

>> **Customer or market:** This scenario is commonly believed to be the right orientation for successful organizations. By focusing on customer needs, your planning process is delivered at the right level of details and balances finances, sales buy-in, and product differentiation.

TIP

If you're serious about helping your company become a more customer driven organization, preplanning is critical. Organize product investments under a coherent strategy, and you get a clearer idea when the product, sales, or financial decisions may be jeopardizing the longer-term goal.

Considering your executives' expectations

Key executives drive most organizations. They have expectations of what your work will look like, and the kind and amount of information they need before they make a decision. Consider the following list of questions about your executives as you begin planning:

>> **Are the executives involved or hands off?**

>> **How do they like to take in information?** Should you speak to them while using visuals; submit a written document/presentation and talk them through it later; give them the information well in advance and have them come back with questions; or give them the information shortly before the deadline (knowing that they won't look at it until the last possible moment)?

- » **Do they use particular language when they accept or reject an idea?** Can you use this language when speaking with them to tilt the conversation in your favor?

- » **How analytical are they?**

- » **Do they empathize with actual customer issues, or are they mercenary in taking advantage of customers in any way they can?**

- » **Do they really know what being a customer is like, or are they just guessing?** When they really know what customers need, do they have the courage to make changes that improve customer experiences?

- » **How much information do you need to (gently) educate your executives?**

- » **Are their communication styles direct or indirect?** Will you know when they've said yes or no?

- » **How decisive are they?** Do they make a clear decision and stick with it, or do they push decisions off?

When you've analyzed their usual behavior patterns, create a communications plan to get your point across. Tie the outcome that your product delivers to the executive goals for the company. Don't leave any crucial parties out of the equation. Getting executive buy-in is critical.

Evaluating investment risk

Investment risk is all about balancing out company resources. For start-ups, the focus is getting to self-sustaining revenue, or growing and achieving market domination as quickly as possible. What many new product managers struggle to understand is how the investment process is perceived at the corporate level. For larger companies with existing products and the opportunity to develop new ones (either follow on products or completely new ones), each project is evaluated differently. Many companies divide their development budgets into two or three categories, as shown in Figure 8-5.

- » **Ongoing product support:** This category is also known as *continuing engineering*. It's allocated to fix bugs and sometimes to enable minor enhancements. Investment risk in this area is low.

- » **New products:** The bulk of what product development spends is here. Typically, many more products want funding than can actually be funded, and prioritization should be strategic. Companies usually decide to balance their investment risk by selecting some projects from the product-market fit Type I category and then a few from Type II or Type III categories. You may find a Type IV category product in here. (See Chapter 7 and Figure 8-3 for more information on these categories.) Again, the idea is that you don't put all your eggs in one basket.

>> **Advanced products:** New technologies fall into this basket. This high-risk category is the "cool new stuff" category. Most of it won't work, but sometimes it will. For example, the touch-screen technology for iPhones came out of Apple's advanced technology group. That said, you can consider most products in this category Type III: technology looking for a market and problem to solve.

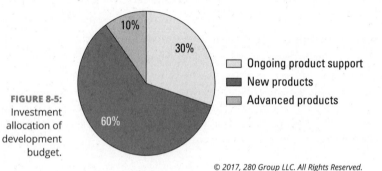

FIGURE 8-5: Investment allocation of development budget.

If you aren't careful to prune your product line, the ongoing product support category may grow too large over time until getting funding for new products is hard. Chapter 16 gives you an idea of the best way to retire products and have more funds to develop new products.

Streamlining the Planning Process with Lean and Simple Planning

Using a Lean approach to planning in product management means not defining all details upfront. It means accepting — and even welcoming — that change will happen and be part of the development process.

Understanding the Lean approach

The goal in Lean thinking for product management is to decrease the time to market and project cost without sacrificing the focus on *customer value*. At the same time, the project has to achieve product-market fit. (See Chapter 7.) In Lean, you investigate the entire system by using a learning cycle. Here are a couple of learning models:

>> Discover Hypothesis Test Learn works well in early stage fluid situations and pairs well with Agile.

>> A/B testing works out which of two chosen options is most effective.

These models are deliberate investigations of the system you originally used to create product and deliver value. With the results of testing, you alter aspects of the system to improve the whole. If, for example, you reduce cost by delivering software faster but the code has so many bugs that fixing it increases time to market, the system isn't optimized. You'd be better off to slow down the coding and have better-working and maintainable code at the end.

With the idea of Lean product management in mind, the next sections cover the product management aspects that need to be in place for Lean to deliver on its promise: more value for less cost and time.

What numbers are you looking at?

Incorporating Lean into the planning process means being honest with yourself. Part of that honesty revolves around the numbers you look at. In today's digital marketing world, you can look at any number of numbers (pun intended). With a product moving through planning, you're developing and testing — and probably selling at some level. Track each step of the process to see, for example, how many people sign on to the service, use it, keep using it, and then pay for it. Look for the big decrease in customers moving from awareness to commitment.

In Table 8-2, 100,000 people became aware of the product; 10,000 showed interest; 1,000 evaluated the product; and 1 person committed. This decrease in customers as they move through each and every step of the sales decision process is huge and needs urgent investigation into all aspects of this product's value proposition. By using Lean thinking, you can run a test like this one and then, in association with an Agile development team, make changes rapidly to correct the situation.

TABLE 8-2 **Analysis of Sell-Through**

	Awareness	Interest	Evaluation	Commitment
Number of people	100,000	10,000	1,000	1

TIP

Beware of looking at numbers that seem to show success (in this case, the high rate of customer awareness and interest) when you know that something isn't right. This approach is called focusing on *vanity metrics*. Instead, start looking for the numbers that will help you find the problems (in this case, the low commitment rate), and then you can start solving problems one by one.

Taking a look at a popular business model canvas

Figure 8-6 is the popular business model canvas. You use it in place of a business plan when you're working in a Lean method with high uncertainty — so not typically for known (Type I) products. As you explore ideas and want to adapt to new information, the business canvas keeps everyone in the loop as to the current thinking, which could easily change tomorrow.

The sections are of a business canvas are in the following list. Turn to Chapter 7 for details on creating business canvases:

>> Key partners

>> Key activities

>> Key resources

>> Value propositions

>> Customer relationships

>> Channels

>> Customer segments

>> Cost structure

>> Revenue streams

Where do you start? With whatever part you believe to be true. You may start with the value proposition that you want to deliver with your product. You can also start with unserved customer segments that you want to target. Then keep filling in the missing parts. If the whole scheme falls apart early on due to an inconsistency or a part of the business puzzle that you can't validate, you've lost only the time spent — not millions of dollars that you may have invested building a product through more traditional planning methods.

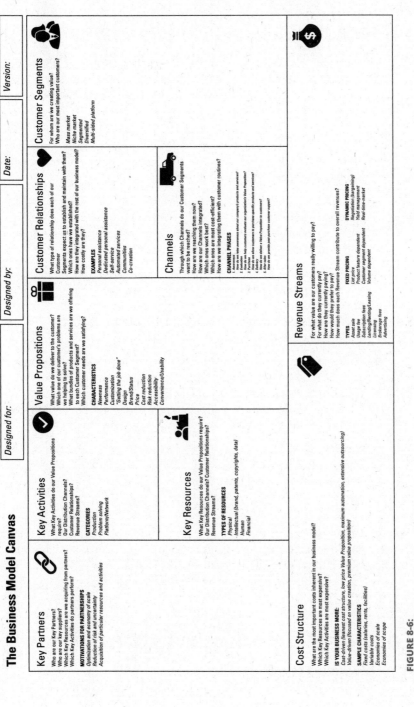

FIGURE 8-6:

The standard business model.

Being prepared to rapidly change and pivot

Lean incorporates the idea of checking and change as part of the process. To implement Lean, it helps to think of the axes on which you can change or pivot your offering, market, price, or communications. These axes may include the following:

>> **Problem:** If you find that customers still aren't interested after you solve a defined customer problem, maybe you need to revisit the problem and make sure that you really understood the underlying need.

>> **Customer segment:** Are you addressing the wrong customer segment or group of customers? Careful analysis may show that a different customer segment would be more receptive to your offering. Use Chapter 5 to help you with customer segment creation and analysis.

>> **Product:** Maybe your customers are using only part of your product. To pivot, you would refocus and expand on the part of the product that is working and de-emphasize or delete the rest. This is what happened with Groupon. It pivoted toward the part of the product that customers were using: deals on products and services.

>> **Marketing:** You may pivot and decide to reposition your product in the market. For example, in one company, the win-loss analysis showed that the product sold more successfully when it was combined with another product. The marketing was then changed to address this target market, and sales efforts were more successful.

>> **Price:** Pricing structure can influence how customers receive and perceive a product. Interestingly, if the offering is positioned as a premium product and brand, one option may be to increase the price so customers understand the value of the offering.

Pivots are a key part of the Lean process. As such, plan to review numbers regularly (on a monthly basis is a good cadence) and decide whether a pivot may be appropriate. Then think along each of the pivot options to see which one or two may offer a change that puts you on the road to success.

Taking a More Thorough Approach: In-Depth Planning

If you're proposing to spend a lot of money on developing a brand-new idea, be prepared to spend a lot of time justifying the investment. Your executives and company may need deep planning and justification, so your planning documents will likely be long and complex.

TIP

In many companies, the trend has been toward using presentations rather than written documents as a form of documentation. Although presentations are faster to create, the deep thinking that goes into a written document creates a more thorough understanding of the issues. Think of a presentation as a movie and a written document as a book. When a writer adapts a book into a movie, she has more extensive background material to choose from; even though she simplifies the book's story in the long run, the final product is still richer because of all that preexisting content. But a tie-in book based on a movie is often very shallow because the writer has far less material to work with. Even if all you are asked to create is a movie (presentation), spend time writing out the book (documents). You'd be surprised at how much thinking you still need to do in order to complete the documents that you didn't have to do to complete the presentations.

Deciding whether to document

Though running an entire project from a business case using only a canvas on the wall may be nice, the reality is that the level of documentation depends on a variety of conditions:

>> **Do you develop using Agile methodology or waterfall?** Throughout Parts 2 and 3, the right documentation for each is specified.

>> **What is the underlying nature of the project you want to document?** If it's a large-scale change in the product, then documenting the market need and corresponding product description in detail is appropriate. If the focus is on changing or adding target markets, then spending more time on the market strategy documents is in order.

>> **What are you trying to create documentation for?** A bug fix or other minor change should be very easy to document and proceed with. But if you're planning to spend $100 million, you'd likely want a detailed and thorough plan that executives are required to read and sign off on. Expect to carefully consider every aspect of the project. Table 8-3 gives you a way of classifying the type of change or project and the corresponding type of documentation needed.

TABLE 8-3   **Comparing Documentation Levels**

Documentation Level	Content	Type of Change or Project	Sign-Off Requirements
Light	Few or no written documents. All critical issues considered in person. Summary email advised to document decision.	Bug fix, minor user interface change.	Informal agreement — even just an email.
Medium	Some or all documents written in short form. Level of detail kept as minimal as possible.	Small-to-medium next revision of an existing product.	Sometimes. May just have direct manager's signature.
Heavy	Complete documents delivered for all phases with extensive detail.	Large and/or new product area, solutions that cover multiple products as part of the offering.	All stakeholders sign off and agree to all documents.

Using key documents and corresponding questions

Chapter 3 discusses documents you use throughout the entire product life cycle. We cover the details of how to think about and create the contents of each of strategic documents in more detail in Chapters 9, 10, and 11. In the planning stage, team members should complete the following strategic documents for a large scale project:

» **Business case:** Captures the reasoning for initiating a project and determines whether the effort should proceed based on profitability and strategic fit. The target audience for this document is management who decide whether a project moves forward.

» **Market needs:** Description of the business or consumer challenges to be solved through an analysis of market needs, user personas (head to Chapter 5), and usage scenarios. The audience is product development and quality assurance organizations.

» **Product description:** A description of the completed solution's feature set, expected usage, and the technology and delivery requirements. Includes initial scoping of product and project costs. Product development typically creates this document, and the target audience is product management, which confirms that the document meets the customer needs as outlined in the market needs document. In some cases, quality assurance uses the document to make sure that all parts of the product are completed.

TIP

Product development is typically unhappy about having to create a product description document. They don't want to take responsibility in case they forgot something or the project doesn't go well because it was described incorrectly. Workarounds include selecting one engineer and, for software, one UX person to work closely with you. Have this work specifically assigned to them through the engineering organization. You can then collaborate with them on the details of the document. Another alternative is to create a version on your own, give it to one person or a small team in product development, and then change it based on what they tell you is wrong. Since this document drives the nuts and bolts of what your product will do, product managers do whatever it takes to complete this document no matter what type of development team they work with.

>> **Road map:** Description of a set of sequential product releases based on scoping, strategy, and objectives. Road maps are used for many internal audiences to explain the longer term direction of a product. A modified and simplified version is used for external audiences. See Chapter 20 for caveats on using road maps with external audiences.

WARNING

When working with Agile teams, product managers often skip an in-depth planning activity. Teams can confuse the planning of a product in the plan stage of the product management life cycle with the scrum planning activities. Both instances use the word *plan*, but the work done is actually very different. To hold the long term vision and strategy in focus, product managers need to have well-thought-out strategic documentation in place at all times. This documentation is quite detailed so the Agile team members are better served by a concise product vision developed on the basis of the strategic documentation which provides a guiding light through the entire project.

Because no development process is truly 100 percent Agile or 100 percent waterfall, many organizations create hybrid processes that retain the flexibility and adaptability of Agile and have the elements of early and deep thought and planning that are waterfall. In Table 8-4, you see that the hybrid method looks a lot like Agile, with Agile requirements (called *epics*) taking the place of large market needs and product descriptions documents. (We discuss waterfall and how it compares to Agile in Chapter 12.)

TABLE 8-4   Comparing Agile, Hybrid, and Waterfall Documents

	Plan Phase Documents
Agile	Business planning/business case Product vision Prioritized high-level user stories
Hybrid (Agile and waterfall)	Business planning/business case Product vision In-depth epics with more direction so that other areas can be sure of achieving certain goals for customers Market needs document (in some cases) to think through the personas, pain points, and customer problems at a more in-depth scale over a longer term
Waterfall	Business planning/business case Market needs document Product description document Project planning

Estimating your time investment

Writing coherently and thoughtfully to clarify your own thoughts and then using the content to influence others takes time, and your time as a product manager is precious. Each page of a document that you write can easily take you an hour or two simply because as you start writing, you realize that you forgot to nail down some of the details and have to go to figure them out. Even a well-written and complete email can eat up an hour.

TIP

You won't likely have the free time to create each of these documents in one sitting. Rather approach the work like a term paper, plan to spend some time each day when you won't be interrupted. Don't be afraid to rotate effort among different documents. In particular, the market needs and market strategy documents are intertwined, and you'll bounce from one to the other. (Check out Chapters 10 and 11 for a more detailed look at these documents' contents.) The most important thing is that you think about all the critical questions that these documents pose well in advance of the project and then update your thinking and assumptions as you go.

One recommendation is to create a very rough draft and then ask everyone's opinion. In that way, you don't spend a lot of time crafting a message only to find that particular issues are still not clarified.

For a detailed project, the time from start to finish for extensive planning may be two to three months as you home in on a solution that works with all internal and external stakeholders. The actual time you spend writing will be much, much shorter than that. But if you're going to be advocating that your company spend a large amount of money developing, launching, and marketing a product, the time you take to answer critical questions upfront and build a solid plan will be well spent.

Chapter **9**

Developing Your Business Case

Before you invest a large amount of time and money developing a new product or service it is best to create a cohesive business case. In product management, a business case has two key components: external market factors and internal product factors. In this chapter, we cover the external factors to consider when devising your business case (see Chapter 11 for information on the internal factors). The business case helps gain buy-in from your company's executives to move forward with developing a product.

Here's a look at what external factors this chapter discusses:

>> Looking outside the company to the problem a customer has

>> Seeking the potential opportunity to profitably address the customer's problem

>> Completing a deep analysis of the market and the competition

As part of your purchase, a Business Case template is included with the Product Management LifeCycle Toolkit (included as a free download with this book; see the Introduction, page 4, for details). The toolkit includes a template and completed sample business case. The sample document is written for a fictitious product which is an always-on, super-connected, hands-free phone in your ear. The code name for this product is "EarBud." We refer to EarBud in this chapter as a way of demonstrating how to put together a business case. Figure 9-1 shows what EarBud looks like.

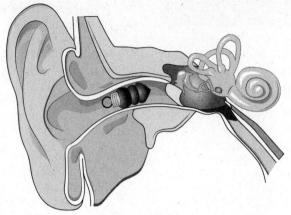

FIGURE 9-1:
Illustration of the
EarBud concept.

Making a Business Case for the New Product or Service

Having a great idea is never enough. You're always faced with a moment of truth: Can you get your management on board and get them to fund the development? Given that executives examine opportunities at a pretty high level, you don't want to bury it in lots of details. You want to clearly tell your story and follow up by convincing management factually that this idea is a worthwhile investment of time and resources.

REMEMBER

Business case or business plan? The tendency is to use these terms interchangeably. However, they're two distinct concepts. A *business case* is made on the product level and gives the reasons creating or modifying a particular product or solution is a good idea for the company for strategic and/or profitability reasons. The business case is intended to get company buy-in and funding for the idea as a first step along a more complex journey. A *business plan* is a detailed plan for the overall company and how it will operate and grow over time.

Recognizing the importance of a business case

The business case is critical in order to get company buy-in. Without it, your company won't give you the funding to get the product out the door. To make your business case easy to comprehend, divide it up by the following three components:

>> **The story:** The why of the problem you're looking to solve. Why is solving it so important for a particular customer set or sets? Tell this part as clearly and as simply as possible. Forget fancy words, and don't go on and on.

>> **The numbers:** The evidence that supports your story. It's nice that you want to solve a problem for somebody. In the numbers portion, you bring the proof — for example, you have this many potential customers, and with a certain amount of budget an expected level of profitability. Again, simplify. You may have a huge spreadsheet of numbers as background material, but focus clearly on the ones that are most important to support your story.

>> **The downside:** These are the risks and tradeoffs that the company need to be aware of. Here's a tip from human psychology: If you admit to the weak parts of your business case, the people who hear you will trust you more. Be realistic; tell your audience about the potential downsides, and you'll actually be better off.

Outlining your business case

Your business case has many components. Table 9-1 briefly outlines the main headings, and we give a more detailed breakdown of each piece of the business case puzzle throughout in this chapter.

TABLE 9-1 **A Typical Business Case Outline**

Document Section	Description
Executive summary	This piece is written last but placed first in the document. It summarizes the entire business case.
Problem and opportunity	What is the problem, and how can your company take best advantage of solving it?
Market landscape	What is happening in the market as a whole that makes you believe solving this problem is the best use of company time and resources?
Competitive landscape	What is happening with competition in your chosen market that makes you believe solving this problem will allow your company to compete and win?
Financial and impact analysis	How much money and other resources does completing the project take?
Risk analysis	What particular risks do you see, and how can you mitigate them?
Assumptions	Are you making key underlying assumptions about the market, economy, and/or internal situation?
Open issues	Does anything (such as a key person, a key relationship, or an unknown technological advance) remain up in the air?
Conclusions and recommendations	What is the bottom line? Why should the company say yes?

Just because a business case has a lot of pieces doesn't mean it needs to be long. Focus on what is important. Don't repeat yourself needlessly. When you're finished writing, put it away for 24 hours and then reread it from the beginning to find any repetition or extraneous information that you can eliminate. Make your goal to cut 30 percent of the content from your completed draft so that you hone in on only the most critical and necessary parts.

Gathering the necessary information

To gather the necessary information for each of the sections of the business case template you'll do market and competitive research (in many cases by the time you are writing the business case you have already completed these). See Chapter 6 for details on how to do these. One good way to make sure that your business case has enough detail and information is to ask your manager and others in your company what the executives expect to see in a typical business case that is presented to them. Check this against the sections of the business case template and add anything that is specific to your company and the management's expectations.

Putting It All Together: Documenting Your Business Case

The following sections contain the main components of a business case as outlined in Table 9-1 earlier in the chapter. Follow the guidelines in each section to create a successful business case.

Part I: Executive summary

Though the executive summary is the first section of the business case, you write it last, after you know what information you're summarizing. The goal is to include the following content: problem statement, vision, project evaluation, risks, return on investment(ROI), and recommendation. The summary should be approximately one page — two pages at most — for a completely new idea. See the sidebar "For Example: Executive Summary" in this chapter for a sample of an executive summary. Here are three reasons for making the executive summary short and to the point:

>> Executives won't read anything that is too lengthy.

>> When you present the business case for approval, you should already have pre-sold the idea within the organization.

>> The details appear in later sections of the business case if questions come up or anyone wants to drill down on the information.

Part II: Problem and opportunity

The problem and opportunity section of the summary addresses what the customer problem is and how your company would solve it. Table 9-2 breaks down the different sections of Part II of your business case.

TABLE 9-2   Problem and Opportunity Questions

Section	Key questions to answer
Problem statement	What problem does a particular customer have? This section can easily be a few paragraphs or a few pages. A lot depends on how complex a problem you're trying to describe.
Vision of the solution	What is your vision of a possible solution? Why is it so great — a compelling must-have for your potential customers? Does your vision have any downsides? Include analogies and similar examples if doing so helps build a strong and irresistible vision.
Current alternatives	What else are people doing today or planning to do at the time the product is available? What do customers do today that you can do better with your proposed solution?
Strategic alignment and business value	Is the opportunity one that aligns with the overall company or divisional goals and adds business value to the company within that context?
Goals and objectives with key performance indicators (KPIs)	What are the numbers that let you know you've succeeded or are on track to succeed?
Window of opportunity	When must this product be delivered in order to capture the market and maximize profitability? Why should the company proceed immediately? What are the impacts of delaying moving forward?
Exit strategy	If it's a temporary opportunity, how do you plan on leaving the market?

FOR EXAMPLE: EXECUTIVE SUMMARY

Based on the EarBud example used in this chapter, the following is a very abbreviated executive summary. You can see how quickly the opportunity is discussed and how the final request is to the point.

"Our company believes that the technology exists to create a discrete wearable audio network access device for many unmet needs. Such needs include completely hands-free cellular phone use as well as the ability to listen to audio information (music, audio casts, directions, and so on). The solution we propose solves many of the challenges by being always on and always accessible.

Our company can best address this market because of our portfolio of patents, especially in the long-distance Wi-Fi space, which form a barrier to entry for other companies to compete. Our company also has unique engineering expertise that will allow us to take advantage of this market more quickly than our competitors. Though we have engineering expertise, we would need to rapidly develop expertise in marketing and sales to reach customer segments that we don't currently sell to.

This is an entirely new market that will develop over the next 5 to 10 years and that will allow us to target consumers as well as specialized B2B markets and government first responders and armed forces.

The potential for this product is a $200 billion business with 25 percent gross margins. We expect to build to a market share of 10 percent. The initial investment is $250 million in development with a further $250 million investment in marketing and sales. The ROI is 10,000 percent.

There are two potential options.

1. Proceed with the initial planning of the project for two months. This requires an investment of $100,000 to further understand the opportunity, develop some initial working technology, determine in-depth market requirements, and create the go-to-market plan.

2. Proceed with the full development proposal for one year at a cost of $250 million with quarterly progress reviews. The result of this work will be a fully functional product that is ready to launch in the market, and the $500 million will adequately fund all development, marketing, sales, and other activities.

The team's recommendation is to proceed with option 2. Given that many other companies are likely to be working on this technology and on similar products, we believe that the window of opportunity for delivering this product and capturing the market is within the next two years, and proceeding with full development will give our company the best chance of success."

Part III: Market landscape

The Part III section contains the following three main components:

>> **Overview:** Provide a general overview of the market. Is it a growth industry, or is it an established market that is growing more slowly? Include a brief analysis of where you believe your product's technology is in its adoption cycle. List the market size, growth, and future projections. Identify any key data points about the market in general. What is the total size of your market? Provide an estimate of the total available market (TAM) in revenue terms if available (total number of potential customers × total number of units per customer × price).

>> **Trends:** What are the top three to five trends you foresee in the industry, both short term and long term? Identify and describe the market growth, competitive situation, trends in consumer or business preferences, and trends in technology in your targeted (and other related) market segments.

>> **Barriers to entry:** Common barriers to entry are high capital costs, high marketing costs, shipping costs, tariff barriers and quotas, brand recognition, consumer acceptance, network effect, vertical integration, training and skills, unique technology, government regulation and patents, unions, and so on. What barriers to entry do you face entering this market?

REMEMBER

In the competitive landscape segment of your business case, you answer the question "What barriers do competitors face that we can put in their way?"

Part IV: Competitive landscape

The competitive landscape section describes who you believe your main competitors will be. It begins by describing what your organization is all about and then provides details about your competitors and their products.

Company background

In the first part of the competitive landscape, the focus is on the alignment between the company and the proposed product.

Begin by defining what your organization is all about. Identify the following factors regarding your company:

>> **Goals:** Goals are destinations. Where do you want your business to be? One example of a goal is to have a healthy, successful company that is a leader in customer service and has a loyal customer following.

>> **Objectives:** Objectives are progress markers along the way to goal achievement. Examples of objectives tied to the goals in the preceding bullet are annual sales targets and some specific measures of customer satisfaction.

>> **Values:** What is important to your company? Certain products just don't fit with the company values, and you need to ensure that your product fits within that scope.

>> **Strengths:** In what areas is your company particularly strong? Are there areas that your company excels in that other companies would find hard to match?

>> **Core competencies:** What are the main things that your company does very well? What defining capability or advantage distinguishes you from other companies?

>> **Barriers:** What existing barriers to entry work for the company and against the competition (or can be reinforced to do so)? What new barriers can your company create? Examples include cost of switching from one product to another when the new product is from a new supplier, customer loyalty, control of resources, economy of scale, pricing, patents, network effect, vertical integration, and so on.

Competitors

In this section of the competitive landscape, you answer the following questions: What companies will you be competing against? What are their attributes? Will they compete with you across the board or just for certain products, for certain customers, or in certain locations? Will you have important indirect competitors? (For example, video rental stores used to compete with theaters, although they're different types of businesses.)

TIP

If you've created competitive analysis using SWOT or Porter's five forces analysis (see Chapter 6), include it in the competitive landscape section.

Competing products

Compare the top three to five competing products. To retain the focus on the customer, include the value or benefit to the customer for each feature listed. In Figure 9-2, you can see a simplified feature matrix comparison.

TIP

Don't make the mistake of comparing your future product to current competitive products already being shipped. You need to project where you think your competitor's future products may be when you ship.

Feature	Benefit	Customer Value	Your Product	Product 1	Product 2
Long battery life	Reduced concern about communication availability	Medium	Yes – 6 months	Yes – 1 month	Yes – 1 month
Hum tones	Can control usage without hands	High	Yes	Yes	No
Ring-fenced communication	No risk of sharing conversations	High	Up to 3 groups	Up to 2 groups	No
Multiple group switching	Greater utility	Medium	Automatic	Manual	Manual

FIGURE 9-2
Simple feature matrix comparison using the EarBud example

Situational analysis

Describe how the company is doing in the context of competitors, life cycle, and from the market's perspective.

Product history

If a product history exists, bring this information to the attention of the decision makers here. How has the company tried to address this opportunity to date? What has succeeded, and what has failed? Why?

Part V: Financial and resource impact analysis

Part V covers the financial and resource impact that bringing your product to market will have on the company. This includes how much it will cost, what the revenues and projected profits will be, and what resources will be required.

Summary

At this point, the rubber hits the numerical road: Will the product make money, and how long will making the company's investment back take? Rather than provide all the details in the summary, cherry-pick the ones that tell the clearest picture and put them here. A simple table or clear graph works best. If necessary, use arrows to point out the information you want to highlight.

The metrics that you will want to include are the following:

- » **Expected revenues:** How much money do you expect to make by selling this product (price/unit × number of expected units to be sold)? Include a one, three and five-year estimate.

- » **Expected profits:** How much profit will you make by selling this product (profit per unit × number of expected units to be sold)? Include a one-, three-, and five-year estimate.

- » **Return on investment (ROI):** How much profit will the company make if it invests to bring the product to market. For example, if the product costs $5 million to develop and market during the first year and you expect to make $20 million in profit, the ROI would be $20 million/$5 million = 400%.

- » **Payback time frame:** How long will it take for the profits to pay back the initial investment. Using the same example, a $5 million investment making $20 million in profits the first year ($5 million every three months) would have a payback of three months.

- » **Break-even:** How many units of the product must be sold in order to break even and pay back the initial investment? If the profit on each unit of the product is $50,000 and your initial investment is $5 million, then $5 million/$50,000 = 100 units. In other words, once you sell the first 100 units you have paid back the entire initial investment.

By providing the financial information at this level of detail, your executives can very quickly see what the risk and reward are for the investment. If they want more details about the assumptions and financials, they can read farther into the document.

Resource impact

Summarize how the project would impact the use of resources (especially head count) at the company. Include all groups that are impacted, such as development, sales, and support. What resources would be required from the various groups, such as development, support, marketing, and so on? What is the availability of those resources?

Cannibalization

No, we aren't talking about eating people! *Cannibalization* for product managers describes a project's possible impact on sales of, or its replacement of, the company's existing products. For example, the Apple iPhone cannibalized sales of the iPod because many customers who would've purchased an iPod instead purchased the iPhone, which offered the same (and more) functionality. Explain the transition plans between existing products and your new product in general terms and specifically in your financial analysis.

Funding

Estimate the required costs to adequately build and go to market with this project. Which internal organizations can the company approach to help fund this service effort? Can it access external financial resources such as other companies that might want to form a strategic partnership? The budget should include all sales, promotional, and marketing communication deliverables.

Part of your calculations should include the human cost of funding, often referred to as *fully loaded head count*. In addition to the cost of an employee's salary, additional taxes, benefits, and even overhead for desk space in the office come into play. A good rule of thumb for calculating this number is to add 25 percent to the average salary. For example, a fully loaded engineer with a $200,000 per year salary actually costs the company $250,000.

Part VI: Risks

Identify the key barriers that could impede the progress of the project in terms of development and bringing it to market. How could the risks affect the company? For each risk, provide an estimate of whether the risk is low, medium, or high. Also include recommendations for reducing the risk. For example, if developing your product is highly dependent on one of your engineers who has deep expertise in an area that no one else in the world does, you might recommend providing a financial incentive to ensure the engineer stays on until the product ships. Keep your answers brief, but make sure you clearly state the risks.

Parts VII through XI: Other sections

Here are some other sections that you can include in your business case for further explanations. Pick and choose from these as needed based on what your executive management is likely to want included.

» **Assumptions:** A business case is about predicting the future, so unless you have a time machine, you have to make a number of assumptions while writing it. Record your assumptions in this section and be prepared to defend them.

>> **Open issues:** Track any open issues that have come up so far in the project. When the issues are resolved, document it. Assign any unresolved issues to a responsible party. You'll likely have a number of open issues, which tend to get resolved as the project proceeds. Identify where in the process these issues need to be resolved.

>> **Conclusions and recommendations:** State your conclusion and justification of the recommendation, including the likely effect of following your proposals. What are the pros and cons? Describe alternative options as well as what may happen if the company pursues this opportunity.

Also identify what will happen if you don't go forward with the project. Every good executive will ask the question "What if we don't do this?" at least once. Be prepared to answer it clearly and coherently.

TIP

>> **Governance:** *Governance* is the process for getting approval and moving forward; it includes who needs to be informed of and approve the decisions. Describe the governance processes and structures within the company. What has happened up to this point, and what are the next steps after a decision is made? Be brief.

List the roles and names of the contributors and key reviewers of this document. Some companies require many signatures and others very few. Some transfer a document electronically, while some create a stapled document that makes the rounds. Keep track of getting full sign-off from everyone that is required so that the project isn't delayed.

>> **Exhibits and appendices:** This is the place for additional or more detailed information that details the core of your argument. Other pieces common to this section are a glossary, profit and loss projection (see Figure 9-3), any supporting data, and external references.

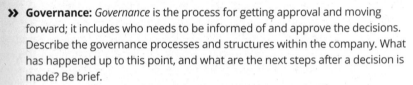
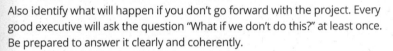

Year	-1	0	1	2	3	4	5
Units sold (1,000s)	0	0	990	4,950	24,750	99,000	198,000
Revenue (1,000s)	0	0	$ 1,165,725	$ 5,828,625	$ 29,143,125	$ 116,572,500	$ 233,145,000
COGS	$ -	$ 1,709,375	$ 338,456	$ 1,692,281	$ 8,461,406	$ 33,845,625	$ 67,691,250
GM	$ -	$ (1,709,375)	$ 827,269	$ 4,136,344	$ 20,681,719	$ 82,726,875	$ 165,453,750
R&D	$ 20,000	$ 40,000	$ 80,000	$ 240,000	$ 720,000	$ 2,880,000	11,520,000
Sales and Mkt	$ -	$ 408,004	$ 2,040,019	$ 2,914,313	$ 12,750,117	$ 36,428,906	43,714,688
G&A	$ 6,557	$ 52,458	$ 104,915	$ 524,576	$ 2,622,881	$ 10,491,525	20,983,050
Expenses	$ 26,557	$ 500,461	$ 2,224,934	$ 3,678,889	$ 16,092,998	$ 49,800,431	76,217,738
Operating Income	$ (26,557)	$ (2,209,836)	$ (1,397,665)	$ 457,455	$ 4,588,720	$ 32,926,444	$ 89,236,013
Cummulative Operating Income	$ (26,557)	$ (2,236,394)	$ (3,634,059)	$ (3,176,604)	$ 1,412,116	$ 34,338,560	123,574,573
Note: All numbers in 1,000s							

FIGURE 9-3: Sample EarBud profit and loss table.

BASICS OF PROFIT AND LOSS

As a product manager, you aren't expected to be a financial whiz. If you are, congratulations. If you haven't had much exposure to financial calculations, check out the following descriptors of a profit and loss (P&L) statement:

- P&L statements show projected revenues, expenses and profits over time. Typically, a P&L is annual, but in faster moving businesses, it may be quarterly or even monthly.

- Revenue = Number of units × price.

- COGS (Cost of good sold) = Number of units × cost per unit.

- Revenue – COGS = Gross Margin (GM).

- Sometimes you'll be asked for a gross margin percentage (GM%), which you calculate by dividing the gross margin dollars by total revenue. Gross margins vary widely by industry as well as by where a product is in the product life cycle. For example, in a mature market with many competitors, the gross margins may be lower due to price competition.

- R&D = Research and development: your product development costs are here.

- Sales and mkt = Sales and marketing: The cost for product management is also usually included here.

- G&A = General and administrative: The cost for HR, operations, buildings and support and anything else is here.

- Expenses = R&D + Sales and mkt + G&A.

- Operating Income = GM – Expenses.

- Net margin (NM) percent is another calculation that you may be asked for. NM percent = operating income ÷ revenue, and it's a measure of what the company really makes on the product in the end.

- You may have questions about the cost per unit you should use in the P&L statement. Your operations and finance counterparts should be able to give you a reasonable estimate of the cost. Cost is never a hard-and-fast a calculation due to a variety of factors. Exchange rates, preplanned component cost decreases, and manufacturing changes that add and remove cost make this figure more of a moving target than many people realize. Find a method of getting a number that you believe is reasonable and that your finance people and executives will see as a good estimate and move on without trying to find a perfect answer for costs.

Work on getting better at reading P&L statements. Quickly calculate the gross margin and net margin percents. What is the average cost per unit sold? What does the level of sales and marketing expenditure tell you about how hard it is to sell this product? Compare different P&L statements from different companies to get some practice.

Getting buy-in for your business case

When the writing is done and you have polished the writing to clarify each part of your business case story, make sure everyone who had input has reviewed it and provided feedback. Your likely next step is to create a short, focused, and compelling presentation to tell your story to your executives to get the funding. The presentation should include everything in your executive summary of the business case. The executives make many decisions every day, so you don't want to make it hard for them to figure out what's going on. The clearer your story is, the more likely your business case is to be approved.

Chapter **10**

Developing Your Market Strategy

arket strategy. Two words and a world of work and thinking behind each of them. *Strategy* in this scenario means creating a high-level plan to achieve goals under conditions of uncertainty. And the word *market* gives some context to the word *strategy*. In creating your market strategy, you're going to create a high-level, market-oriented plan under uncertain conditions. This task may sound hard, and doing it well certainly is challenging. In this chapter, we break down the components that create a great market strategy. Taking the results from the work in the later section "Grasping the Importance of a Market Strategy" creates a really compelling and comprehensive plan for your product as it comes into the market.

TIP

If you have no background in marketing, this chapter (along with Chapter 15) is for you. In Chapter 5, we discuss different customer-oriented concepts such as personas. This chapter shows you how to take these concepts to the next level as your customer interacts (psychologically speaking) with your product. You're answering these key questions:

>> Which customers are most interested in my product?

>> What do I want them to believe about my product?

>> Are there any other partners in this process of communicating with my customer that I need to bring on board and how am I going to do that?

Three bullet points. Sounds easy. To really understand this process, you need to dig deep into other people's thought processes and actions. And then decide how best to influence their actions so that they choose to buy or help you sell your product.

Grasping the Importance of a Market Strategy

In our practice, the 280 Group consults with many organizations. Most of them wait too long to develop their market strategy; the strategy is an afterthought either as the product is heading off to be developed or, worse, just as it's being completed. Developing your market strategy early in the product life cycle at the plan stage can dramatically increase your product's chances of success. See Chapter 3 for a review of the product life cycle.

REMEMBER

If your organization splits the role of product management and product marketing management, the market strategy often is the responsibility of the product marketing manager. If you don't have direct responsibility for developing the market strategy, you'll still be a key contributor to the contents. So, keep reading.

Developing a market strategy involves a few components:

>> What is your plan of action to bring your product to market, and why will it result in your beating the other competitors in the market?

>> What is the entire product that you're offering, including service and support?

>> Which market segments are possible for you to reach and which target markets are you going after?

>> What is your positioning? See the later section "Positioning" for more information on this topic.

>> How is your positioning supported in your messaging? What are the messages for each target market?

>> At a high level, what will it take to launch this product? Check out Chapters 13 and 14 for more information on launching.

>> How much money (rough estimate) will be necessary for your product to build enough initial awareness and then to continue to grow sales and revenues?

Setting Yourself Straight on Strategy Tools

Marketing strategy involves a lot of moving parts, but with the right tools, you can navigate the process with confidence. The following sections show you the importance of a go-to-market strategy and give you a variety of options for determining your strategic market position.

Go-to-market strategy

Developing a coherent go-to-market strategy is a critical success factor for your product. Take a close look at Figure 10-1, starting over on the left-hand side with your market analysis. A core role of a product manager is to define customer needs and analyze the market topics which are covered in many earlier Chapters like 4, 5, and 6. The business case (which we discuss in Chapter 9) outlines your company's capabilities; Chapter 6 covers competition. Chapter 15 has info on collaborators and partners, marketing mix, customer acquisition, and distribution

REMEMBER

Go-to-market strategy is the approach and plan you use to succeed in the market and ensure your product is as successful as possible both short term and long term. Think of the go-to-market strategy as the marketing perspective you need to support your product throughout the seven-phase product life cycle (Chapter 3). From a marketing perspective, it involves addressing each of the four parts of Figure 10-1. Much of this book is written so that you can complete your market analysis, make choices on which markets you choose, and clarify what your message to these markets is. This chapter focuses primarily on the market selection process. In Chapter 15, the focus is on marketing mix and customer acquisition.

FIGURE 10-1: Strategic marketing framework.

Market Analysis:	Marketing Selection:	Marketing Mix:	Customer Acquisition:
• Customer needs • Markets & market dynamics • Company capabilities • Competition • Collaborators & partners	• Market segmentation • Market selection • Segment targeting • Product positioning	• Product • Price • Place/ distribution • Promotion • People • Process • Physical evidence	• Awareness • Interest • Evaluation • Commitment • Referral/ customer loyalty/ retention
What does the market look like?	Whom do we go after and how?	What do we sell? Where do we sell it? How do we sell it? How do we gain & retain customers?	

Strategy models

Determining your strategic position in the market is much easier when you use a few strategy models. The tools in this section help you identify your situation with respect to each model. The strength of using these models or strategy tools is that the analysis and conclusions take so many possibilities off the table. Then you can focus on the best opportunities given your strategic context.

Boston Consulting Group (BCG) matrix

The Boston Consulting Group developed the matrix shown in Figure 10-2 in the 1970s to analyze different business units and make decisions about strategy and investment. It's also a tool to evaluate different product lines. To use it, you take a product line — for example, incandescent lightbulbs — and determine where it fits into the matrix given its growth rate and market share.

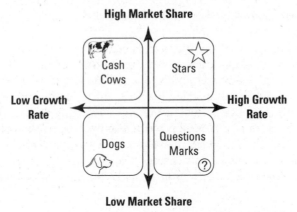

FIGURE 10-2:
Boston Consulting Group matrix.

Incandescent lightbulbs (the old type of lightbulbs that give off a lot of heat and are banned in many places) have a low market growth rate (in fact, it's negative). Following the axes in Figure 10-2, if you're a market share leader (have high market share), this business is considered a *cash cow*. If you have low market share, you categorize your product in the *dog* quadrant. On the other hand, LED lightbulbs, which are replacing incandescent bulbs, have a high growth rate; depending on your market share, you can classify your product line as a *star* (high market share) or a *question mark (low market share).* Your quadrant determines your strategy and tactics. You decide to invest more or less in the product's success. The best way to understand how to use the BCG matrix is to apply it to your own products. Classify each product according to their market share and the growth rate and then put the product into the correct quadrant in Figure 10-2.

We cover the BCG matrix in this book because as a product manager, you need to know what quadrant your product is in. The BCG matrix is a good, simple tool to use as the basis for your strategy.

REMEMBER

The BCG matrix has a downside and isn't always very helpful. Why? Product lines can be successful because of reasons other than growth rate and market share. If you have a niche product that is critical in a particular industry where you have a low overall market share and the growth rate is low (a product in the dog quadrant), you may have customers that are loyal to your product and brand. You may still be able to continue developing, marketing, and selling the product very profitably. The key question is whether you should do so at the expense of other products that may be in the star quadrant with high market share and growth rates.

Product life cycle chart

The product life cycle is how a product goes from "I think I have an idea" to an actual product (see Chapter 3 for details on the entire product life cycle). There are two kinds of product life cycles:

>> Life cycles for products from the time they're an idea until they no longer exist (that is, the seven phases in the Optimal Product Process we describe in Chapter 3).

>> Life cycles for the overall market after the public is allowed to know about the product. These phases are the introduction, growth, maturity, and decline phases. This life cycle is also known as a product life cycle or sometimes as an industry life cycle.

When you work on your market strategy, one great tool for the product/industry life cycle (PLC) is the product life cycle chart shown in Figure 10-3. Using the chart, you combine knowledge of where you are in the product/industry life cycle with what should be happening in your market and what actions you should take. A good example is the smartphone market. In most parts of the world, the smartphone market is considered mature. Read down from the word *Maturity* into the figure. With respect to the marketing objective, market leaders in this field want to keep you loyal to their brand. There is a lot of competition and a very full product lineup. Companies with good market share, such as Apple and Samsung, defend the market through promotions and by encouraging you to switch to their models and brands. The promotions don't involve a lot of explaining what a smartphone is; instead, the ads remind you that your favorite brand is still around and you can buy the products anywhere. This scenario is a far cry from the early days, when the smartphone market was in the introduction and growth phases. At that time, the idea of a smartphone and why people needed one required a lot of explanation.

A useful exercise is to figure out where all your products are on the basis of the criteria in Figure 10-3. Are they in the introduction phase, growth phase, maturity phase, or simply in decline? If you have a lot of products in mature markets, the

PLC shows that you are profitable. However, if you don't have any products in the introduction or growth phases, your company may not be investing enough in upcoming products that provide the next wave of revenue growth.

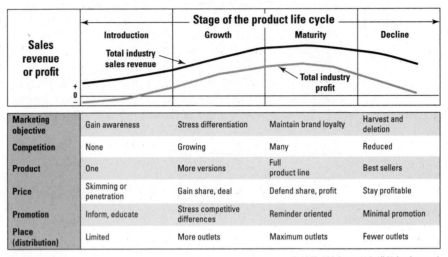

	Introduction	Growth	Maturity	Decline
Marketing objective	Gain awareness	Stress differentiation	Maintain brand loyalty	Harvest and deletion
Competition	None	Growing	Many	Reduced
Product	One	More versions	Full product line	Best sellers
Price	Skimming or penetration	Gain share, deal	Defend share, profit	Stay profitable
Promotion	Inform, educate	Stress competitive differences	Reminder oriented	Minimal promotion
Place (distribution)	Limited	More outlets	Maximum outlets	Fewer outlets

FIGURE 10-3: Product/industry life cycle chart.

One great benefit of having a successful product in the market is that your customers are already familiar with it and (hopefully) loyal to your version of the product. In many industries, such as food, sales really only grow with population. In the United States, population growth is minimal. To take advantage of known brands and products, packaged goods companies like Proctor & Gamble, Nestle, and Unilever develop a slightly different version of a successful product. They re-segment their markets so that they can more finely address a customer's needs with a slightly different version of a successful product. This is called creating a *product line extension* and the effect is to increase product line revenue and extend the length of time that a product remains in the maturity stage.

One example is salad dressing. The customer already buys ranch dressing, so the product line extension may be a variation on salad dressing, such as blue cheese, or bottles of ranch dressing in different sizes: large for large families, smaller for individuals and couples. The possibilities are endless. You may decide you want to pursue this strategy for your products.

Chasm model

The *chasm model*, as shown in Figure 10-4, shows how different types of customers adopt a product over time. The chasm model is shown in the shape of a bell curve and is built from two theories:

>> **Adoption of new ideas and technology:** This concept came out of work done in the 1930s when U.S. agronomists tried to get farmers in the Dust Bowl to change their farming habits and reduce topsoil loss. A few farmers took to the new ideas readily, but most farmers needed to see how it worked elsewhere. They were the *pragmatists*. The agronomists classified people according to their willingness to adopt new ideas; the most willing were innovators, followed by early adopters, pragmatists, conservatives, and then laggards who had to adopt new technology because the old stuff wasn't around anymore.

>> **Geoffrey Moore's work in the book *Crossing the Chasm* (HarperBusiness), which deals with today's issues in technology adoption:** The first two categories of customers adopt new ideas and technologies almost solely because it's a "cool" new idea, technology, or product. However, to gain real market acceptance, achieve longer-term profitability, and reach the pragmatists, the new technology must deliver real customer value. This concept drives much of product management today. It's why the mantra of listening to your customer as you move from innovators and early adopters to pragmatists is so critical. Without delivering real customer-focused value, products won't be able to cross the chasm and reach wider customer acceptance — and longer-term viability and profitability. To cross the chasm, marketing messages change from a focus on product technology to a focus on what problems the product solves for the customer.

As a product manager, you have to answer four questions, then:

>> Do you understand the different needs of each of these kinds of customers?

>> How are you communicating with each of these customer types?

>> Which primary customer type (innovator, early adopters. . .) are you communicating with at this point time?

>> Has your product delivered real customer value over and above the cool technology solution so that you can cross the chasm?

Ansoff's opportunity matrix

Another way to look at the opportunity that you're working on is to use Ansoff's opportunity matrix, shown in Figure 10-5. The matrix is both simple and powerful. The basic concept behind it is that you can choose to address either existing or new markets, and you can address your chosen market with either existing products or new products.

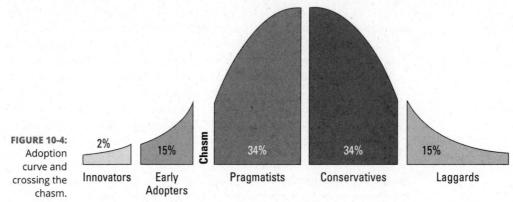

FIGURE 10-4:
Adoption
curve and
crossing the
chasm.

2% | 15% | Chasm | 34% | 34% | 15%

Innovators | Early Adopters | | Pragmatists | Conservatives | Laggards

This matrix leads to the four corresponding growth strategies:

>> **Market penetration:** Following a *market penetration* strategy means your goal is to sell more of your existing products to your existing markets, which is generally less risky than the other strategies.

>> **Product development:** In pursuing a *product development* opportunity, you create new products for the markets you already know how to address. In many cases, this approach means your sales force and channels can stay in place and you simply add more products to the portfolio of things they can sell. This method has more risk than a market penetration strategy. Operating in the product development quadrant may cost more and take more time than market penetration, but many companies successfully use this strategy.

>> **Market development:** With this growth strategy, you decide to bring your existing products to new markets. For example, you may have a database product that you currently sell into a healthcare market. Now your company extends the use of this product into financial services markets. The new market may also be a new geography or country. In market development, the product doesn't change (much), but the sales force and channels may have to change. Depending on how you proceed, your risk is about the same as with a product development strategy.

>> **Diversification:** In diversification you're changing both the market and the product focus at the same time. Your chances for mistakes are much higher. Some companies, like conglomerates, make this strategy work because they don't care very much what business they're in. They operate a very closely controlled profit model and let the individual companies they own take care of the rest. The individual companies owned by the conglomerate don't diversify; the diversification takes place at a higher corporate level where day-to-day usual modes of operation aren't as critical to success.

	Existing Products	New Products
Existing Markets	Market Penetration (low risk)	Product Development (medium risk)
New Markets	Market Development (medium risk)	Diversification (high risk)

FIGURE 10-5: Ansoff's opportunity matrix.

WARNING

Proceeding without understanding which quadrant you're choosing in the Ansoff matrix may expose you to significantly more risk than you realize you're taking on. This is often the case with start-up companies that have a product that looks revolutionary and requires simultaneously developing both a new market and a new type of product.

Porter's five forces in competition

Porter's five forces is another strategic tool that allows you to evaluate where your risks are. (Flip to Chapter 6 for a full description of this tool.) Using Porter's five forces is critical for understanding how vulnerable you are to the competition, your buyers, and your suppliers — and from what direction the challenge will come. Fill in the five cells in Table 10-1 under "Porter's five forces" with the answers to the questions you developed in Chapter 6. Then you can plan how to counteract these threats.

Collecting all strategy information in one place

When all the strategic analysis is in place, gather all the information into Table 10-1 filling in the placement, opportunities and challenges column on the right-hand side. This information is important as you plan and document your market strategy. Read what you have written when you are done and look for common threads, areas to avoid competing, areas where you have more strengths and opportunities. Discuss your findings with your boss or mentor to see what additional insights they have. This exercise provides you with the strategic thinking and background to make great decisions. It also positions you as the internal expert on the market and strategy for your product or product line with your team.

TABLE 10-1 **Strategy Modeling Results Table**

Strategic Model	Sub-classification within strategic model	Your placement/opportunities/challenges
Ansoff's matrix		
BCG matrix		
Product life cycle		

(continued)

TABLE 10-1 *(continued)*

Strategic Model	Sub-classification within strategic model	Your placement/opportunities/ challenges
	Marketing objective	
	Competition	
	Product	
	Price	
	Promotion	
	Place (Distribution)	
Chasm model		
Porter's five forces		
	Bargaining power of customers	
	Bargaining power of suppliers	
	Threat of substitutes	
	Threat of new entrants	
	Intensity of competitive rivalry	

Considering Other Components of Marketing Strategy

Many factors go into your market strategy, from what you call the product to how you price it and beyond. The following sections cover important marketing strategy concepts that you should be aware of.

Whole product offering

Chapter 1 discusses the *whole product offering*, a concept is built around the idea that customers buy your product not only because of its intrinsic features and their associated customer benefits but also because of the augmented product features like service, support, and financing. As a product manager you own the overall success of your product and are most likely the only one looking at the whole product offer to make sure it fits with your customer strategy, and your product and brand promise. Your responsibility is to influence all parties in your company to ensure the whole product offer is compelling and consistent with your strategy.

Brand promise

A *brand* is a promise of benefits. It may consist of word(s), image, and supporting tagline. Try this. Close your eyes and think of Nike. What image comes to mind? What is the tagline? What emotions does it elicit? Now try the same thing with Coca-Cola, Apple, and Tesla.

In each case, you register a core promise that you believe the products sold by these companies would deliver if you used them. That is the power of brand. Now close your eyes again. Say your company name. What image, thought, belief, and feelings come to mind? Is that what your customers think about your company? Is that what you want them to think about your company?

A *product promise* is the implicit assurance that you're making to your customers about the experience and benefits they'll gain from purchasing or using your product. If your promise is ease of use and your whole product offering fails to deliver it, whether your product has the right features won't matter. Your customer may be very unhappy.

TIP

Later in this chapter, we also discuss positioning. The relationship between a brand and positioning depends on whether a product falls under a known brand or is defining or redefining the brand.

>> **Known brand:** The Coke brand defines the positioning for Diet Coke. It's Coke without the sugar. The Coke brand speeds up the customer's understanding of the Diet Coke positioning.

>> **Undefined/redefined brand:** A few years ago, the Tesla brand was unknown. Now, with more electric cars on the road and people's increasing familiarity with Tesla, the positioning of Tesla as a provider of advanced electric cars has created brand awareness the company now uses to offer new products such as solar batteries for industrial and home use.

Pricing

The most important factor in setting your price is determining how it fits into your overall strategy. Are you a luxury brand, in which case you may want to set your price very high to convey the fact that your brand is very exclusive and that not everyone can afford it? Are you a low-cost brand like Walmart, in which case, you want to keep your price low and sell on volume?

Pricing is a critical success factor for your product. Set your price too high, and you may stall or kill initial sales and create a perception in the market that your product is overpriced. On the flip side, if you set your price too low, you may be leaving profits on the table, and your product may be perceived as inferior because the price is so low compared to some competitors.

You can approach pricing in two primary ways:

>> **Cost plus:** What a product costs, plus a markup. This internal method of focusing on pricing doesn't really take into account what the value is to the customer, but it's a way to ensure the profit that you desire for each unit of the product that is sold.

>> **Value-based:** What is the product worth to customers? Are you solving a big problem that they have or providing them with something that they really want? How can you tell? How much is it worth to the customer independent of the cost to provide the service? Determining value-based pricing is very complex. For the rest of this section, we will give examples of scenarios that help you analyze your own situation. A general rule is that you break down each piece of the additional value that you provide over and above today's solutions and then calculate what the total adds up to. Then you test it with various audiences to see what happens when customers are faced with a buying decision at that price. Another great piece of advice is to bring in a pricing expert.

Here's a simple value pricing example. You take a small child to a petting zoo, and she wants to feed the goats. You put a quarter in the goat food dispenser. From a pricing perspective, there is the cost of the goat food — about two cents. Then there is the amazing value you get from watching your child grinning as she feeds the goats. You take pictures. It's so cute. Okay, what was that worth? $5? $10? You're going to show this picture at her wedding reception 20 years from now, right? $100? The petting zoo charges you 25 cents. It's a deal. The petting zoo is most likely using cost–plus based pricing, when it could charge a much higher amount because the value of that particular moment is very high for parents.

Now, think of your product and the problem it solves or what it provides to the customer. Does the customer get to go home earlier at night? Does she not worry about her work so much? If you sell security software to an IT manager who is then able to manage the software more easily and work shorter hours, then the value to her may be very high. What value does your product provide? It isn't in a list of features; it's in the benefits (often defined in emotional terms) that your product provides to your customers. How much is each benefit worth compared to what the customer does now?

Pricing based on market position

The fundamentals of pricing are based in how your product is perceived in the market. Are you a market leader with a differentiated product? If so, your price most likely sets the benchmark for the market. All other products will be valued against yours. If you have a less dominant position, you may find that lowering the price below that of the market leader is the only way to compete. If you have a specialized niche, you may be able to charge even more than the usual rate because the value is so much more. For example, think of products for the military. If your company builds products that can handle harsh conditions such as extreme heat and sandy environments and there aren't that many specialized suppliers of the product, the military is going to be willing to pay you a higher price.

Pricing based on quality

In Figure 10-6, *Kotler's pricing strategy model* offers another way to look at your pricing choices by comparing the quality of your product offering and its price. Each of these may be low, medium, or high. If you have a high-quality product and offer it at a medium price, then you have a *high-value strategy.* Your customers will feel great because they have a great product at a reasonable price; this situation may lead to a longer-term relationship with them. However, if you charge a lot and the quality of your offering is low, you're using what's called a *rip-off strategy.* If you're selling low-quality products in an airport with lots of transient tourists, chances are you'll get away with it. If you want repeat customers, the rip-off isn't a great long-term pricing strategy. Above all, understand where you want to be, be consistent with your pricing strategy in all that you do, and, if it isn't working, deliberately and carefully move to another position in the pricing strategy table.

	High Price	Medium Price	Low Price
High Quality	Premium Strategy	High-value Strategy	Superb-value Strategy
Medium Quality	Over-charging Strategy	Average Strategy	Good-value Strategy
Low Quality	Rip-off Strategy	False-economy Strategy	Economy Strategy

FIGURE 10-6: Kotler's pricing strategies.

Which price and where?

When you create a product, you're often not the one selling it directly to customers. Customers are often getting it from resellers who buy from distributors. Each step along the chain between the producer and the consumer takes a cut of the money that eventually comes from the customer. Table 10-2 shows you what this pricing stack looks like for a 25-pound bag of goat food.

TABLE 10-2   **Pricing Stack through Distribution**

Goat Food Distribution Chain	Margin = (Selling Price – Cost)/Selling Price
Goat food manufacturer manufactures for $2.00.	
Manufacturer sells it to goat food distributor for $4.00.	100% for manufacturer
Distributor sells it to local agricultural reseller for $4.80.	20% for distributor
Reseller sells it to customer for $10.00.	52% for reseller

The numbers in the table may be overly generous (margins are dependent on the specific market and type of products), but they make it easier to see where the profits go. In reality, the following is true for our goat food example:

>> **Manufacturers:** Goat food is a commodity. You get low margins on commodity products because a competitor can offer the same thing at a lower price. In the end, each manufacturer just scrapes by.

>> **Distributors:** Distributors typically make about 10 percent margin. They operate efficient transport centers and try to hold onto any product in their centers for as little time as possible. They may even have terms and conditions that ensure any unsold product can be sold back to the manufacturer for slightly less than they paid for it.

>> **Resellers:** Resellers often do mark up prices quite a bit (in Table 10-2, the reseller markup ((selling price-cost)/cost) is over 100 percent). They have to pay for the product up front and then may hold onto it for some time before a customer buys it. They have costs for their storefront, employees, and so on. Sometimes they have to write off damaged products that can't be sold at a loss. Another factor to keep in mind: Customers who buy a lot of a product will ask for a discount. The reseller needs to keep enough margin in reserve to make the end customer feel good with a 25 percent discount and still make money.

As a product manager, you need to understand not only your price but also the price up and down the line of your distribution channel — and in some detail. What margins can each channel partner accept and still have a viable business? If you don't know it today, go and do this research. You'll need it soon enough.

Additional pricing guidelines

Pricing is a very complicated topic, and entire books have been written about it. We are only covering a small amount of what is a very important topic. There are a few additional considerations we recommend as you're determining your price:

>> Read additional *For Dummies* content about pricing in an article at www.dummies.com/business/start-a-business/business-models/ten-pricing-models-to-help-raise-margins/.

>> Remember that it's virtually impossible to raise your price after the product has been released. The market will rarely accept it. The opposite, however, is true. You can always lower your price if need be.

>> Most pricing decisions are made on a gut-feeling basis. By applying some strategic thinking you'll be ahead of many companies as well as your competitors.

Segmentation

Segmenting your audience means you divide your customers into groups depending on the attributes (common needs, interests, and priorities) they collectively share. Chapter 5 provides more detail on segmentation. In developing your market strategy, your segmentation provides a target for each positioning statement and the messaging platform top of the positioning. If you don't know which segment you are speaking to, you can't complete your market strategy — and get the targeted customer to purchase your product.

Positioning

A common positioning phrase is "My product's position is X," but *positioning* actually refers to what the product means in the mind of the customer. For example, Heineken sells beer in the Netherlands (its home country) as well as in the United States. If you buy Heineken in the United States, you pay more for it because it's positioned as a premium export beer. U.S. customers treat themselves to Heineken. In the Netherlands, Heineken is an everyday beer — much like Budweiser is in the States. Dutch customers don't pay more for Heineken. The liquid in the bottle is the same in both places. The only difference is its worth in the mind of the U.S. versus Dutch consumer.

Positioning is a powerful tool. It's the base on which all your product decisions — your marketing, your development, your sales channels, all of it — will be based. Figure 10-7 shows that the positioning supports the key messages, which are then used to create all the marketing and sales enablement material known as *marketing artifacts*. See the sidebar on these particular marketing artifacts in this chapter. Chapter 15 covers marketing artifacts or collateral in more detail.

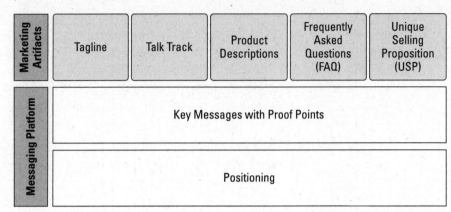

	Tagline	Talk Track	Product Descriptions	Frequently Asked Questions (FAQ)	Unique Selling Proposition (USP)

Key Messages with Proof Points

Positioning

FIGURE 10-7: From positioning to marketing artifacts.

If you don't know the position that you want your product to occupy in your target segment's mind, you're going to find it tough to create the messaging, proof points, and then the marketing artifacts. Read on to find out how to decide on your product's position.

Positioning format

For each segment of your market, you should develop a positioning statement. Here is the format to use:

> For [target customer] who [statement of the need or opportunity], the [product name] is a [product category] that [statement of key benefit/compelling reason to buy].

> Unlike [primary competitive alternative], our product [statement of primary differentiation].

A good positioning statement can take a lot of time and effort. Here is a positioning statement example for a fictitious high-end department store named Grexper (short for Great Experience).

> "For trend-conscious, upper-middle class shoppers who are looking for high-end products, Grexper is a fashion-focused department store that provides a unique, comprehensive, and exciting shopping experience.

> Unlike other department stores, Grexper provides personalized service in a compelling shopping environment."

Creating powerful positioning statements

Creating a positioning statement can more accurately be called crafting a positioning statement because it's usually a repetitive and creative process. You write one draft, edit it, and put it away for a day. You edit it again and then have some-one look at it and discuss every point. Tweak it a bit. Then show it to a larger audience.

Here are a few questions to answer before you start creating a positioning statement:

>> Who are you (as a company)?

>> What business are you in?

>> Who are your target customers?

>> What are your target customers' (key) needs?

>> Who are your competitors?

>> What unique benefit(s) do you offer compared with your competitor?

One useful tool is to compare your products to the competition on an *x-y* axis chart. Figure 10-8 shows a blank format for you to play with. It's up to you to develop the names on each axis, but common choices include performance, func-tionality, and ease of use. The names should reflect the various axes on which customers decide between different products in your market.

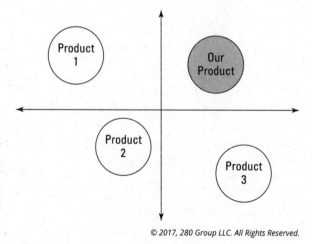

© 2017, 280 Group LLC. All Rights Reserved.

FIGURE 10-8:
Blank four-quadrant
positioning
matrix.

Once your four quadrant positioning is complete, you can use the names of the axes and the relative position of each of the companies or products to complete the competitive comparison part at the end of the positioning statement. Using Figure 10-9, a positioning statement draft would be

"For the value focused customer who is looking for a range of clothing and house-hold goods, Kohls provides . . . .

Unlike other full-range department stores, Kohls' products have low prices every day."

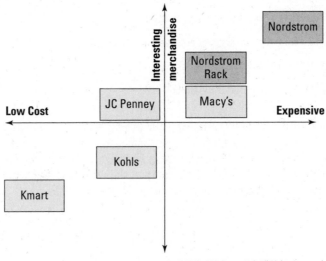

FIGURE 10-9:
FIGURE 10-9: Four-quadrant positioning for U.S. department stores.

TIP

Avoid the following missteps while creating your positioning statement:

>> Is it too vague?

>> Is it focused on features rather than benefits? (This complaint is the number one item we hear in people's first efforts.)

>> Is it too narrow, such that few customers will identify with the product?

>> Is it too broad; does it claim too many benefits?

>> Is it difficult to believe?

And when you're critically reviewing the positioning statement, see whether it satisfies the following criteria:

>> It's memorable, motivating, and focused on the target market.

>> It's believable to your target market coming from your company.

>> Your brand can own it. You can develop a competitive advantage, which will help your company grow.

>> Customers can decide to buy or not on the basis of the positioning.

TIP

Classical music buffs close their eyes to more deeply listen to the music. You can do the same thing when you're listening to a positioning statement. As someone else reads it, listen for the benefits. Benefits "feel" different from features and answer the question of "What's in it for me?" If you have a feature-laden positioning statement, the emotional sense will be the same as reading a phone book: nothing. If, however, you have benefits at the core of your positioning statement, they'll resonate at some emotional level.

Why is this so important? Because people don't buy because of facts. Do you buy a car because it has brakes, air bags, and a sun roof? No, you buy a car because you want your family to be safe and have a fun driving experience. If you have the benefits in place, the rest of the marketing communication naturally pulls these stories out and causes your customers to want to buy your product.

Naming your product

Your product name needs to support your positioning and match your messaging (see the next section for more on messaging). Choosing a product name is one of the most critical success factors for your product. Finding a name that is available and meets all of the possible criteria is challenging, but a necessary task.

Following are the criteria you want to consider when choosing a name:

>> Memorable.

>> Easy to pronounce/not confusing.

>> Available worldwide after doing full trademark search.

>> Has website URL available.

>> Is three syllables or fewer (otherwise, people will make up an acronym or shortened name of their own).

>> Inoffensive and doesn't convey negative aspects in foreign languages/countries that matter. The classic case is the car called the Chevrolet Nova; in Spanish, *no va* means "doesn't go," which doesn't exactly inspire confidence in an automobile.

>> Doesn't confuse customers with a competitive product (otherwise, they may purchase the competitive offering).

- >> Clarifies things for the customer:
  - Describes what the product does.
  - Conveys a benefit.
  - Provides immediate and compelling reason to buy it.
  - Describes who should buy it.
- >> Creates both logical and emotional appeal.

Alternatively, you can use a name that is a unique word or concept unto itself and conveys some intrigue, emotional appeal, or logical connection. Examples here are Excel, iPod, Acrobat, Zune, Tivo, and Napster. However, this approach requires an immense amount of marketing and negates many of the benefits of the criteria listed previously.

Messaging

Positioning is the base of your marketing efforts. However, it's too abstract to build marketing artifacts on. And build you will. In Chapter 14, your marketing programs and the corresponding collateral, web content, and product demos take form on the basis of your positioning and messaging as you present your product to the world.

At this point in time, you want to make sure that you have a customer-oriented story worth telling. The method for breaking the positioning statements into workable chunks it to create *messaging statements*. Each messaging statement will then have associated *proof points*. The proof points are where your customer case studies and features come into play.

TIP

Be prepared when someone — typically sales, marketing or anyone in management — asks you for your "messaging." As shown in Figure 10-7, they mean your messaging platform. A messaging platform is built on a base of your positioning statements and then expanded with more detail with fully blown out messaging statements and proof points for each of the messaging statements.

Unlike the positioning statement, messaging statements don't have a particular format. Here are a couple of examples from the Grexper positioning statement that may help you get started. The top level is a messaging statement and the bullets underneath each are proof points.

1. Grexper stores are exciting and different places to visit and shop.

   - Pianos are playing.

   - Clothes are laid out in a manner like designer clothes stores.

2. Shopping at Grexper means that we've done the hard work to make sure that you can find everything you want in one place.

   - Grexper offers a wide selection of hard-to-find but unique merchandise.

   - Grexper shoppers actively seek out up-and-coming designers as well as established middle-range designers.

   - Each department ensures that the offerings are comprehensive in terms of a head-to-toe clothing offering and the equivalent in other departments.

3. Grexper ensures that each shopper feels special with his or her unique needs identified and catered to.

   - The children's shoe department has lots of highly experienced staff so that children don't have to wait long to be served.

   - Individual sales representatives have named business cards.

Now it's your turn. Start with your positioning statement. Break it into individual, benefit-focused messaging statements.

TIP

You may find that you start listing features rather than benefits as your messaging statements. Use the "which means that" trick. For example, "pianos are playing" is a feature, not a benefit. To get to the benefit, add "which means that" and fill in the answer:

> Pianos are playing, which means that the stores are exciting and different places to visit and shop.

Now you've got the first messaging statement from the example.

Experiment with a few messaging statements and list at least one or two proof points for each one. Put this first draft away for a day or so. Come back to it with fresh eyes and start revising.

At the second check, answer the following questions: Do the benefit statements have an emotional aspect that a customer can describe back to you? Are the proof points in the right place? There are no rules, so you can put a given proof point under more than one messaging statement if necessary, but keep this practice to an absolute minimum.

MARKETING ARTIFACTS

Marketing artifacts are marketing pieces that tell the product or marketing or product story to a particular audience or in a particular circumstance. In Figure 10-7, we mention five different marketing artifacts. These are by no means the only marketing artifacts. There are a lot more in Chapters 14 and 15. Here is a description of each of the five:

- **Tagline**: This is a very brief and memorable statement of the product's value for the customer. It should be just a few words that identify the product and a compelling reason to buy.

- **Talk Track**: An expanded version of an *elevator pitch*. An elevator pitch is your product story that can be told in the time it takes an elevator to travel ten stories. The talk track is the next part of the conversation in which a sales person breaks down each of the product benefits and then provides one to three proof points of each benefit.

- **Product descriptions**: Chapter 14 has more details on how to develop these 25-, 50-, 100-, 200-, and 250-word descriptions of your product.

- **Frequently asked questions (FAQ)**: Often made available to customers online so that the customer can answer their own questions without any personal involvement from the company. More about this in Chapter 14.

- **Unique selling proposition (USP)**: This is a short description of what makes your company and/or product different from any other in the marketplace. Yes, any other company or product. If you don't have a unique selling proposition, customers don't know why they should choose you instead of your competitor.

Putting Your Market Strategy in Writing

When you've collected the information in the earlier sections of this chapter, the next step is to document your market strategy so that you can get agreement from all parts of the organization. Table 10-3 lists the key elements of the market strategy document. In addition to these sections, you also fill in the risks, assumptions, open issues, and, of course, your conclusion and recommendations.

The following sections cover just how to fill out each portion of Table 10-3.

TABLE 10-3   **Market Strategy Document Outline**

Section	Description
Executive summary	A summary of the entire market strategy.
Whole product offer	What is the whole product offer? Which components of the actual product and augmented product are most critical?
Pricing	What is the proposed price of the product? What is the strategy and rationale for setting this price? If it's too far in advance, do any pricing boundary conditions need to be met, such as margin or cost? What happens if these boundary conditions aren't met?
Segmentation	Which are the target market segments that the product addresses? Why are these segments the best fit for your product or solution?
Positioning	What is the overall product positioning? Are there additional positions for channel partners?
Messaging	On the basis of the positioning, what are the key messages? If you don't have all the proof points, put in what you have now and build on it in subsequent versions.
Strategy	What is your strategy for taking this product to market? In what way are you the leader? And how does this strategy align with your company's overall strategy and market position?
Launch programs	What are your top-line launch programs and initiatives? What are the key launch milestones?
Budget	How much is the likely cost to successfully bring the product to market? This figure isn't product development cost; it's the marketing and sales costs.

Part I: Executive summary

Complete this section after completing all other sections of your market strategy document. This section should be brief — no more than one page. You can treat it as a stand-alone document. Explain the "why," "what," "where," "who," and "when" of your approach to the market for your product.

You should have separate paragraphs for the following topics:

>> **Overall strategy:** Based on the current situation, objectives, and budget, what is the overall recommended strategy? What will generate the most demand? What will create the most value in the customer's mind? What will differentiate the product from its competitors?

>> **Objectives:** State the key objectives the market strategy plan will achieve. These should be in direct support of the product and/or company objectives and should contain some quantifiable metrics. One example is to achieve 10 percent market share and $100 million in revenue. Another example is to be perceived as the technological market leader.

>> **Risks:** What are the risks with your chosen approach? Do you have resources missing, or are you stretching the company too thin among all the projects under consideration?

>> **Recommendation:** What is your overall recommendation?

Part II: Whole product offer

Briefly describe the value the product brings to your customers as benefits of each of the features. Add in the augmented features such as warranty, support programs, installation, standards, and any additional software and hardware. (Head to Chapter 1 for a more complete discussion of augmented features.)

List a few key features as they address the problems that your customers have. Refer to Chapter 11 for more on both these concepts.

TIP

One of the biggest mistakes that product managers make is to describe the features of the product but not convey why customers should care about them. For example, most customers couldn't care less that a product runs on the Linux operating system. However, if you relate this feature to a benefit and state that the product "runs on the Linux operating system so that you can be assured of a high level of security," customers know what is in it for them and why it matters.

What is a key theme for this product? Security? Performance? And how is that valuable to the customer?

REMEMBER

Often, the terms *product* and *solution* are used interchangeably. The reason is that a product should provide a solution to a customer problem. Sometimes, the term *solution* in fact refers to several products that together provide a more important and valuable solution. Market strategy documents are often created to explain a solution and the products that are needed to support that solution, and then each product is defined in its own market needs and product description document (Chapter 11). Common sense is needed to make sure that the right story is told at the right level.

Briefly describe how the product or solution identified aligns and supports the company's vision, mission, and strategy. How does this whole product offering take advantage of the company's core competencies to create a unique and sustainable competitive advantage?

Does this product release or version create an end-of-life decision for an older version of the product or for a different product? If so, a separate end-of-life plan needs to be written. Chapter 16 has details on retiring products and end-of-life plans.

Part III: Pricing

Refer to the "Pricing" section in this chapter to describe your pricing model and strategy. What are the parameters that impact price? List and briefly describe the assumptions underlying the pricing targets. What are the objectives of your pricing strategy?

List all major product configurations to be offered. What is the manufacturer's suggested retail price (MSRP), also known as *list price,* and expected *street price* (actual price that customers purchase a product for)? What are the channel discounts?

TECHNICAL STUFF

The trick with street price is actually determining how to calculate it. It can vary by channel, region, and country. For example, the street price of gas is affected by state and local taxes (which can vary dramatically), costs to get the gas to more remote locations, and a host of other factors, so customers pay different street prices in different locations. The simple workaround to get to a street price estimate is to choose a typical discount off of MSRP. Depending on your industry, this default street price may be 5 to 25 percent lower than an MSRP. In most places, the original supplier of a product can't fix the final price of a product to a customer without serious legal problems. That's called *price fixing* and carries stiff legal penalties.

WHAT ON EARTH IS A PORTFOLIO?

A *portfolio* of products is officially all the products that a company offers. For product managers, the most common use for a portfolio is to describe a set of products that are related to each other in some way — for example, low-end, mid-range, and high-end versions of the same product. There is a relationship among the three of them in terms of price and features. The following figure is an example of how portfolios are explained to customers.

	Low-end product	Mid-range product	High-end product
Feature 1	✓	✓	✓
Feature 2	✓	✓	✓
Feature 3		✓	✓
Feature 4			✓
Feature 5			✓

Part IV: Segmentation

Segmentation (which we discuss in Chapter 5) is a critically important part of your market strategy. In this section, you describe the segmentation strategy for the company, and how it supports selling your product to your chosen market segments. By answering these questions, you clarify who you are selling to and how, very specifically, they buy your product. Use your segmentation information to answer the following questions:

>> Does your product/solution target a niche, or does your solution provide coverage for everyone in the market? As an example, if you open a fast food restaurant, you could target a niche market with vegan food or provide coverage for almost anyone and anywhere the way McDonalds does. Does the company have a full portfolio of products the way a department store provides bedding products at a range of prices, or does it specialize in specific segments like high end bedding boutiques?

>> What are the size and growth attributes of the given market segments?

>> How does each target market segment buy? Do customers buy direct or through a channel? If so, which channel partners are best to reach your target markets?

>> Is the buying cycle seasonal? If so, describe it. What is the average length of the sales cycle (more about this in Chapter 15)? What are the key selection criteria for the sales decision? Are there any deal killers in being able to complete the sale?

>> Is the buying decision made by a technical decision maker, a financial/ business decision maker, the channel representative, or outside consultants? Check out Chapters 5 and 11 for more information about defining different kinds of decision makers.

These are hard questions to answer well. When you do get answers, you may uncover a lot of problems in actually getting your product in the hands of customers. These issues are much easier to address the earlier you uncover them.

Part V: Positioning

Place your positioning statement in this section. Make sure you include information on

>> Whether you're leveraging off an existing brand or creating a brand with your offering

>> Whether the company is going to be a product leader, a low-cost leader, or a customer-satisfaction leader

TIP

If this offering is part of a portfolio of products, describe how it will be positioned relative to the portfolio.

Part VI: Messaging

Put the messaging that you developed earlier in this chapter here. Make sure your messages clearly differentiate your product from competitors' offerings and messages. Make sure the messaging in this section covers all of your critical audiences, including customers, the channel, and press and analysts.

>> **Customers**: Include the messages that highlight the value proposition, positioning, features and benefits, and product differentiation.

>> **Channel partners**: Include specific channel-oriented messages that articulate the value proposition and how your channel partners can be successful with their customers. Can they use your offering to differentiate themselves from their competitors?

>> **Press and analysts:** List specific messages for the media. These external messages should be focused on differentiation and relevancy.

For each of your audiences, create a very brief statement about your offer. It needs to be clear, concise, and memorable. It should answer the following questions:

>> What is your competitive advantage?

>> Who is behind the company?

>> What is your revenue model?

>> What is your product or service?

>> Who is your target market?

>> Who is your competition?

Part VII: Strategy

Using the strategic tools in this chapter, you can explain why you've made certain choices and why you have made the product, segmentation, and messaging decision that you have. Then fill in the details about how you'll actually achieve what you've planned.

Marketing objectives

When you have the strategic context documented, describe your marketing objectives. Marketing objectives should be high level (for example, "build awareness among X target audience," "drive upgrades among loyal users," and so on). They should contain at least one or two quantifiable metrics (such as "increase market awareness from X to Y percent" or "proliferate X trials/downloads worldwide"). Your best bet is to keep the total number of objectives at three to five so that the direction is clear and not overly complicated.

Communications strategy

Briefly describe the communication strategies for all parties. Given your current situation, objectives, budget, and target audience, what is the overall recommended strategy? For example, if you have a limited budget, you may focus more on viral programs or online marketing versus expensive activities like trade shows or print advertising. If applicable, include the communications strategies of your channel and partners in your communication strategy.

If you already have a loyal customer base, you may focus on strong upgrade promotions or "tell a friend" campaigns. You can assign different approaches to different audience segments if that's helpful.

Sustainable leadership

Describe why your overall strategy will allow you to create a sustainable leadership position in the market. This should be supported by the overall positioning and development activities, and should be in line with the marketing objectives and strategy.

Company performance claims

Describe the high-level corporate and product marketing objectives. How do objectives map to high-level business goals? Describe the short- and long-term objectives. They should be in direct support of the product/company objectives, which you can also state here.

Barriers to entry

Describe the barriers to entry the company can create that work against competitive forces. Identify barriers that are already in place to support the company's competitive position. Some typical barriers include high capital, marketing, and/or shipping costs; tariff barriers and quotas; brand recognition and consumer acceptance; and government regulation and patents.

Part VIII: Launch programs and activities

Briefly summarize the anticipated launch activities (see Chapter 14) and programs associated with this product. What are the main channels for marketing communications (see Chapter 15)? Some possibilities include the following:

» Blogs

» Press

» Advertising

» Direct mail and email blasts

Make sure to answer the question, "Why are we choosing these particular communication vehicles over other options?"

List both short-term (6-to-12-month) and long-term (12-to-18-month) marketing milestones such as retaining, acquiring and growing the customer base. Focus on marketing goals. Describe how the effort aligns with the overall company's marketing and business goals.

Part IX: Budget

List the overall budget for major programs and metrics. This figure will be used to validate estimates given in the business case in the sections on marketing and sales expenditures. Take your budget estimates from your business plan in Chapter 9.

Part X: Concluding sections

In this section, you provide a risk analysis, assumptions, open issues, and finally conclusion and recommendation sections.

» **Risk analysis:** Identify the key barriers that may impede the market strategy's objectives and how likely they are (for example, low, medium, or high) to affect your company. How will you overcome these barriers? Keep your answers brief.

» **Assumptions:** List any assumptions made in this document.

» **Open issues:** Track any open issues during the creation of this document. When the issue is resolved, document it. Any unresolved issues should be assigned to a responsible party.

» **Conclusion:** State your conclusion and the justification of the recommendation. This section should include the likely effect of following your proposals.

Chapter **11**

Developing a Plan: Market Needs, Product Description, and Road Maps

Transforming a customer's need into a product is the basis of product management. It's an exciting process that offers great rewards. Along the way you can encounter breakthroughs and challenges. In this chapter, you discover how to successfully document your market needs, work with product development to translate a need into a product description, and lay out the future of the product with a road map.

Uncovering Market Need and Creating Product Feature Descriptions

Any tension between product management and engineering is often traced to whether the discussion is taking place in the problem space (where product managers focus) or the solution space (which engineers and many others find to be more comfortable). The terms used to describe issues changes depending on what the focus of the conversation and discussion is. Here is a clarification of the terminology and how it can help your team work more effectively simply by choosing the right words.

The problem space

A *market need* is a customer-oriented and clearly articulated understanding of the problem a customer needs to solve. It's also often referred to as a *customer need* or *customer requirement* and *market requirement.* For the purposes of this chapter, we will use the term *market need* to mean all four terms.

The solution space

A *product feature description* is an explanation of a feature or features in your product that will address one or more of the market needs. Again, the following terms are often used interchangeably: *feature, product feature,* and *product requirement.* For this chapter, we will use the term *product feature* to describe something that is part of the solution space.

WARNING

The issue with the word *requirement* is that it can be used in both the problem and solution space. If your company uses the term *requirement,* use either *customer/market requirement* or *product requirement.* In addition, the term *feature* is often used instead of *product feature.* This can sometimes lead to features being confused with what the customer wants. Select words that specifically indicate that you are in either the problem or the solution space and insist that others in your team follow the same convention.

Comparing market needs and product features

To clarify market needs versus product features, here is an example:

> A salesperson has a need to quickly and easily be able to dial the top three people in a major account she manages. She calls them all several times per week, often from the car or while on the move. She doesn't want to have to look them up in the contacts in her smartphone.

The market need is "call the three most important people in my major account easily." Giving the product development department a well-constructed market need rather than a product feature is very important. Your engineers often come up with something that is far more creative than what they'd create if you just offered up a product feature such as "have the top three contacts at a major account on speed dial."

Some product features that may meet this need include the following:

>> Show a list of favorites, including people she calls frequently, so she can tap once to see the list and then tap once on the person's name to dial the call.

>> Allow her to add the three people from the major account easily to her speed dial list so she can use speed dial.

>> Have the smartphone suggest creating a new speed dial group with these three people after she's called them a certain number of times.

By stating market needs rather than communicating product features, you gain lots of benefits as a product manager:

>> Harnessing the creativity and brilliance of your engineers

>> Fostering more of a team spirit with your engineers

>> Ensuring that people understand the importance of their roles and feel valued in what they contribute

>> Coming up with better solutions for your customers

>> Being perceived as a product leader who can influence without formal authority without having to come across as being dictatorial

WARNING

In some engineering teams, delivering only market needs isn't an effective strategy. If a group doesn't have a sense of teamwork with product management, or your company has a culture of engineers not wanting to take ownership for deciding product features or simply believing that features should be delivered by product managers, you may have to define specific features for them. In this case, expect to provide the product features and even write a detailed product description to support each feature.

TIP

One approach for helping foster creativity while providing guidance is to state the market need and then provide one or two potential product feature descriptions that would solve the problem. With these as guidelines, you can challenge your team to come up with something even better that will meet the market need. This way, you're giving them more guidance but aren't coming across as telling them exactly what they must do.

For any particular product, a market need and a product feature don't necessarily correlate one to one. The relationship is closer to that in Figure 11-1. Market needs 1 and 3 are resolved by feature 2. Market need 3 also needs product feature 4 to be complete. Don't expect to have one market need be solved neatly by one product feature.

FIGURE 11-1: Relationship between market needs and product features.

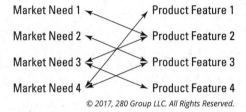

Keeping discussions clear

In the world of market needs and product features, clear terminology can make sure that you and your team are on the same page. It's a relief to know that simply agreeing what certain words refer to can solve so many problems.

TIP

One of the frequent statements that the 280 Group hears from organizations is "We don't know how to write effective requirements." Usually, the underlying problem isn't that they can't write down what's needed but that until the language itself is untangled and closely defined, resolving the requirements-writing issue is tough. Sometimes, they forget that words are a poor substitute for images and, more critically, discussions.

In Figure 11-2, you see the effect of poorly defined and poorly understood requirements — both customer and product. The longer the misunderstanding continues, the higher the probability that the possible solution delivered won't meet market needs.

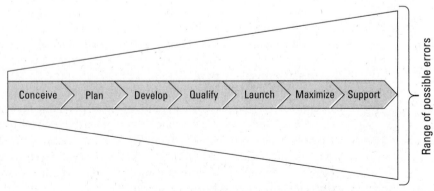

FIGURE 11-2: Requirements errors over time.

Documenting Market Needs

Documenting market needs is the first step in communication and negotiations with product development. If you skip this step, you're at a significant disadvantage when working with product development. The documentation of market needs keeps you on track, providing a road map of where the product begins and ends. Then you'll be able to tell if you've gone off route sooner rather than later.

Questioning why "why" is so important

Simon Sinek writes and talks about leadership and management. One of his great ideas is keep to the reason "why" you are doing something top of mind at all times. Figure 11-3 illustrates this simple, powerful concept.

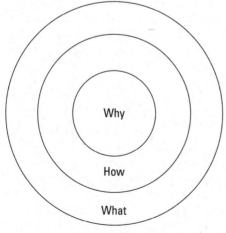

FIGURE 11-3: The golden circle of starting with "why."

© 2017, 280 Group LLC. All Rights Reserved.

Here's a breakdown of how starting with "why" translates to product management:

>> **Why:** The core of what motivates people is the purpose, the central belief, and the reason your organization exists. For a product manager, the "why" translates into the real driving vision — the reason the customer will find the product offering and solution so compelling.

>> **How:** Around that core belief and meaning is the "how." What's the special way your company and your product can deliver value?

>> **What:** And then you have exactly "what" (the products and services) you deliver.

Companies that have a strong "why" often have much better stock market valuations and an easier time of making decisions on a meaningful basis. Their product strategies and long-term success are often far greater than their competitors. And everyone on the team is more likely to be on the same page.

Your understanding of market needs protects you from wavering from solving the actual problems that your customer has. It's your guiding light that gives you direction in the middle of the day-to-day discussions that may otherwise consume all your energy and cause you to lose focus on your original purpose. What is your why? What is your company's why?

GETTING THE SKINNY ON MRDS AND PRDS

The market needs document is also known as the market requirements document (MRD). The MRD has historically been used in waterfall and phase-gate development processes rather than Agile and is designed to capture a deep description of the market needs that customers have. In many Agile cases, a short MRD is an effective way to capture and understand the market needs before diving into writing user stories and cranking out features in the product backlog as fast as possible.

The MRD is accompanied by the product requirements document (PRD). Oftentimes, the company is so excited and pressured to create the product rapidly that many organizations do away with the MRD and jump right to the PRD (or, in the case of Agile, simply put together a list of product features as a backlog, write user stories, and start developing the product without discussions or a deep understanding). The PRD includes a section to explain why the customer needs the product. If you aren't going to produce an MRD or a PRD, make sure that you at least have an in-depth discussion and get agreement with your team about the "why" of the product, what the true market needs are, and how the product features will solve that need. You'll have much greater product and career success as a result.

Gathering the necessary information

Developing a market need involves collecting information that gives the context of the problem, who experiences it and when the experience occurs. Four key components that you need to understand thoroughly in terms of market needs are

>> Personas

>> Problem scenarios

>> Customer journey/workflow

>> Market needs statements

Creating personas

The idea is to begin with the customer in mind, and the most common method is to define the personas that your product interacts with. Check out Chapter 5 for a full discussion of personas. For the purposes of this chapter, you just need to know that personas are archetypes of people that share similar characteristics. Table 11-1 shows how to define a persona. Figure 11-4 includes a completed user persona.

TABLE 11-1 **Information Needed for Creating Personas**

Persona attribute	Attribute explanation	Example
Name	Name each persona.	Fred
Role	What is the persona's role in the product purchase decision?	User, buyer, influencer
Goal	What problem is the persona trying to solve that your product provides some or all resolution to?	Enter data for manager to track work
Background	What is the persona's background that informs how it reacts to your product?	Earns $/year, college educated
Attitude	What is the persona's attitude toward the product or actions that you're asking it to take?	Intimidated by new technology
Behavior	What is the persona's observable behavior with respect to your product offering?	Reluctantly uses iPhone; scared of Android phones
Insight	Do you have any other insights into the persona's reaction to your product that hasn't been covered elsewhere?	Feels stressed when out of control

Characteristic	Description
Quote	• With my iPhone I should no longer need to carry a laptop
Goals	• Quick and painless input of his sales data to satisfy management • Access to customer account information with minimum disruption to his job
Role	• Sales Representative Power User
Background	• 35, male, San Jose, college graduate, $97,000/year in enterprise software sales • Used Salesforce.com at previous employer • Understands and uses Windows at work, prefers his Mac at home • Mac Airbook, Firefox, Mac Office 2011, WiFi at work and home, iPhone
Attitudes	• Doesn't trust most web sites with personal information of any kind • Didn't see a personal benefit of CRM but management required it as part of his job • Values style and elegance
Behavior	• Often uses the iPhone to browse the web while mobile • Often buys latest gadgets and software • Loves to brag about his technical competency
Insights	• Will be quickly frustrated • Product must be slick and optimized for his usage

FIGURE 11-4:
Sample user
persona: Steven.

Problem scenarios or problem statement

When you've defined all the personas associated with your products (as we discuss in the preceding section), you need to create the problem scenarios that cause them to need your product. The product should be the "Aha, you fixed my problem!" solution to the problem.

Problem scenarios contain the following information:

>> **Primary goal:** What is the primary goal of the customer in this particular situation?

>> **Persona(s):** Who has this problem and is trying to reach this particular goal?

>> **Background:** What is the background situation regarding why the customer want to achieve the goal? Think of the difference between a person trying to park on a wide-open street with few cars on a sunny day versus someone parking at night in a crowded muddy lot during a rainstorm. The background is important.

>> **Frequency:** How often does this problem happen? Every day? Once a year?

>> **Trigger:** What causes this problem to arise?

>> **Description:** What if any other details do you have that describe the problem in its entirety?

Here's a very quick example:

> You decide to make potato salad. You buy potatoes, and now they need to be peeled. You can use a knife. The downside is that you're frustrated by how much potato comes off with the peel. Your market need is to peel potatoes without removing anything but the skin. Aha! A potato peeler is just the product to resolve your problem. It shaves off only the potato peel, leaving the potato flesh behind. And you can push down hard on your potato peeler to give you more control over the peeling process for different results.

If the definition of the customer and persona who has the problem changes, another solution may arise. For example, think about a new persona — an older person, Suzanne, with arthritis. The problem definition changes, and the market need does as well. Now, you need to add in an aspect of comfort in using the peeler while still being able to retain control and apply pressure. That's why a company named Oxo makes a range of kitchen implements with soft, comfortable grips. Oxo extended the problem space to account for this different persona.

Problem statements and *problem scenarios* are two similar-sounding terms. A *problem statement* is a short version of a problem scenario. In the potato peeler problem, because the problem as written is quite short, it's closer to a problem statement. Here is the same information written as a problem scenario with more context and color:

> A grandmother, Suzanne, decides to peel potatoes for the Sunday family lunch. Ten people are coming over to eat, and she wants to make mashed potatoes because it's a family favorite. She doesn't believe in waste and prefers to peel off as little potato skin as possible. She knows that the vitamins are in the outside of the potato and wants to feed her family well without peeling away these nutrients. Recently, her arthritis has really been bothering her, and when she uses her standard metal peeler, her hands hurt. It feels like either the potato or the peeler will slip and she'll injure herself.

This problem scenario has much more detail, both qualitative and quantitative, about the actual situation that the persona faces before the product solution is developed. This approach helps the group developing the product imagine more easily all the challenges the grandmother faces and create a wonderful solution. Though you wouldn't want to write up a problem scenario for each little detail of the customer problem, there is a strong case for creating at least one or two key problem scenarios that can guide your product development team.

Customer journeys and workflows

Customer problems aren't always a single-point situation. In many instances, particularly in a sequence of software interactions, an overall goal is achieved by resolving a series of problems along the way. The sequence is either defined from the customer's perspective using a customer journey or the sequence of tasks that the software needs to help different users navigate from start to finish. The more technical the sequence and the more people involved at each step, the more likely that a workflow point of view works better. The more generic the process is for any customer, the more likely that a customer journey is useful. The most common and generic of the two is a customer journey, so we'll describe the process of creating one here.

Start by defining a customer journey using two pieces. Define the overall goal of the customer and then the specific problem points along the path to problem resolution. At each stage of the journey, identify the following from the customers' viewpoint:

>> What action do they need to take to get to the next step?

>> What is their motivation (or lack thereof) in moving to the next step?

>> What questions do they have at this point in their journey?

>> What barriers are in the way of them completing this particular step?

For an example, consider navigating paying a tax bill online with the IRS. Given the level of tax jargon, navigating the IRS site is likely going to be confusing for customers. They have little positive motivation, other than to pay their taxes and avoid a penalty. Each user has many questions along the way and, when faced with a barrier more complex than providing a name, address, and social security number, may simply give up and pick up the phone to call instead of using the website.

By mapping out the customer journey and workflow, the IRS can get a deeper sense of how the customer is going to interact with the website. It can anticipate what the questions and barriers may be and then build a solution that minimizes challenges and makes it far more intuitive for the user. And in the end, it can save a significant amount of money because users will be able to accomplish what they need to by using a self-service website rather than the IRS having to pay an agent to answer the phone.

TIP

One way to map out a customer journey is to pull out some old favorite tools: sticky notes in different colors and marker pens. Write down each step along the way on larger sticky notes and put them in sequence at the top of your workspace (such as a whiteboard, wall, or flip chart paper). Then fill in the actions, motivations, questions, and barriers along the way. Workflow situations vary tremendously, but with a little thinking, you can experiment and discover the key components that need to be solved at each step. Document the sequence for your team using drawing software to show the overall story and then break the story down into each separate step. A personal favorite is simply to draw it out in PowerPoint and then share it with the team.

Market needs statement?

When you've sorted out your personas, worked out what problem you're trying to solve for each particular persona, and determined where they are in their journey toward solving their problem, your market need becomes much easier to write. Various useful formats can make the process easier.

The simplest format is this one:

> The [Persona role], [Persona name], must be able to [achieve a result] OR [solve a problem].

Consider Suzanne, the arthritic, potato–peeling grandmother from the preceding section, as an example:

> The user, Suzanne, must be able to remove the skin of six 3-inch-diameter potatoes without experiencing pain or losing the nutrients in the outer part of the potato just below the skin.

Detailing your market needs document

Documenting your market needs uses a simple format based on the data you collect. Remember that the market needs and product feature descriptions are intricately linked. As you work to resolve the differences between the two points of view — that of the product manager and that of the product development organization — remain flexible. Here are the parts of the market needs document; the following sections explain them in more detail.

>> Executive summary

>> Personas

>> Problem scenarios

>> Market needs

>> Success criteria

>> Assumptions, open issues, exhibits, and appendices

Executive summary

Complete this section after completing all other sections, even though it comes first in the document. It describes the three to five main problems to solve and the personas who have these problems and lays out the main problem scenarios in two or three sentences. The executive summary should ideally be just one page — certainly no more than two. You can treat it as a standalone document.

Personas

One or two personas should always be the primary focus for the design even though you may have five to seven personas total. Describe the personas representing the different user types within the targeted markets.

>> **Buyer personas:** This section describes the buyers, made up of the financial and technical decision makers. These people are often found at businesses (B2B) and are distinct from the users who directly interact with the product. Buyer personas are often very concerned with aspects of the whole product offering as described in Chapter 1.

  ● Financial decision maker (CFO) persona(s): These are the personas that determine whether to buy the product or not. They may not have a great understanding of why the product is so important to the user.

  ● Technical decision maker (CIO) persona(s): These personas worry about the technical standards used and support for the product. They are concerned how the product fits with the rest of work done at the company.

>> **User personas:** These are the personas who interact with the product. They allow the development team to live and breathe the user's world. By always asking, "Would Jim (or whichever persona) use this?" the team can avoid the trap of building what users ask for or what the company may think is cool rather than what customers will actually buy and use. Constantly evaluate designs against the personas and resolve disagreements over design decisions by looking back to the personas.

Problem scenarios

This section describes various scenarios related to the market need(s), relative to the personas' goals. Problem scenarios describe the current state, not the solution state (also known as a use case).

Market needs

In this section, you describe the customer needs, the solution to which an architect or designer later documents as product features. Market needs are described from the customer's perspective and use the voice of the customer; they're never about product capabilities. Use the INVEST criteria for creating great market needs. INVEST is described in Chapter 12.

For each need in the next sections, give the following information:

>> **ID number:** Assign the need an identifying number.

>> **A description:** "As a [persona] I want to [do something] so that I can [derive a benefit]".

>> **Acceptance criteria:** What are the high-level criteria that measurably determine the success of this need? Use the "given, when, then" format as follows: "Given [condition], when [event], then [testable outcome]."

>> **Objectives:** What is the value or overall benefit provided to the customer with this ability?

>> **Personas:** Who are the personas who have this need?

>> **Problem scenarios:** Which problem scenarios are involved with this need?

>> **Priority:** What priority is this need? Check out the sidebar "Different ways of saying 'maybe'" for optional market needs.

TIP

In addition to the following sections, you can also add customer journey and/or customer workflows sections depending on your industry and solution.

FUNCTIONAL

What is the functionality the customers seek? What do users need to do to achieve their goal? Most of your market needs end up here.

COMPATIBILITY

What are the platforms and systems the solution must be compatible with (for example, browser version X and above or Windows version Y and later)? Do customers require interaction with other systems using APIs or certain programming languages? *APIs* are application program interfaces which specify how your program shares information with other software. What document formats do customers need? If this is a new version of an existing product, what compatibility needs do customers have?

SECURITY

What are customers' security needs? Do customers require the data to be encrypted? What type of standards do they need to comply with? If a legal or some external requirement mandates this customer need, describe it in the legal, regulatory, and compliance section.

PERFORMANCE

Many times, the market requires, or expects, performance needs. Don't use this section to describe how the solution may be designed. If industry standards exist, name the specification instead of describing its details. Don't make up criteria. It must be based on market research.

USABILITY

Include ergonomic and accessibility needs. Is the product to be used by the elderly, people with poor eyesight, or those with difficulty lifting? Ergonomic and accessibility needs should be based on known user experience standards (for example, a progress bar will be shown for any operation taking more than x seconds). Wherever possible, simply reference the company's user interface (UI) standards instead of describing them here.

OPERATIONAL

For hardware products, this section includes manufacturability and serviceability needs. It may include environmental issues such as "operating at temperatures up to 120 degrees Fahrenheit." The performance of many electronic parts degrades (officially the term is *derate*) at certain temperatures and start to behave erratically or even stop working. For example, clothes dryers use electronics, so knowing the upper temperature of operation is an important design factor. Does the product need to conform to environmental needs, such as disposal or recycling programs? Does the solution need to include data capture and reporting on usage (analytics or other diagnostic criteria)?

Do customers depend on the company's internal operations — for example, a software service that needs to be maintained by internal operations? Does the customer need for service occur during business hours or 24/7?

INTERNATIONALIZATION

In what languages and countries will the proposed product be used?

DOCUMENTATION

What forms and types of documentation are needed? (This is documentation for product usage. You capture marketing materials in the market strategy and marketing plan documents.) Documents may include a user manual in printed or online format and/or a one-page quick-start guide. Include the needs of the channel, partners, and resellers.

SUPPORT

What are the needs placed on the support organization? What do customers expect from support: hardware replacement, return and repair, email responses, phone calls?

LEGAL, REGULATORY, AND COMPLIANCE

Define all of the legal and regulatory requirements customers need. This information may be security for the military or privacy data for a financial company. It may be accessibility requirements as defined by Section 508 of the Rehabilitation Act of 1973.

DISTRIBUTION AND PACKAGING

What are customers' distribution and packaging needs? Do they require overnight delivery? Is the product sold at retail stores; if so, what are the needs of those resellers?

MISCELLANEOUS AND ADDITIONAL TOPICS

Describe any other market needs not defined previously.

Success criteria

Describe what success is for customers. How do customers measure success — an improvement in productivity, a reduction in errors, or elimination of eliminating a manual process (just to name a few)? Are there specific and measurable tests of success?

Assumptions, open issues, exhibits, and appendices

Writing about a future product is all about prediction. You've made a number of assumptions while writing the market needs document. Record your assumptions here and be prepared to defend them.

Track any open issues during the creation of this document. When the issue is resolved, record it. Any unresolved issues should be assigned to a responsible party. You'll likely have a number of open issues, which tend to get resolved as the project proceeds. Identify where in the process these issues need to be resolved.

For other data that isn't easily included in this document, cite the references to the external documents.

Prioritizing detailed features and market needs

TIP

Be sure to include detailed information on prioritization in your market needs document. Prioritization is a way to pare down ideas into what will work to eventually solve the market need and what won't. For a large software project, feature requests and ideas can reach into the thousands. If you work in Agile, the list of user stories grows too, and having prioritization tools and methods will help you be efficient at making the right choice about what to build next. The prioritization matrix in Chapter 7 is especially useful given the large number of trade-offs you need to make. Check out other prioritization tools while you're there.

REMEMBER

In this section, the term *feature* has crept back into use because it's the common terminology for this type of work and using these tools. The same tools and techniques work with market needs.

DIFFERENT WAYS OF SAYING "MAYBE"

Prioritizing features, needs, and requirements is possibly one of the hardest decisions that a product manager has to face. What absolutely needs to be part of the product, and what is optional? If something is optional, how optional?

Here are a couple of common methods that teams use to assign the relative importance to a feature:

A simple but effective method is to allocate each optional feature into three buckets.

- **High:** Highly desirable in this release
- **Medium:** Nice to have in this release
- **Low:** Can defer to the next release

The MoSCoW prioritization includes prioritization for features that both have to be included as well as three decreasing distinctions for less important features.

- **Must:** Requirement must be satisfied.
- **Should:** High priority item that should be included if it's possible. Critical requirement, but can be satisfied in other ways.
- **Could:** Considered desirable, but not necessary. Include if time and resources permit.
- **Won't:** Will not be implemented in a given release, but may be considered for the future.

Whipping Up a Product Feature Description

You've come a long way. You know your customers, their problem, and when and why they have it. You've documented or communicated this information to your development team members, so now it's time to turn the work over to them.

Figure 11-5 shows you how the who and why become the what and how and points out two important considerations for you to think about:

>> **The line between product management and product development is porous.** Your conversations about what your customers need and what product development proposes as a solution is a discussion. During this discussion, you as a team come to the best possible solution. In fact, the discussion is critical to any relationship between product management and product development in order to ship great products.

>> **The "how" part of the product development isn't the product manager's responsibility.** As a product manager, it isn't up to you to be involved with the guts of how a product is actually made. Your development team determines what development tools, programming languages, and processes to use to build the product. You as a product manager simply don't have that expertise (and if you do, it still isn't your responsibility), just like your engineers don't have the business background and expertise to create the product strategy or business plan.

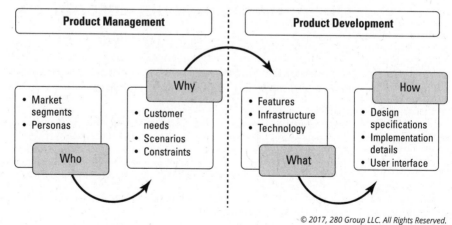

FIGURE 11-5: How customer needs become features.

USE CASES?

In many companies, product managers create or assist in creating use cases. These aren't the same as problem scenarios because use cases contain design-level details and are focused on the solution space. Use cases also don't have the holistic vision that customer journeys, workflows and story mapping (see Chapter 12) give the development team. The major difference is that a use case includes a description about what the system will do (typically a sequence of steps) as the user interacts with the proposed solution.

Unfortunately, you can't find a standard formulation of a use case. It's usually a mix of product and customer information that makes it slightly easier for developers to understand how to solve the problem. The downside is that this mix of information can overwhelm or shut out the customer need. The 280 Group recommends avoiding use cases, but you may not have much choice if your team uses them. As you develop a use case, clearly identify which parts are oriented towards the problem space and which turn the focus to the solution space. Guard against changes to the problem space topics because those are where the market need shines through.

REMEMBER

A small caveat to this discussion: Product managers are smart to learn as much as possible about their products. For example, are some plastics prohibited for regulatory reasons? You want to know that. Do you need to know what the actual formulation of the offending plastic is? No. But you do need enough technical and product knowledge to know whether the decisions being made are sound.

Outlining the product description

A best practice is to have your product development folks create the product description as a response to your market needs document. Then you can have a team discussion to determine what is achievable. Here's a basic outline of the product description; the following section breaks these parts down in more detail:

>> **Executive summary:** This rundown includes the product vision, objectives, scope, and risks.

>> **Product features:** This detailed section defines the following list of product features. In Agile, this section will be at the level you know today. Agile accommodates change later on in the process. Add to the list if needed and delete what isn't applicable:

- Release planning
- Functional

- Compatibility

- Security

- Performance

- Usability

- Operational

- Internationalization

- Documentation

- Support

- Legal, regulatory, and compliance

- Distribution and packaging

- Miscellaneous

>> **Architectural vision:** What is the structure of the entire development project? What tools and processes will be used to create the entire product?

>> **High-level scope:** This section outlines the needed resources, tools, dates, and milestones.

>> **Risk analysis, assumptions, and open issues:** As with all documents, provide a risk analysis and note your assumptions and open issues.

>> **Conclusions and recommendations:** What is your conclusion and recommendation?

>> **Exhibits and appendices:** Any supporting documents and further details are placed here.

Completing the product description document

The product description document is where the product itself appears. As you or your development team creates the document, use the market needs document as a constant check to make sure that all needs have been accounted for, even at a high level for those who work with Agile. It isn't the length of the document, but the quality of the thinking that counts.

Executive summary

Complete this section after completing all other sections. This section should be just one page; you can even treat it as a standalone document. Explain the why, what, where, who, and when of the product.

PRODUCT VISION

Briefly describe the highest-level description of the product and the overall goal of building the solution. What are the three to five key features designed to be in this release of the product? What is the long-term vision of the product? This section provides the directional statements to help guide detailed product and design specifications. Even if your engineers are creating the product description document, this is the one section which is directly guided by product management.

OBJECTIVES, SCOPE, AND RISKS

Who are the features designed for, and what key problems, as described in the market needs document, do they solve for the customer?

What are the required resources? What is the time frame for the release? How will this impact the development team and other groups? What was identified in the market needs document that is out of scope for this release? You can use a product description document for multiple releases or add short versions of new documents for future releases. If items are out of scope are they documented in a road map? *Out of scope* here means features that unable to be developed in this release.

What are the main areas of risk and what are the associated mitigation plans?

Product features

Describe each of the features with the associated costs necessary for product management to make the trade-offs on the basis of the value-based priorities. These have been identified in the market needs document. This section also informs marketing team members what the solution will provide so they can create the appropriate market strategies. The format of a mandatory functional product feature in waterfall is:

The product MUST be able to perform <function> or provide <function> or have <function>. Check out the sidebar "Different ways of saying 'maybe'" for optional product features. Use the INVEST criteria for creating great product features. INVEST is described in Chapter 12.

RELEASE PLANNING

The purpose of *release planning* is to establish a plan and goals that the development teams and the rest of the organization can align to for the project. Release planning answers the questions, "How can we turn the vision into a winning product in the best possible way? How can we meet or exceed the desired customer satisfaction and return on investment?" It also establishes a probable delivery date and cost that should hold if nothing changes.

What is the goal of this release? What are the major risks and the overall features and functionality? For each feature, define the following: a unique ID, the description, the acceptance criteria and the cost in engineering terms. Use high, medium, or low or the point system that your Agile team uses to determine how much effort a feature is to develop. Agile point systems are often eclectic and use relative values of, for example, t-shirt sizes (S, M, L, XL).

FUNCTIONAL

What functionality does the product provide? How will this functionality help customers achieve their goals?

COMPATIBILITY

What are the compatibility features of the product? Does the feature need to be compatible with another product or system?

SECURITY

What are the security features of the product?

PERFORMANCE

What are the performance capabilities of the product?

USABILITY

What are the usability features of the product? If needed, put *wireframes* (sketches of what the user will see on the screen) and other drawings in here.

OPERATIONAL

What are the product's operational capabilities? What operational requirements does it place on the company? For example, the product may have data center, application servers, and/or website implications.

INTERNATIONALIZATION

What languages will the product support? Does it need to meet any other legal or regulatory compliance to deliver product in particular countries or regions? Note them here and under the legal, regulatory, and compliance section, if necessary.

DOCUMENTATION

What form of documentation will be included?

SUPPORT

What support capabilities will be provided?

LEGAL, REGULATORY, AND COMPLIANCE

What legal, regulatory, or compliance requirements are going to be supported?

DISTRIBUTION AND PACKAGING

How will the product be packaged and distributed?

MISCELLANEOUS

Describe how the other customer needs will be met via the product features.

Architectural vision

Briefly describe the long-term objectives of the product. What architectural issues exist? Are new technologies or tools needed, and, if so, do they need to be obtained? Is the company likely to build, buy, or partner? What engineering is necessary during the product's future set of releases that needs to be addressed now? Can technologies be reused or created for reuse? What would the technical road map look like? Is this project part of a platform or portfolio of products, and how do they integrate? If this project is a platform, how will it develop over time? How do the new capabilities of this project support the business objectives and vision of the company?

High-level scope

This section gives scoping estimates to communicate to the key stakeholders (upper management, product management, product marketing, and engineering). These are initial (rough) estimates. You determine more specific details during the project's planning that takes place between engineering and finance.

RESOURCES

What are the resources needed to complete this release?

TOOLS

If new tools are necessary, how long will it take to have them available and integrated into the development process?

EXPECTED RELEASE DATE AND MILESTONES

What is your best estimate, given all the features and needed resources described in this document, for the product's release? What are the key milestones for the project, such as a prototype that can be tested or a beta version for customers to install? When can the project start?

Risk analysis, assumptions, and open issues

Identify the key barriers that may impede the processes and/or services provided by the project. How will you overcome these barriers? How may the following affect your company? You may simply flag the probability as low, medium, or high. Keep your answers brief. Also identify the risks to the company of not doing the product and the product development risks like technology hurdles that need to be overcome.

Record your assumptions here and be prepared to defend them. Keep tabs on any open issues and document them as they're resolved. Assign unresolved issues to a responsible party and identify where in the process these issues need to be settled.

Conclusions and recommendations

State your conclusion and the justification of your recommendation. This section should include the likely effect of developing the product in the specific way outlined in the document. Describe alternative product development options. What are the pros and cons?

Exhibits and appendices

Include larger detailed analysis, which may best be shown in table or possibly graph form. For other data that isn't easily included in this document, cite the references to the external documents. Make sure all appendices are items the main document text mentions.

Plotting Your Product's Path to Success with a Product Road Map

Products evolve over time. Road maps are a great way to document planned changes for product strategy, direction, and features. Chapter 21 has a lot more detail on different types of road maps that you may find useful.

Documenting your plan to deliver product features over time is critical for getting management buy-in, project funding, and customers who agree to buy it ahead of production. This document is called a *product road map*, and it shows what you'll deliver and when and how the product features will support your strategy and achieve your long-term vision.

Product road maps are a core deliverable for product managers. Here is a simple eight-step process to make sure that you don't miss a step.

1. **Decide the detail level and amount of time to spend depending on your audience and the purpose of the road map.** Should this be a "quick and dirty" road map that you create in half an hour, or is it something that warrants you spending many hours on? How much detail do you want to include? Does it need to include details on all of the features in each release or can it be more high-level?

2. **Assess the competitive moves, market, and tech trends that are the background into which you are developing your product.** This will help you as you plan your product strategy and determine what a winning road map will look like.

3. **Gather and prioritize your requirements.** See Chapter 7 for prioritization tools.

4. **Decide on the appropriate timeframe.** Will your road map be short-term and just show three, six, or twelve months? Or is it a longer-term road map that is one, three, or five years?

5. **Choose an organizing strategy.** Use themes, golden features, timed-release, or other ways of organizing the releases on your road map. Refer to Chapter 21 for details on themes, golden features, and timed-releases.

6. **Build an internal road map.** This should include enough details to help educate your team and others about where the product is headed and what to expect in the future in terms of product releases.

7. **Get buy-in and finalize your road map.** Share the road map with your team and executives as you are developing it. Make sure they understand your logic and thinking using the organizing strategy and other data. Once you have a final draft, get sign-off from the main stakeholders.

8. **Create an external road map.** Use the internal road map as a basis and then remove the appropriate level of detail and specifics so that it can be shared more widely outside of your company to give major customers, the press, and industry analysts an idea of how you will achieve your vision.

Eight steps seem so simple. In practice each step may involve a lot more in-depth thought.

3

Building and Maximizing Product Success: From Development to Retirement

Identify the success factors for the most common development methodologies your engineering team is likely to use.

Validate your product so you know when it's ready for your customers to use.

Find out what makes a successful launch and how to decide which type of launch is right for your situation. Execute the launch effectively to make sure your product achieves or exceeds the goals you've set.

Discover how to take advantage of each part of the marketing process to maximize your sales.

Ensure that, when appropriate, you quietly and efficiently remove a product from market while keeping your customers satisfied.

Chapter **12**

Shepherding a Product Idea through the Development Phase

You've got a great idea that meets all the criteria for success. Your plans are in place, and your development team knows who the personas are (see Chapter 5), understands the use cases (see Chapter 11) and/or user stories (discussed later in this chapter), and is ready to build a great product. Now the work of creating that great product begins, and you as the product manager need to step up and lead the team through any bumps in the road that come up.

Getting the Lowdown on Waterfall/Phase-Gate versus Agile Development

The two general development methodologies used for developing products are waterfall and Agile. Waterfall is a phase-gate (also called stage-gate) process (see Chapter 3), and Agile comes in many flavors, such as scrum, extreme programming, Lean, and kanban. We cover the key principles of waterfall and Agile in regards to product management here so that whatever method you choose (or is chosen for you), you can be successful.

Waterfall: Measure twice, cut once

The philosophy behind waterfall development is that you do all the planning up front in large batches. Product managers give developers an inclusive list of features and market needs (see Chapter 11) from which developers can build a completed product for release. Development in waterfall can take six months, a year, or even several years.

REMEMBER

The waterfall approach is typically used for physical products, large-scale software releases, and products that have very strict regulatory or other legal requirements. It works very effectively for products where requirements, the market, and competition don't or won't change often.

In waterfall development, the product manager delivers a market needs or market requirements document (MRD) before development starts. The MRD includes everything about the market, personas, use cases, customer and market needs, window of opportunity, and anything else the engineers need to completely develop the product. It's often a formal document that key stakeholders (such as management, development managers, the product manager, and anyone else in the company that will be affected) have signed off on. Only after sign-off of the comprehensive MRD in the plan phase does development then begin. See Figure 12-1 for a look at the progression of phases.

FIGURE 12-1:
In waterfall, development begins only after MRD sign-off in the plan phase.

Conceive ▸ Plan ▸ Develop ▸ Qualify ▸ Launch ▸ Maximize ▸ Retire

Gate Gate Gate Gate Gate Gate

© 2017, 280 Group LLC. All Rights Reserved.

The advantage of waterfall is that the product manager can take an extensive amount of time to put forth a carefully thought-out MRD. It avoids the company's rushing to market and potentially building features that may be trendy this month but meaningless in the long-term. It also avoids asking engineering to change priorities constantly; under waterfall development, everyone has to get on the same long-term page. The product manager has more time for strategic planning and for maximizing the overall success of the product.

The disadvantage of waterfall is that it lacks the flexibility to change plans because the MRD has to be revised and the stakeholders have to be informed of the changes, agree to them, and sign off accordingly. Thus, new features can't be added easily, and they aren't delivered to customers as rapidly as they are in Agile since the planning and release cycles are much longer with waterfall. Market and customer needs may change during development, and with waterfall, the team can't respond quickly.

Agile: Plan and deliver rapidly

Agile is the opposite of waterfall (which we discuss in the preceding section). Agile development uses a lot of very specific terminology. You may hear terms such as scrum, scrumban, kanban, and extreme programming (XP) to refer to different development methodologies. The most common Agile development framework in use is scrum, which is the one we focus on here; Figure 12-2 shows its structure. Agile is excellent for software products, especially for smaller applications, software as a service (SaaS), and web-based applications.

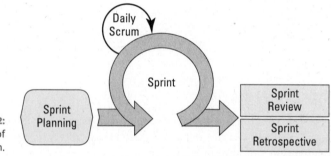

FIGURE 12-2:
A view of
Agile scrum.

© 2017, 280 Group LLC. All Rights Reserved.

Sprinting to the finish

Under scrum, development occurs in short, defined periods called *sprints*, which are up to two and no longer than four weeks long. The goal of each sprint is to create code in an iterative and incremental way and complete a particular piece of work. This process is repeated (iterated) while the product is progressively built (increments).

For each sprint, the development team takes work from the top of the product backlog (discussed in detail later in this chapter) focusing on the top priority items that can be developed during the allotted time. The team breaks down the work for each sprint into *tasks* and then executes each task. Quality assurance occurs *in parallel* (simultaneously). If a task won't be completed in its given sprint, it's pushed out to the next sprint.

However, each sprint can be released to customers as soon as it is complete. Alternatively, several sprints are often bundled together and provided to customers in a larger product release. Figure 12-3 shows the cascading relationship between tasks in a sprint, sprints, and a product release.

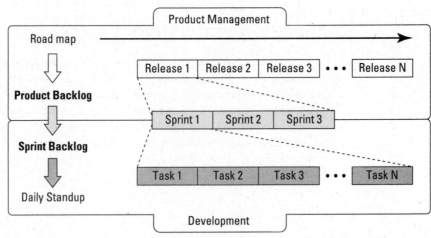

FIGURE 12-3: Breaking down the work within a sprint.

Telling (user) stories

In Agile, you communicate the requirements through simple *user stories* to the engineers instead of writing and signing off on a comprehensive MRD as in waterfall. User stories can be simply written on a 3-x-5-inch notecard, or they can be captured electronically in a database or Agile development software system. The focus is on communicating and working as a team while minimizing documentation. The user stories convey to the engineer what the customer need is and what the user is trying to accomplish. Once the engineer has discussed the user story with the product manager or product owner and fully understands the meaning of the user story, the engineer then builds the feature.

The format of a user story is as follows:

> As a <persona>, I want to be able to <customer need> so that I can <benefit of requirement>.

Figure 12-4 is an example of a user story.

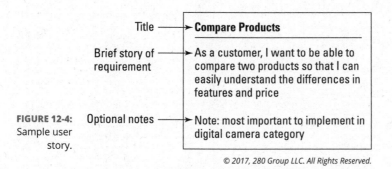

Title ──────► **Compare Products**

Brief story of ──────► As a customer, I want to be able to
requirement   compare two products so that I can
       easily understand the differences in
       features and price

Optional notes ──────► Note: most important to implement in
       digital camera category

FIGURE 12-4:
Sample user
story.

Creating the backlog in Agile

To understand how the entire product is eventually divided into user stories, you need to start up at the top with the overall scope of the entire product and work your way down into the details of the user story. Two key tools you use are story mapping and product backlog prioritization.

Story mapping

Story mapping is a technique, developed by Jeff Patton, of mapping out the particular activities that need to happen in the product to make sure a customer accomplishes her goal. The wonderful thing about a story map is the clarity it gives you and your development team about what completely addressing a customer need will take. In the best case, you bring everyone together in one room and work the story from beginning to end. The process generates significant learning and understanding on all sides, which leads to less confusion for the duration of the project.

To create a story map, you can use sticky notes, markers, dots, colored masking tape, and a blank wall space. In Figure 12-5, you can see how you start by creating a backbone of user activities at the top. These can be logging into the software, selecting a product, and going through the check-out process. Under each of these activities are tasks (not necessarily the same as the tasks which drive development work within a sprint). Under each task, the development team fills in all the subtasks, user interface, and other details that the user needs to complete the tasks. Once all the development tasks have been documented, the list of tasks is divided into what absolutely must be done to bring the product to market. This *first slice* is your minimum viable product. The work done in future releases is allocated to the next slice.

Prioritizing the backlog

REMEMBER

As we know, in Agile, the basis for a development team to create a working piece of software is a *user story*. It's the smallest block of development. The next size up is a *feature*. And even larger is an *epic*. (In Europe, the term for an epic is a *saga*.) So remember: user story < feature < epic.

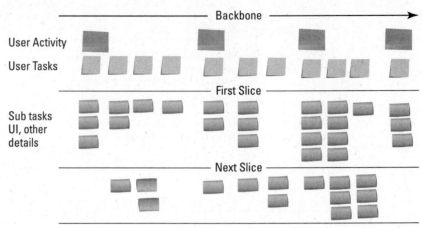

FIGURE 12-5: An illustration of a story map.

Here's an example of an epic, feature and user story for an online store selling shoes. The epic has a larger scope of work than the feature which is again, more work than the user story. The user story is the smallest slice of work that the product manager typically works with.

>> **Epic:** As a customer, I want to be able to purchase shoes online so that I easily compare a wide range of shoes from the comfort of home.

>> **Feature:** As a customer, I want to be able to purchase the shoes I have selected so that I don't have to look around a lot of shops.

>> **User story 1:** As a customer, I want to be able to pay by a range of most commonly used credit card options so that I can choose a convenient payment option.

>> **User story 2:** As a customer, I want to be able to input the city where the shoes will be delivered so that I can receive my shoes.

User stories 1 and 2 both address parts of the feature, but not all of it. And the feature addresses some of the epic but again needs other features to complete all aspects of the epic.

As you can see in Figure 12-6, your *product backlog* consists of many of these user stories, features, and epics. As you investigate proposed development work, you realize that some work has more customer value than others. This work should then be done earlier. The reality of development is you simply can't get to the level of detail needed for the entire product upfront. You would spend a huge amount of time upfront in development breaking down each and every piece of work to be done while developers twiddled their thumbs. Instead, you prioritize the proposed work by customer value and create a prioritized product backlog, most often referred to as a *prioritized backlog* or more simply *backlog*.

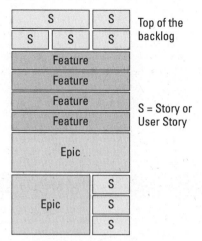

FIGURE 12-6: Prioritized backlog.

At the top of the backlog, you have your user stories that the development team are just about to start with; below that are your features and then your epics. As features and epics come to the top of your backlog, you break them down into user stories that your development team can work on.

So what do you work on first? A lot depends on what you're building. If you're just starting out, building out a software structure or architecture for what comes later is usually most important. For an ongoing product, the items at the top of the backlog are most definitely what has the most value both to the customer and your company. The reality is that sometimes you have to prioritize a bug fix or solve a larger structural issue with the software, which is referred to as *technical debt*.

The beauty of a product backlog is that one person is in charge: the product owner (or product manager in the role of product owner). That is an absolute within scrum. This person decides what the development team works on next. That said, it would be a poor product owner who didn't get feedback to make sure that the development team lets her know what would make most sense to complete next.

Documenting the product backlog

The issue with tracking an Agile backlog is that the volume of information is huge. Most teams move quickly away from documenting each piece of information with index cards and switch to software written for this purpose. A side benefit of using software tools is that tracking is integrated so it's also easier for you to figure out what stage each piece of work is at. When you know what software your development team is using, spend the time to learn all the ins and outs so that you can use it to efficiently document the product backlog.

Invest in features

When you write down your product features, a good rule of thumb to see if you're headed in the right direction is to use the acronym INVEST (kudos to Bill Wake for this idea). Table 12-1 tells you all the aspects of a good product feature or user story. The "small" rule is critical to Agile only. The rest are applicable to both waterfall and Agile requirements.

TABLE 12-1   **INVEST in Good Features**

Aspect	Explanation
Independent	Avoid dependencies between features and user stories.
Negotiable	User stories are reminders to collaborate.
Valuable to the customers	Avoid requirements that have only technical value.
Estimate-able	Can estimate how long it will take to complete.
Small (Agile only)	The requirement should take no more than two days to complete.
Testable	The requirement has defined acceptance criteria.

When is a feature really a constraint?

In creating a product, you sometimes have features or user stories that are really hard to write. They don't seem to fit into the usual user story pattern. These are better written as *constraints.* For example, how long should a task take? What operating system(s) should it operate under, or what temperature range should it operate within? Simply write down the limits of what the product needs to do without reference to a customer and move on.

Examining Agile's manifesto and key principles

Agile in all of its different forms was created based on the principles stated in the Agile Manifesto, shown in Figure 12-7. The Agile Manifesto was created by a group of software developers who were looking for a more optimized way to develop products and bring features to market faster. Over time Agile has started to be applied to many types of products beyond just software.

Agile has 12 key principles shown in Figure 12-8.

We are uncovering better ways of developing software by doing it and helping others do it. Through this work we have come to value:

Individuals and interactions over processes and tools

Working software over comprehensive documentation

Customer collaboration over contract negotiation

Responding to change over following a plan

That is, while there is value in the items on the right, we value the items on the left more.

1. Our highest priority is to satisfy the customer through early and continuous delivery of valuable software.

2. Welcome changing requirements, even late in development. Agile processes harness change for the customer's competitive advantage.

3. Deliver working software frequently, from a couple of weeks to a couple of months, with a preference to the shorter timescale.

4. Businesspeople and developers must work together daily throughout the project.

5. Build projects around motivated individuals. Give them the environment and support they need, and trust them to get the job done.

6. The most efficient and effective method of conveying information to and within a development team is fact-to-face conversation.

7. Working software is the primary measure of progress.

8. Agile processes promote sustainable development. The sponsors, developers, and users should be able to maintain a constant pace indefinitely.

9. Continuous attention to technical excellence and good design enhances agility.

10. Simplicity — the art of maximizing the amount of work not done — is essential.

11. The best architectures, requirements, and designs emerge from self-organizing teams.

12. At regular intervals, the team reflects on how to become more effective, then tunes and adjusts its behavior accordingly.

Assuming typical responsibilities

Whether you're working with a team doing waterfall development or Agile development, getting clarity on the roles and responsibilities of each of the team players is critical.

SPEAKING THE SCRUM VERSION OF AGILE

Agile development using the scrum framework has a lot of very specific language (check out *Scrum For Dummies* by Mark C. Layton [Wiley]). Here are a few additional terms you may encounter. Figure 12-2 may help in giving you context for the different sprint meetings.

- **Sprint planning meeting:** Happens at the start of a sprint. The product owner and the team first decide on a sprint goal. During the meeting, the product owner describes each user story, and the team then asks questions and plans the group's work for the sprint. Don't confuse sprint planning with the product management planning activity. Sprint planning focuses on the work required to complete the user stories the team committed to for the sprint. Product planning is a strategic activity that provides long-term direction and spans an extended time period.

- **Sprint goal:** A brief one or two sentence description describing what the Agile team is planning on accomplishing during the sprint.

- **Daily scrum:** The daily synchronization meeting that takes place within the team. The team includes all the engineers. Product owners and scrum masters are optional attendees. Each person stands and answers the following three questions: What did I do yesterday toward the sprint goal? What will I do today toward the sprint goal? What's getting in the way of me doing my work to achieve the sprint goal?

- **Sprint review:** Meeting at the end of a sprint where the product owner reviews the sprint goal with key stakeholders and has the engineering team demonstrate the completed product increment.

- **Sprint retrospective:** A separate meeting from the sprint review; it can exclude anyone outside the development team. Typically, product owners join this meeting. During the meetings, the team reviews lessons learned and improvements that can be made. Ideally, the team commits to making at least one change in the way that they work.

Typical responsibilities for the product manager include the following:

>> Acts as a market expert

>> Defines and drives strategy

>> Owns the product vision and road map

>> Bridges the gap between engineering and marketing

>> Develops and creates the business case

>> Presents customer needs

>> Makes feature, schedule, and cost trade-offs

>> Brings products to market

>> Is responsible for value delivery through business ecosystem

>> Is responsible for all aspects of product success

Typical responsibilities for the product owner are these:

>> Is responsible for managing and ordering the product backlog

>> Optimizes the business value of the development effort

>> Ensures product backlog is visible

>> Ensures the development team understands each item in the backlog to the level needed

>> Facilitates setting the goals for each sprint

>> Is available to the development team at all times

Unlocking the Secrets of the Product Development Trade-Off Triangle

Product development involves a well-known concept called the development trade-off triangle. Figure 12-9 shows the trade-off choices: features, quality, and schedule. The idea is that you can aim for two vertices of the triangle, but three is usually unattainable. If you want more features and want to keep the schedule fixed, you need to lower quality. If you want more features, and want to keep quality fixed, you have to increase the amount of time for development and slip your schedule. And if you want to shrink the schedule, you have to give up scope or quality. The challenge is to make these trade-offs in the best possible manner so that the best product ships as close to schedule as possible with the features that it needs to be successful.

The bottom line in terms of the triangle is that no set formula exists for making these tradeoffs. Making a decision on what to give up is highly dependent on your product's situation. You as the product manager have to constantly monitor the team's progress, get feedback from your testers and the competitive environment, field pressure from your management, and account for other factors; and make the most informed choice that you can.

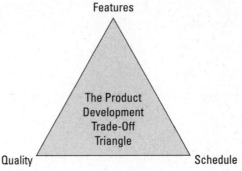

Features

The Product
Development
Trade-Off
Triangle

Quality   Schedule

© 2017, 280 Group LLC. All Rights Reserved.

FIGURE 12-9:
Product
development
trade-off triangle.

WARNING

In a waterfall development environment, the trade-offs are typically more diffi-cult than when doing Agile development because all the planning takes place upfront and development then occurs on a long schedule. Having the schedule and release dates already set far in the future puts pressure on keeping to the original schedule. This time crunch pressure leads to sacrifices in quality or a reduction of features when the development team can't deliver what was initially promised. To add to the difficulty of waterfall development, additional information is flowing into the product manager while the product is under development: competitive information and product change requests from management, sales, and other stakeholders. Adding or changing features once again adds to a trade-off between the schedule and the quality level. Often the amount of testing is also at risk. The product manager is the only person in a position to understand from a market, competitive, and customer needs perspective what the right trade-offs are between the schedule, features, and quality.

When you're working with a team doing Agile development, the trade-offs aren't necessarily easier; they're just different. The schedule is usually fixed in terms of the length of the development, and the quality assurance is built into the sprint schedule. The easy thing to do is simply remove features. In other words, if a fea-ture isn't ready during the sprint, it simply gets pushed to the next sprint.

One challenge is that if you're combining sprints to complete a major release, critical features may not be included because the team ran out of time to develop them. This scenario can put your product at a competitive disadvantage or make it not compelling enough for customers to purchase. The product manager and the development team have to plan carefully to ensure that difficult-to-develop fea-tures make it to market.

Maintaining Best Practices during Development

Staying informed and engaged with your team during development of the product is crucial. Critical questions about how to implement features and what trade-offs to make come up on a daily basis. As a leader for the product efforts you must step up and be there to help the team do the right thing for the customer.

REMEMBER

Depending on the type of product that you manage, you may spend a lot or a little amount of time in the develop stage. Understanding and then succeeding with your partners in the journey of product creation is important to your success as a product manager, regardless of how much time you spend on the task.

Here are a few best practices and tips for being as effective as possible during this phase:

» **Make sure you're easily accessible and available to your team.** Often, decisions need to be made rapidly; if the team members can't ask your opinion, they may proceed with whatever they think is best.

» **Continue to monitor the market, competition, and other factors.** Communicate what's going on with customers and the overall market to your team so that they view you as the de facto expert and are able to make the best product decisions. Update your strategy and plans accordingly. You know your engineers view you as the true voice of the customer when they come to you with questions like "Do you think customers would prefer A or B?"

» **Whenever possible, use data in all your decisions and communications.** Engineers love data and logical decisions, so make sure they understand where your decisions and opinions are coming from.

» **Resist the temptation to cry wolf.** During development, your salespeople, executives, and others will often come to you with a sense of urgency or panic. They want to change plans, add features, and pull in the schedule. If you react to these requests by constantly asking your team to make adjustments, you lose credibility and eventually severely diminish your ability to lead the team. Save your requests for times when changes are mission-critical. Give thorough explanations to your team if changes need to be made so that team members know that when you ask, it really matters.

» **Don't fall into the trap of wanting to get the product out at all costs.** This decision is often based on the assumption that any remaining issues can be fixed easily with a product update soon after launch. It may be tempting as you near the end of development and everyone on the team is tired, but don't do it. If your product isn't good enough, you may cause irreparable harm to your product and brand reputation.

Chapter **13**

Gearing up for Your Product Launch: The Qualify Phase

Y ou and your team have been working hard on creating a great product. You identified the target personas, chose the best opportunity, prioritized the features, made challenging trade-offs, and have been in development for quite some time. The next step in the Optimal Product Process is to prepare for running a beta program, getting the near-finished product into customers' hands, and ensuring that it's ready to be released to a wide range of customers.

Getting Up to Speed on the Qualify Phase

Many times, you may be tempted to skip or shortcut this phase because of schedule and time constraints, but don't make this mistake. Use this phase to be absolutely sure the product meets the quality level you need. Then you can be certain the features and benefits it provides are more than adequate for customers to justify paying for the product. Beta testing (along with your own internal quality assurance and testing efforts) lets you know that the product is ready to shine when released to customers — or that you have more work to do.

TIP

Alpha refers to the first phase of internal testing after some of the features are in place and the quality assurance team can begin testing it for problems and bugs. *Beta* refers to the phase when the product has all its promised features complete and the internal quality assurance team (as well as external testers) are looking only for areas where the product doesn't function correctly. Don't start testing with external users during the alpha phase; the product will generally be too unreliable, and the testers will get frustrated.

Ensuring internal and external quality validation

As you go through development, your internal quality assurance team develops a testing plan and tests the product. As the product manager, you should read and approve the plan to make sure quality assurance is testing the most common customer scenarios. Make sure that the plan includes a rigorous variety of common scenarios and setups that the target customer is likely to have in their environment. For example, for a web software product, make sure your internal testing team includes a variety of operating systems and browsers in their testing that are representative of what you customers use.

Rigorous internal testing will find many of the problems with your product. So why test externally at all? Because even with the best possible internal quality assurance engineers and testing, circumstances arise where real-world customers use the product in a different way that internal testing can't anticipate.

Figure 13-1 helps you determine how big a need for a beta program your product has by asking you to evaluate the potential risk any post-release bugs pose to the customer against the difficulty of fixing them. For some products, such as consumer web software where the risk to the customer is low, you may want to run an open beta program for anyone. Google popularized this approach years ago as a way to release products without the company having to be responsible for bugs, problems, or things that didn't work as advertised. In fact, many Google applications have never left beta.

For an application where the risk to the customer is low or for products that can easily be changed and updated rapidly after customers begin using them, the strategy of running a large open beta for anyone can be viable. For products that are mission-critical for customers or for products that can't easily be changed — such as hardware, physical products, financial services software, or other applications that deal with sensitive data — it may not be a viable approach.

High	Must run at least a limited beta program	Must run comprehensive beta program
Low	May be able to release product in beta form to general public or limited audience	Must run at least a limited beta program
	Low	**High**

Difficulty Changing the Product Once Released

Risk for Customer

FIGURE 13-1:
Difficulty
of change
versus risk.

WARNING

For all types of products, the risk you run in not holding an adequate beta program is that you may damage the brand reputation with customers and the market if the product isn't solid. Even if it's a web-based application, customers who have a negative experience may never be willing to use it again. Too many companies have put out products too early without getting adequate beta validation, and they simply could never recover.

Creating a beta plan

The beta plan is critical in that it helps formulate plans well in advance and ensure the corresponding beta program based on the plan will adequately achieve the desired results. The Product Management LifeCycle Toolkit (included as a free download with this book; see the Introduction, page 4, for details) includes a beta plan template you can use in creating your plan.

Beta programs take a lot of time and effort to execute in order to be done effectively. Table 13-1 suggests a timeline for each part of your beta program. Plan on 9 to 12 weeks from when you start planning the program, and make sure you have an employee or contractor dedicated at least half-time to running the program. Planning, recruiting customers, gathering feedback and suggestions, running an exit survey, and tallying the results to determine whether the product is ready to be released are all time-consuming yet critical activities that need to be covered.

TABLE 13-1

Beta Program Timeline

Task	Amount of Time
Set goals, write plan, and sign off	1 week
Recruit and receive applications	3 weeks
Select, notify, and send agreement	1 week
Run program	3–6 weeks
Conduct exit survey, tally results, and write final report	1 week
TOTAL	9–12 weeks

Dodging typical beta testing mistakes

The most common mistakes made in the beta program are as follows:

» **Not building enough time into the schedule to do adequate beta testing with real-world customers:** Development almost always takes far longer than expected, and the company is anxious to release the product on time. As a result, the time set aside for beta testing is often reduced dramatically at the very end, resulting in an ineffective (sometimes nonexistent) beta program.

TESTING WITH AGILE

A note to consider if you're working with Agile development teams: You may be releasing new versions of the product at the end of each sprint. This scenario generally occurs with small apps or web-based software where a small subset can use the product in real-life circumstances and then it can be released to a wider audience. The great thing about these types of products is that you can easily roll them back to the prior version if a significant problem crops up.

If you have a mission-critical application or one that you can't roll back easily, you may want to combine sprints into a master release. Salesforce.com is a company that routinely does this; it develops its software in monthly sprints and then puts out small quarterly releases and one big release once a year. The advantage of using this approach is that you have more time for a larger set of customers to test the beta and make sure everything is working correctly instead of trying to release software rapidly after every monthly sprint.

- **» Choosing beta testing customers that don't represent the actual customers and personas:** Friends and family often beta test. Though these people can provide some good feedback, don't assume that they're representative of how your actual customers will use the product or of the kind of environment customers will use it in on a day-to-day basis.

- **» Running a beta program without predefined goals and metrics:** If you don't establish what the goals and metrics are prior to running the program, you won't be able to determine whether the product is actually ready to release. Having some concrete metrics in place can help make your decision to cut corners at the very end of development a far easier decision.

- **» Underestimating how difficult recruiting participants for the program will be:** Many times, companies incorrectly believe finding customers who are willing to spend time beta testing the product will be easy. In real life, finding people who are dedicated, and willing to spend the time and effort required to provide useful feedback is often far more difficult.

Putting a Beta Program in Place

Once you have a comprehensive beta plan ready you can execute your beta program. To do a thorough beta program well requires a lot of time and effort, but the feedback you get from customers letting you know whether the product is ready for primetime makes it well worth it.

Setting appropriate goals

Make sure you define your goals upfront and early. What are you really trying to accomplish? Do you want a broad cross-section of customers to spend extensive amounts of time using the product to prove that it's ready to ship? Or is your existing quality assurance (QA) work extensive, and you just need a few customers to validate readiness with some hands-on customer usage? Do you want to gather early feedback for the next version? Or do you just want to find a group of customers willing to talk to the press or provide you with quotes or testimonials?

Making your goals concrete

REMEMBER

The earlier you set your goals and the more concrete they are, the better. When you don't define success upfront, creating your overall plan and knowing that you have reached your goals are difficult. In addition, if the testing shows that the product isn't ready to ship, you need concrete goals that allow you to push back on the team and delay launch.

For example, your goal may be that a certain number of customers must have installed the product, used it for N days (or N hours or number of times) successfully, and found no major crashing bugs. One goal should be that you'll survey the beta testers at the end of the program and find that a certain percentage of them (for example, 90 percent) indicate they believe the product is ready to ship. Flip to the later section "Exit surveys" for details on the survey part of the process.

Other goals may include finding three to five customers that are willing to give you quotes and talk to the press if reporters ask for references. A real bonus is if a customer is willing to create a blog post for you or recommend the product on your website or in social media. You may want to set a goal that the number of bug reports must show a decreasing trend to an acceptable level before the product can be declared ready to ship. Obviously, you can use a number of metrics.

Recruiting participants

Your success at recruiting customers depends on a number of factors, including whether it is a brand new and unknown product or an upgrade from a previous version, how well known and prominent your company is, and how popular your products are. For example, Apple could probably find iPhone beta testers pretty easily. Other factors include how easy finding your target customers is and how much effort and time you're asking them to put in.

If you have an enterprise software application from a new, completely unknown start-up company that will require the beta customers to go through a lengthy installation (or worse yet, installation may affect their other mission-critical systems), you may have a difficult time recruiting. On the other hand, if you have a consumer application that takes little time to install or try out and provides immediate benefits, you may find recruitment easier.

Depending on all these factors, you need to gauge what kind of recruiting program you need to do and how strong the incentives need to be (see the section "Incentives" later in this chapter). You may need to make personal phone calls and visits in order to convince customers to participate. Or you may be able to use email or even a form on your website.

Sources for recruiting include the following:

>> Current customers

>> Prospective customers that didn't purchase before

>> Venture capitalists and investors who can refer you to representative customers

- Your personal network (but be careful using friends and family; see the earlier section "Dodging typical beta testing mistakes")
- Your sales force and leads
- Advertisements (online, in the local newspaper, and so on)

Incentives

In terms of incentives, you can offer participants many things. Certainly the "Help us improve the product" angle works to some degree. If you're lucky and have a fanatical user base, you may actually have to fight off customers wanting to participate. You may also want to offer free or reduced pricing or upgrades. Another option is to have a contest to keep users motivated. For example, you can run a program called the "Great Bug Hunt" where for each valid bug submission the beta tester receives an entry into a drawing for a tablet or some other prize. This approach not only encourages testers to sign up but also gets them enthused to continue using the product throughout the course of the program.

Response rates

You need to contact customers to get them to participate. The response rate you get in terms of participation and actual usage for a beta program varies widely based on a number of factors, including these:

- Popularity of the product
- Whether the product is completely new and unproven
- Who your company is (well known or unheard of)
- How personal and compelling your recruiting approach is
- How stringent you are at selecting customers that fit your profile
- Whether your product will affect mission-critical systems of the customer
- How much time and effort you're asking the customer to put in

Just how many customers do you need to contact to get an adequate number that agree to be part of the program? More importantly, how many will actually end up testing the product and doing what they've promised for the duration of the program? To give you an idea of the range of actual participation you can expect, here are some numbers from actual beta programs that the 280 Group has run for clients.

For an existing (versus brand new) product that is very popular, is low-risk to install and use, and doesn't take a lot of time and effort, you may be able to get away with contacting only 25 people initially. If your targeting was accurate, expect that 20 of the 25 would likely fit your criteria and 15 may sign up. Of these, you can expect 8 to 10 to actually use the product enough to give you some valid beta feedback. Your success rate is roughly 30 percent of the initial number contacted.

On the flip side, for a brand new unknown product from an unknown start-up that has a high risk and time commitment for installation, you may contact 100 customers initially, find 40 that are interested, have 20 sign up, and in the end have 5 to 8 that are actually active. And that's a success rate of roughly 5 to 8 percent of the initial number contacted.

Beta agreements

When you've got participants on board, you'll want to have them sign a beta agreement. It doesn't have to be a formal agreement. Recognize that in bigger companies (either yours or theirs) you'll be forced to use an actual contract. Focus on clearly stating what the commitments and expectations are, including maintaining confidentiality until the product is released publicly. Make it as simple as possible. Include details such as length of program, incentives and rewards for participation, responsibilities of participants, expected amount of usage, and support that will be provided. Getting participants to actually sign an agreement makes their commitment much more real. After they've signed, you have a higher probability that they'll actually use the product and provide feedback.

Kicking off the program

After you've lined up all of your participants and gotten them to sign a beta agreement you're ready to kick off the program. The most important thing at this point is to do everything you can to avoid a false start. If the participants have a bad first experience with the product, your chances of getting them to continue putting in effort are much lower.

To avoid a false start, make sure you've agreed with your team about what the criteria are for starting the program. For example, you may all agree that the program can't begin until all fatal/crashing bugs have been fixed or until N users have been running the product internally with no major problems for at least a week. And you may agree not to start the program until all participants are signed up.

The other approach you may want to use is to deploy with one or two participants who are more technical and/or whom you know better than the others. You may even want to go to their company if they're local and watch them get up and running so that you can figure out where any of the likely bumps in the road may be for other participants.

TIP

Make sure all components of the product are solid before deploying anything. Check and double-check the installers, prepare a FAQ document so that participants won't have to contact you to get answers, and include documentation and help system content if at all possible.

After the program has started, communicating regularly with both the participants and your internal team is critical. For smaller programs, you should call the participants at least once a week to check in and make sure they're using the product and having no issues. For larger programs, send regular email communications. Make sure you communicate about the overall status of the program, bug fixes/new versions that testers need to install, updated FAQs, and details about contests or incentives. If the participants hear from you regularly, they'll be reassured and be much more likely to continue putting in time and effort to help you with the product.

Also make sure to communicate internally with your team. Provide a weekly status report, including number of bugs reported, usage by participants, whether you're meeting the stated goals, and what you need from the team to continue to be successful. Keeping the team informed is crucial so that as the program gets ready to wrap up, everyone knows the status and no one experiences any surprises or disconnects about the results.

Exit surveys

When you're ready to end the beta program, have the participants complete a short exit survey. You can send it via email or through an online survey tool such as SurveyMonkey or Google online forms. Ask the participants how much they used the product, what their overall impressions are, whether they believe the product is ready to ship, and what can be improved. Also ask them to rate the features of the product on a scale of one to five (five being the highest ranking).

TIP

If you offer an incentive or a contest, make it a requirement for participants to complete the survey in order to qualify.

Final report

Take the results of the survey and deliver a final report to your team. This account should include a short testing summary, bug trend information, information on whether you met the original agreed-upon goals, and a summary of customer opinions and feedback. Deliver this report to the team prior to making the decision to ship the software; it's a fact-based tool to make an informed choice.

Making the Decision to Ship the Product

You set your goals, recruited participants, and have run a thorough beta program. You've got the data in hand about how successful customers have (or haven't) been using the product and whether they recommend that it's ready to release to the general public. Now you have to make the final decision about whether the product is ready.

This point can be a challenging time for the product manager for a variety of reasons. Your engineering team is tired and most likely wants to ship the product and take a short break, your management wants the additional revenues associated with the product, and your customers may be hounding you for it. Yet you still must carefully consider whether the product is ready because releasing a product that has severe deficiencies can not only kill the product's revenues but also severely limit your career.

Some of the key factors to consider when making the decision include the following:

>> What percentage of the beta testers believe the product is ready to be released?

>> What's your confidence level in how solid the product is? Are you 50 percent confident? 95 percent confident? Is either of these numbers acceptable?

>> What is the risk if you know there are problems, and how quickly can they be fixed?

>> Do you have the luxury of waiting, or will your competition steal too much market share from you if you wait?

The great (and also challenging) thing about being a product manager is that you're where the buck stops. You own the decision about whether the product is ready to be released to customers. By all means, explain your decision to the development and management team. Don't be afraid to make the right decision at this point. After all, your biggest responsibility is to make sure the product is as successful as possible.

» Establishing quantifiable launch goals

» Determining what type of launch to execute

» Writing a launch plan and comparing it with your goals

» Making sure your launch team and milestones are in place

Chapter **14**

Liftoff! Planning and Executing an Effective Product Launch

Your team members have been hard at work developing a great product based on the winning strategy and customer needs you provided them. Now comes the exciting part where you get to show customers and the rest of the world what you've been working on and give them a chance to purchase the product.

Launching your product is just as important as developing a great product. If you don't do the launch effectively, customers won't be aware of your solution and may have a bad impression of your product, and you may not hit your revenue and profitability goals. As such, planning early is critical. When you're in the qualify phase (or even as early as partway through the develop phase), you want to be planning the launch of your product so that when the product is ready for sale you will be ready to effectively execute a launch that meets your goals. (Head to Chapter 3 for more on the phases of the product life cycle.)

TIP

The Product Management LifeCycle Toolkit (included as a free download with this book; see the Introduction, page 4, for details) contains a launch plan template and a sample launch plan completed for a fictional product called EarBud. Use these tools to make sure you've thought through all the most important questions and aspects of your launch and to help communicate to others the details, budget, and resource commitments needed for the launch.

Unlocking the Do's and Don'ts of a Successful Product Launch

It's simple: Make a great first impression by planning the launch early. Sure, many factors go into a successful product launch, but if you follow the rule of early planning, you get off to a great start. Read on to find out the importance of a positive first impression, the impact of a negative first impression, and the elements of a successful launch.

Understanding the importance of first impressions

We can't state strongly enough how important making a good first impression as part of your launch is. Here's what making a good first impression can do for your product:

» **It sets the competitive stage.** If you're entering a crowded market, a good impression gives you a chance to be considered against the competitive alternatives. If you're entering a new market, a positive impression gives you the chance to set the standard against which all new products will be judged.

» **It gives you a positive presence online and bolsters affirmative word-of-mouth responses.** Customers rely on word-of-mouth, social media buzz, and information on the Internet more than ever before.

» **It allows for positive press coverage and stellar product reviews.** The press and customers love to tell others about products they love.

Conversely, a bad first impression can really damage your product's image and your bottom line. Here's what happens when you create a bad first impression:

» **It puts a bad taste in customers' mouths.** By launching a product that isn't ready for the market, you're opening the door to a whole host of problems that customers may encounter with a not-ready product. Customers are demanding. Giving them a bad experience will taint your brand, and they may never be willing to try your product — or even your company — a second time.

» **It creates a poor online presence.** A bad impression could live on forever via negative postings on the web.

» **Sales often stall.** If the first experience that customers have with your product gives them a bad impression word may get out to other potential customers who will choose not to buy your product, and you may not be able to meet your revenue projections.

Detailing the elements of a successful product launch

The elements of a successful product launch are many:

» **Planning:** Follow a plan to make sure all elements of your launch are in place.

» **Communication:** Communicate with all the parties internal and external so that awareness of your product is broad.

» **Timing:** Planning launches typically requires three to six months. The sequence of events is staggered depending on how close they are to the customer: internal departments first, partners and press next, and finally customers and the general public. Your aim is a seamless meshing of internal operations readiness, sales and marketing readiness, and product readiness.

» **Effective marketing program mix:** Have you chosen the right mix of activities, such as online advertising combined with product reviews and a social media campaign? Creating the correct marketing program mix generates the sales results that you've agreed to with your company.

» **Compelling messaging:** What messages are going to motivate customers to buy your product? Do you need to deliver those messages in a particular order to be more effective? Have you tested them with potential customers?

» **Budget to achieve goals:** If you have big sales goals, your marketing and launch budget need to give you the ability to reach customers with appropriate marketing tools.

» **Message reach:** Make sure the marketing activities you put in place reach the customers that you want, and avoid spending money reaching those that aren't your target market.

» **Product readiness:** Your product must be ready at the quality level that customers expect. If it isn't, you've wasted a lot of money attracting people to a product that either isn't available or disappoints customers.

Keeping these in mind can help make sure you do everything possible to run a very successful launch and have the best possible chance of achieving your revenue goals.

Setting Launch Goals

Getting clear on what you're trying to achieve with your launch is important. Your launch goals guide all the other elements of your plan, such as how much you're going to spend, what marketing programs you'll be running, where and whether you want to get exposure through public relations, and what type of launch you'll want to run.

REMEMBER

Choose goals you can measure. Otherwise, you won't be able to do upfront analysis to determine whether your plans will meet your goals. For example, if your goal is to generate 1,000 leads, you can analyze how much exposure your launch activities will give you and estimate whether it's enough activity to get to the goal. Of course, using concrete numbers also means you can measure after the fact whether you achieved your goal.

You may simply have one goal, or you could have multiple goals, depending on what you are trying to achieve with your launch. Here are some examples of different types of goals:

>> Identify 700 well-qualified leads, 3 percent of which purchase the products, generating 21 unit sales and $600,000 in revenue.

>> Get to market with a *minimum viable product* (MVP), which has minimal features and functionality, to get customer feedback and quickly improve the product.

TECHNICAL STUFF

Releasing products with an MVP goal is a common strategy in start-ups as well as companies bringing new products to market by using Lean startup and Agile development methodologies. Chapters 8 and 12 have explanations of Agile and Lean concepts.

>> Become the de facto perceived market leader by getting 12 positive reviews and mentions in a targeted list of publications and websites.

>> Within 3 months, get 20,000 subscribers to sign up, use the service, and refer at least one friend.

>> Have 90 percent or more customers indicate that they'd recommend the product to a colleague or friend.

Checking Out Different Launch Types

The range of launch possibilities varies from an app update every couple of weeks to a full-scale launch every year or two. Read on to see the advantages and disadvantages for different types of launches and what will work best for your product.

Launches under Agile or very frequent releases

Some products don't need any formal launch marketing activities. For example, if your product is web-based and you release new features to customers online once a month, you may need to do very little other than notifying your customers with a pop-up about what the new features are. This kind of launch strategy is common with teams doing Agile development. If the new version of the product contains major features, you may want to update your website and marketing materials to include the new features as well. The downside of this kind of approach is that launches are usually so small that getting any kind of press coverage or generating much excitement is difficult because everything you do is a minor launch.

TIP

Make sure that your launch cadence takes into account how quickly your customers want to have to learn and get used to new features. If you change your product too often, even if the new features provide value, your customers may become overwhelmed and unhappy. This point is particularly true if the new features change how users perform any of the most important and critical tasks that they routinely do with your product. If your customers have to re-learn how to do basic tasks, they may become frustrated and turn to a different product. A strategy for combating this feature-release fatigue — and helping you generate excitement, buzz, and awareness about your product — is to hold off releasing smaller iterations of your product when their development is complete. Instead, combine a larger set of features into one major release. A company that uses this technique well is Salesforce.com. Although the company does fully Agile development, it saves up the features and does bigger releases less often so its customers aren't inundated constantly with new features and the company can get websites and analysts to write about the new versions of its products.

Easy does it: The soft launch

The first type of launch is a *soft launch*. A soft launch is when the product is launched without a lot of corresponding launch activities to generate widespread awareness. Sometimes companies do this type of launch if their product isn't fully ready and they want to deploy to a limited set of customers who may have special agreements to delay payment until the product is deemed final. Start-ups often use soft launches because they don't have the financial and marketing resources to do much more. They may have a need to get the product out quickly, capture some customers and revenues, and then use results to go to venture capitalists for additional funding to expand their sales and marketing efforts.

The other reason for doing a soft launch is that a company wants to get the product into customers' hands rapidly to get some quick feedback and improve the product. For products that are a brand-new type of offering, this type of early feedback may be necessary in order to make course corrections to get to a version 2.0 or 3.0 that truly meets market needs.

The downside to soft launches (when a product is fully ready and the company's goal is to maximize revenues) is that, more often than not, they generate little or no revenue. Because a soft launch doesn't have the momentum of a big push behind it with the corresponding marketing and PR activities, the launch often creates little or no press coverage, and the company finds itself weeks later wondering why it was unable to generate more interest in the product and why it missed its revenue targets. Once the product is launched, the company can't go back and re-launch it because it has been available and is old news. So they must create extensive and expensive marketing programs to attempt to make up for the lack of awareness created by the soft launch.

A small effort: The minimal launch

A *minimal launch* is something you want to consider when you have a small launch budget and few resources to work on the launch. Your product may not be that important to your company's strategy and overall success, or you may be coming up with a minor revision and only want to make your existing customers aware so that they upgrade.

Companies also often use minimal launches because they've failed to plan early enough and then have to scramble for a minimal launch because they've run out of time. Another scenario is that companies mistakenly think they need only a minimal launch to meet their goals. This happens because of unrealistic expectations about how important their product is to the market and the assumption that the product will sell itself.

Minimal launches can be very effective if you use your resources wisely. For example, instead of trying to do a *horizontal launch* to make the entire industry aware of the product, a company may want to target a specific *vertical market,* such as the insurance or health care industries, with a combination of email blasts, PR, and seminars. If the product is a good solution in that vertical, it may provide the company with the revenues necessary to expand the marketing campaigns later on.

REMEMBER

Minimal launches can have the same downsides as soft launches (see the preceding section). When a company has minimally launched the product, it may have to spend an extraordinary amount of money to build the revenue momentum it needs, if it can at all.

Going all-in: The full scale launch

A *full-scale launch* is designed to maximize awareness, generate as many leads and sales as possible, and let the industry know who your company is and why you matter. You spend more money on a full-scale launch, but, spent right, each dollar is much more effective because your marketing programs build on each other and provide synergy. For example, imagine you place dozens of product announcements in publications, follow them up with advertising that reaches the same readers, receive excellent product reviews, and then send your target customers a direct-mail piece. Each one of these exposures to the potential customer creates additional awareness and credibility and builds on the others, ultimately enticing your prospects to act and buy your product.

REMEMBER

Full-scale launches can be broadly horizontal in nature or can target one or multiple verticals. The choice depends on your product and chosen marketing strategy.

A full-scale launch gives your product the best chance of success, though most companies are afraid to spend the money to execute one. Even though they may have spent millions of dollars developing a product that is going to change their customers' lives, when it comes down to spending a few hundred thousand dollars they aren't realistic that this amount may be required to generate the millions in revenue their plans call for.

Choosing a launch type: Key considerations

An excellent strategy for planning is to use a full-scale launch as the starting point. If you're budget, resource, or time constrained, scale back the plan and use a subset of the programs listed in Figure 14-1 (and even more options listed in Chapter 15) to run a more minimal launch. This gives you the best chance of success, ensures you don't forget to consider all the options, and allows you to make educated trade-offs about how you're going to reach your goals. Use Figure 14-1 to look at the trade-offs in results and Figure 14-2 for relative costs for each kind of launch.

	Soft Launch	Minimal Launch	Full-Scale Launch
Budget and resources required	Low	Medium	High
Risks	May not generate enough awareness and may cost significantly more to do so at a later date	May not be sufficient to meet aggressive or unrealistic goals	Product or market may not be ready and money and resource investment could end up not paying off
Brand and product awareness generation	Low	Low	High
Possible reward	Low, unless the goal is to generate a small amount of awareness due to the product not being fully ready to delight customers	Medium to high, if the product completely delights customers it may go viral through word of mouth	High due to the fact that this strategy generates as much possible awareness and target customers are likely to positively hear about it many times in a short time period

FIGURE 14-1:
Launch type trade-offs.

Item	Soft Launch	Minimal Launch	Full-Scale Launch
PR firm for six months or press release only	$1k	$1k	$120k
AdWords campaign	$4k	$4k	$5k
Sales enablement:training, collateral, demo	$5k	$10k	$25k
Email blasts to purchased lists		$10k	$20k
Print advertising			$250k
Trade show and launch event			$30k
Channel marketing program			$50k
Guerrilla activities via in-house staff	✓	✓	✗
TOTAL	**$10k**	**$25k**	**$500k+**

FIGURE 14-2:
Launch type costs.

TECHNICAL STUFF

Guerrilla marketing activities are things the employees and friends of the company do to promote the company. They can include wearing product t-shirts at an event, writing blogs, posting on Twitter, and liking and sharing the company blog article about the release on LinkedIn. All these activities cost little or nothing. They often have minimal impact as well, but when you don't have a lot of budget, you get very creative. Guerrilla marketing activities have such a low impact on full-scale launches, it's as though they never happened.

Running a Smooth Product Launch

You have a solid plan designed to realistically meet your goals. The critical thing now is executing a flawless launch so that things go as planned (though you can adjust the plan where/if necessary) and the company and launch team give you the support and cooperation that you need.

Some companies have groups that are dedicated to running product launches, while others have specific launch processes with clear roles, responsibilities, and timelines. However, some have none of this infrastructure in place, so you may have to step up to create and implement it for this and future launches. Don't be afraid to define some best practices and a simple process that states who does what and when. Doing so will reduce future stress and position you as a knowledgeable leader who has the company's best interests at heart. The team will likely welcome a simple process that minimizes failure, fire drills, and bumps in the road.

Building your launch squad

Make sure you identify who will be on the launch squad from each of the respective departments, including operations, marketing, support, engineering, public relations, quality assurance, international, and any other pertinent groups. While sales can be part of your launch squad, they are often not in the office. It's easier to keep sales informed or ask them for specific participation as you need it. Meet with squad members at least three months prior to launch to have a kickoff, walk through the plan, and set expectations of what you need from them. If you meet resistance, this point is the time to address it and make sure you have full commitment.

TIP

Let your company and a broader audience of stakeholders and executives know who is on the launch squad so that the squad members feel happy to be included and publicly committed to the success of the launch. Acknowledge the role of each squad member and the specialty skills they bring as being critical to the plan and show that you have confidence in the team to deliver.

Tracking milestones and ensuring accountability

Build out a chart of milestones and a table with key activities, such as collateral and website content being completed, showing who is responsible for them. Include due dates so that you can track progress on a weekly basis. Hold launch squad meetings as often as necessary so you can hold the team accountable and make sure nothing is slipping through the cracks.

Make sure you communicate the status in a brief report to a wider audience, such as your executives and channel partners, so they're aware of the effects of how the plan is being executed. For example, if the launch slips, let them know so they can plan how they need to respond in their area. Share any bad or challenging news with them, and highlight positive happenings — giving your squad credit, of course!

Arming your sales team and other key stakeholders

A highly effective tool during the early part of your launch is a product launch one-pager like the one shown in Figure 14-3. This short, simple document gives your sales team and other key readers the critical, need-to-know information. Creating this document and making it readily available can save you dozens of hours answering questions and explaining (and re-explaining) the product details.

Product/Code Name One-Page Overview Company Confidential	
100-word product description	
Target customers	
Positioning	
Tagline	
Top three features	
Unique selling proposition	
Pricing	
Availability	
Distribution channels being used	
Promotions	
Estimated availability Beta: Golden Master (final released software):	
Competition: Top three	
FAQ: Top three to five	

FIGURE 14-3:
One-page product description.

TIP

Early on in the launch process, create 25-, 50-, 100-, 150-, and 250-word descriptions of your product. You'll need descriptions with various word lengths for web, brochures, ads, and partner sites. Getting them all done at once saves a lot of time later on.

As you approach launch, you want to train your salespeople so they know who the product is for (that is, the personas; see Chapter 5), what's in it for each of the people in the buying cycle, why it will be compelling and easy to sell, and what's in it for them. (*Tip:* Make sure salespeople see how they can meet their goals and make their quota and commissions easily!) Train the support staff and, if your product is replacing an existing one, let the appropriate people know the end-of-life plans for the retiring product. (Chapter 16 has details on end-of-life planning.) And train and inform anyone else who will be critical to keeping your product launch engine running smoothly as the launch starts and progresses.

Creating a Product Launch Plan

Your launch will tell your company and stakeholders what you are planning and how it impacts them. The process of creating it will help you think about the different aspects of the launch so that you are well-prepared to execute on the plan.

Recognizing the importance of the launch plan

As with all things in life, spending some time upfront planning your launch will likely pay off with great success. If you have an idea of what your goals are and have a well-thought through plan, you're at least headed in the right direction.

In our consulting practice, we can't believe how many companies spend lots of money developing the next killer product yet devote little or no time determining how to launch it and get the revenue and profit engine going. They simply assume customers will flock to the product. Instead of simply relying on assumptions, make sure you're ahead of the game so that your sweat and labor building that great product don't go to waste.

Your planning for launch happens during the develop and qualify phases (which we discuss in Chapters 12 and 13). To make sure you cover all the key questions, use the launch plan template included in the Product Management LifeCycle Toolkit (included as a free download with this book; see the Introduction, page 4, for details). *Note:* Be sure to revisit documents you've already developed, such as the market strategy document; they already contain some of the elements that would typically be in a standalone launch plan (such as the total available market, market segmentation, positioning, and unique selling proposition). You can update them now based on any changes in the market and/or product and include them in the launch plan if others in your company need to know about and/or approve them.

Filling out the launch plan template

The launch plan template includes a brief back story to the launch. Most of the launch plan is a long list of launch activities and reasons for each of them. The better you can tell the overall launch story and how all the pieces fit together, the better you can defend your launch plan.

Executive summary

Summarize the goals of your campaign: company messages, product audience, goals for the launch, and how you'll measure the launch success. Identify key features of the product you're launching here, including features, functions, and system requirements. You can take some of these items from the market strategy document.

Product description

Include a brief description of the product (two to three paragraphs) that describes what the product is, the main features and benefits it provides and how it solves customer problems. This is a synthesis of the information that you created in the market needs document along with the solution as defined in the product description document.

Target audience

Who is your target customer? Who are the product personas? What are your target market segments? What business segments are you targeting? Identify here the differentiating factors for your products and the important customer needs they're satisfying. Identify customer value and total cost of ownership issues.

Key messages

What are your key messages for the product? For your company? This information comes from the messaging platform that you created as part of the market strategy document discussed in Chapter 10.

Critical success factors

Include the specific criteria that indicate that the launch has been a success. Include concrete and measurable goals such as revenue targets, number of press articles/mentions, number of partners carrying the product, channel availability, and competitive perception in the marketplace.

Critical dates and milestones

List all critical dates and milestones including product availability, finalizing product name, budget, positioning, and press activities.

Internal commitments and owners

List all necessary commitments you need from individuals or groups in your company required for success and call out who owns each.

Marketing communications

What key marketing vehicles will work best for you given your budgetary constraints and your target audience? Following are some components that product managers need to consider:

>> **Collateral materials:** What types of materials, such as product fact sheets, brochures, and so on, do you need to support the launch? Are corresponding company materials required? Do company-wide collateral pieces need to be updated?

>> **Press event/conference:** Do you want to hold a press event/conference for your product? Which key press members do you need to invite? You can decide on the specific press you want to target based on your key messages.

>> **Trade show or event:** Do you want to have a presence at a trade show or event where your target audience will be in attendance? What does that presence look like — a booth, a suite, or one-on-one meetings with customers? Who from your company do they meet with?

>> **Press releases:** Send out quotes from premier customers/beta customers to target publications.

>> **Publications:** Create key articles to target publications. Either submit articles written by someone in the company or be available for interviews by publication and online writers.

>> **Product evaluations:** Will you perform product evaluations? Will you publish benchmark data? What reputable sources will you quote?

>> **Online communication:** How will you communicate online? What online advertisements will you develop and use (banner ads, email campaign, and so on)?

>> **Company web pages:** Will you update your company web pages? Which ones? Will you provide demos of your products? Via a web page?

Milestones

List an overall timeline of all activities in the launch plan that need to happen.

Financials and launch budget allocation

What is the budget for your launch plan? Provide a pie chart of how you're allocating the launch budget (Figure 14-4) and give the details in a table. Include a short explanation of why you're allocating the funds the way you are.

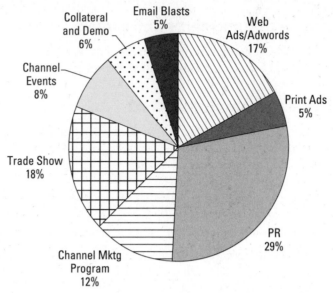

FIGURE 14-4:
Sample launch budget allocation.

Launch budget and ROI

What is your launch budget? What do you expect each line item to contribute to the overall launch ROI? Your launch sales don't usually recoup all the product development costs. Ideally, you want the sales generated during launch to reimburse the launch expenditures. If you're working for a start-up or have very long sales cycles, recouping your investment during the launch may not be possible. Figure 14-5 shows a typical launch plan ROI calculation. Refer to Chapter 9 for more information on ROI calculations.

Program	Cost	# Exposures	# Leads	Closed Sales	Profit
Webinars	$75,000	1,200	24	3	$9,600
Adwords/Online Advertising	$100,000	500,000	12,500	1,250	$125,000
Online White Paper Distribution	$75,000	40,000	4,000	40	$160,000
Trade Shows	$140,000	6,000	2,400	240	$384,000
Email Blasts - Known Customers	$75,000	3,000	300	30	$120,000
Channel Marketing Program	$35,000	10,000	1,000	70	$160,000
TOTAL	$500,000				$958,600
Total Profit	$958,600				
Less Total Cost	$(500,000)				
Net Return	$458,600				
ROI	92%				

FIGURE 14-5:
Launch budget with ROI.

Risk analysis

Include information on all possible risks, including critical decisions not being made, product slips, competitive landscape changes, and so on. How will you overcome these barriers? How might they affect your company? Is the probability of these risks low, medium, or high? Keep your answers brief.

Assumptions, open issues, and governance

List any of the assumptions made in this document. For example, you may have a formidable competitor that is due to release a new version of its product and your launch plan may assume that you will launch your product six months prior to the competitor's launch.

List all open decisions, including final budget and anything else that needs to be resolved to move forward. Track any open issues during the creation of this document. When the issue is resolved, document it. Any unresolved issues should be assigned to a responsible party.

Describe the governance processes and structures within the company. What has happened up to this point, and what are the next steps? Be brief.

Document approval

List the roles and names of the contributors and key reviewers of this document.

Core project team

Specify what commitments are required from each of the departments involved. Which named individuals are part of the launch team? What are their roles in the launch?

Validating the Plan against Your Launch Goals

As you near finishing up the plan, make sure to do a reality check to determine whether it can meet your stated launch goals. Answer the key questions, such as whether the launch type, budget, resources assigned, and company commitment are enough to accomplish what you must achieve to make the launch and product successful.

One of the most common goals is to achieve a certain level of sales, revenue, profits, and/or customer adoption and usage. Carefully analyze your launch plan to determine whether your activities will drive enough potential customers to awareness and consideration that even as some of them fall away you end up with a total number in terms of unit sales and revenues that is realistic given your goals.

TIP

Do an analysis like the one shown in Figure 14-6 and present it to your executives and stakeholders so that you can either get the support and resources you need or set expectations for how the results will likely compare to the company's goals. Otherwise, you may be expected to deliver on unreasonable goals — and blamed for a lack of results if things don't work out. By including assumptions, getting everyone to walk through them and understand the calculations, and then tracking results, you can use data to build your case and lead the company to launch success.

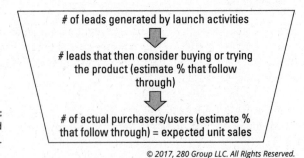

FIGURE 14-6:
Launch lead funnel.

© 2017, 280 Group LLC. All Rights Reserved.

Use Figure 14-6 to work through the following example from the bottom up. The company has agreed that your goal is to sell 1,000 units in the first three months during the launch. So 1,000 is your expected unit sales. Now start at the top. Your marketing generates 10,000 leads (people who want to find out more about your product). Your estimate is that 5 percent (10,000 × .05 = 500) of those leads then learn more and consider buying. In the next step you estimate that 10 percent of the 500 who consider purchase actually do complete the purchase; that's 50 (500 × .10) unit sales, nowhere near your target of 1,000 units. Working the math back the other way, if your target is 1,000 units sold, then you'd have to have 10,000 people who consider purchasing (1,000/.1) and 200,000 (10,000/.05) leads. That's a 20 times increase over the 10,000 you had planned. And now you need to explain that you'll need more marketing budget to make the sales targets.

After the launch is well underway, analyze how you're doing against your stated goals and make adjustments to how and where your marketing funds are spent. Hold a formal review with the launch squad to evaluate how the launch process worked: What went well, and what could be improved? Did you meet your goals? What did you learn in terms of assumptions, roles and responsibilities, and schedules? Capture the results formally and share them with the company. If you hold a formal review, share the results and help the company to constantly improve; you'll not only have greater success and buy-in for your efforts but also begin to be perceived as a true product and company leader.

Chapter **15**

Maximizing Your Product's Revenue and Profits

This chapter discusses the phase that your product is likely to stay in the longest: maximize. Many products in the mature phase of the four-phase product life cycle (see Chapter 3) stay there for years or even decades. Maximizing revenues requires working through all aspects of marketing to continually improve the message, marketing programs, pricing, channels, and possibly the product itself.

Marketing is a vast topic, and it's covered in-depth in books such as *Marketing For Dummies* by Alexander Hiam (Wiley). In this chapter, we focus on the marketing knowledge and tools that allow you as a product manager to have an effective conversation with your sales and marketing colleagues. In the end, product management, marketing and sales all want to maximize sales and profits. This book can't possibly cover every possible situation and all the in-depth concepts of marketing, so this chapter concentrates on core marketing concepts.

By getting some basic marketing know-how, you can effectively contribute to the marketing plan and track whether the marketing campaign is a success. This chapter introduces the fundamentals of both marketing and forecasting and shows you how to put them into practice after your product has launched.

Grasping the Basics of Marketing

Marketing basics give you the vocabulary to talk to the folks in your marketing department and effectively work with them. You often work closely with marketing people (more often known as *marcom*, short for marketing communications), so speaking their language is important.

The following sections give you some insight on what goes on in the marketing department so you can be an active participant.

Marketing mix

Marketing mix is the interplay of several different factors you can act on to change how your customer perceives your total product offering. The marketing mix is traditionally known as the four Ps, although there are actually seven Ps worth considering. We spell them out in the following sections. As you work through your marketing plan, you look at all aspects of your whole product offering and adjust it so that everything works together to tell your story to the customer.

When you plan your marketing activities and all the associated services (or review a plan being created by someone else), keep these seven marketing mix variables in mind as you build up a picture of how to best both sell the product and have customers remain satisfied with it after purchase.

The four core Ps

The four traditional Ps are *product, price, place* (which is really *distribution,* but that word doesn't start with a *p*), and *promotion.*

PRODUCT

To better address your target markets' needs, you can vary or adjust your product in the following common ways:

>> **Variety:** How many different kinds of product do you offer? One common way to vary your line is to have a series of products that correspond to good, better, and best.

>> **Quality:** Do products offer different quality levels? Is one longer lasting than another?

>> **Design:** Products can be designed to look more or less expensive or scale to cater to more or fewer users.

>> **Features:** What features are available? Which ones aren't available in a lower-end product?

>> **Brand:** A high-end, luxury brand brings an expectation of a higher product quality than a non-branded product.

>> **Packaging:** What story does the packaging tell? Is it luxurious for a high-end product? Simpler for a lower-end one? Does the packaging itself form part of the value of the product? One example is the circus box of cookies. The string that goes across the top is what children use to hold the box, and any product manager who takes over that product is told, "Don't mess with the string!" The string is such an inherent part of the part of the experience that it's untouchable even as other parts of the package may change.

>> **Services:** Are any services associated directly with the product or available in addition to the core product?

Most product changes are made earlier in the development process. But as you sell your product, new target markets arise and you should be ready to adjust your offering accordingly. You would typically go back to the beginning of the product life cycle process and start with conceive. Instead of marching through every step of the detailed process, however, you would quickly move through the phases to reach a final product because you are basing your revision on a pre-existing underlying understanding of the market.

PRICE

To get the base price, start with the manufacturer's suggested retail price (MSRP). Most products are then discounted depending on volume and location. One additional service product to consider offering customers is financing. Financing enables customers to buy big-ticket products and pay them off over time. This increases the number of customers who can afford your product. For a more in-depth look at pricing, head to Chapter 10.

Sometimes prices are discounted for a certain time only. This promotional pricing creates artificial urgency, meaning customers will tend to buy earlier than they otherwise would because they want to take advantage of the good price. Each industry has its own special pricing vocabulary. Your salespeople are great sources of information on how they vary price to generate sales faster.

Product managers have more or less control over pricing depending on regulation, complexity of pricing in a particular industry, and the amount of control that the finance organization demands over pricing. When product managers are able to, they recommend pricing which is then approved by management and finance.

WARNING

Pricing is driven by your market positioning. If you're a high-end brand, moving to a lower price point confuses your customers. Let your brand and product strategy drive the price, not the other way around.

PLACE (DISTRIBUTION)

Your product is typically distributed according to where your customers are used to buying your type of product. If you don't have (or don't want) direct relationships with everyone who sells your product (such as stores or online sites), you can use distributors. Distributors sell a range of products through to the outlet that sells your product to the end user. A strong interplay exists between distribution and what the end user pays because a distribution partner introduces one more intermediary. The more intermediaries requiring margins and profits from the product, the higher the price to the end user.

Product managers do not decide which distribution mechanism a company uses. Sales is the key decision maker on distribution. However, you should know how much information customers need to be comfortable buying your product from a particular reseller, channel partner, or website. In high-end goods, the type of experience that customers get from the reseller is also a factor. For example, you may find a product cheaper on Amazon, but you don't get nearly the retail experience as you would through a high-end retail shop, which may handle returns or product setup or allow you to try out the product more easily. Certain high-end brands have extremely limited distribution because in their cases, being hard to find is part of the attraction.

Another distribution issue has to do with logistics and inventory. If you don't want to pay to keep your product in your own warehouse and don't want to have the hassle of dealing with stores and resellers directly, the distributors will do it for you. This distribution service is paid for with the margin that they take as they sell the product on.

PROMOTION

Promotion is probably what you first picture when you think of marketing: ads, sales campaigns, and press tours, among others. Yes, promoting your product is fun. It's even better when you're really clear on the message that causes customers to buy (quickly, and at the highest reasonable price) and you communicate that message through the right marketing vehicle. It's a complicated juggling act — one you get better at it over time. Look to "Fitting into the sales and marketing funnel" later in this chapter to better understand all the parts of the promotion sequence.

The three additional Ps

If you work with service products like airlines, banks, churches, and car rentals, the following three Ps are also very useful. In fact, they're useful for any product because virtually any sale requires an interaction which relies on one of these Ps. For service products, however, understanding them can mean the difference between success and failure since these three Ps represent the only interaction that a customer has with the product.

PEOPLE

The employees who deliver a service to your customers are sometimes the only contact a customer has with your product or brand. Your people (employees) and their ability to consistently and carefully deal with a wide range of customer requests determine the success of your company. Training in how to treat customers consistently and well is critical to your success as a service.

PROCESS

Because a service is by and large intangible, consistency in how you provide that service makes your customers feel confident that you know what you're doing. If they call to accomplish a task, they want to be able to expect certain procedures and processes are being followed. For example, if you call your bank, the correct process is to verify your identity through a variety of checks. Calling a bank isn't the core banking product; however, by following a consistent process, customers are confident that their bank can be trusted with the entirety of the banking products that they use. The bank, is after all looking after the customer's money! If you receive lots of negative feedback from customers, dissect how your people are following the given process. The process may need to be updated, improved, or simply followed more closely.

PHYSICAL EVIDENCE

In today's online world, you have very little evidence that a transaction has taken place. The physical evidence (or even the user interface or online receipt, for that matter) is the only manifestation that a transaction occurred. If the evidence available is unclear in any way, it substantially devalues the product that was provided.

Here are a few examples of physical evidence supporting the value of a service product:

>> A customer at Nordstrom interacts with a salesperson at Nordstrom and is handed the salesperson's business card. This reinforces the high-end brand value of Nordstrom.

>> Your anti-virus software works in the background. Occasionally a window pops up to let you know how many viruses have been blocked.

>> You use a coupon service at a store. Once a quarter you get an email outlining how much money you saved.

Keep physical evidence in mind for anything that the customer looks at. The physical evidence is what determines their assumption of whether a product is good, viable, and valuable.

Working with marcom and creating marketing collateral

Marketing collateral refers to all the virtual, printed, videoed, and other pieces you use to communicate about your company and your product. Your marcom people know how best to create the entire pack of materials in the most cost efficient way. For example, if they insist that a piece of collateral be a particular size, it may be because they know that increasing it by half an inch doubles the cost. They know how long it takes to create and print something or make a web page available online — including design time. They know the role of fonts, layout, and design and how best to communicate the message so the customer can actually understand and use it. Work closely with them; you'll gain a huge appreciation for their specialized skills, and they'll help greatly in your product success.

Much like picking out an outfit for a special event, the marcom person will propose a range of marketing materials to choose from. Marcom creates some of the collateral items. Some items like the product presentation may be created by you, the product manager. However, marcom's catalog of the most common marketing items created can guide you as to what salespeople find useful. If you aren't convinced by what marcom has proposed, go ask a few salespeople directly what they find useful. Based on our experience sales never even uses about 40 percent of all marketing material, so you may be able to save money by researching what exactly sales and customers need and then just focus on key marketing pieces.

The following team prepares marketing collateral

>> **Product manager:** Responsible for core content, technical facts, initial drafts, and final technical checks.

>> **Product marketing manager (if available):** Wordsmiths initial drafts to ensure customer-focused language. Checks final layouts prepared by marcom. If you don't have a product marketing manager, the product manager does these tasks.

>> **Marcom:** Takes initial texts and adds images and graphics. Creates a layout of the information that adheres to company collateral standards. Checks with product management and product marketing that the final versions are correct and arranges for the materials created to be posted (web) or printed (hard copies).

Here are a few possible collateral pieces:

>> **Datasheets and brochures:** Datasheets are the source point for product information that is shared with your customers. Often it's the first piece of collateral generated and the one most frequently referred to. The trick to an effective data sheet is to have enough data and information but not so much you overwhelm potential customers with detail. One good idea is to focus the beginning of a datasheet on customer benefits and work toward the most technical bits at the end. Brochures join several products to tell a larger story about your company's solutions. The information in a brochure is an abbreviated version of the datasheet or tells the story of a solution that the product solves.

>> **Success stories or case histories:** More commonly used in B2B settings, these items are written-up stories of actual customers who agree to promote your product or solution. Essentially, they're testimonies of how your product or group of products (solution) helped a customer solve an actual problem. Success stories are used to convince prospective customers that your offering solves their need. Success stories are very powerful sales tools, so keep working on getting a few of them for your salespeople, especially if you see your competitors have them.

>> **Product demonstrations:** A great product demonstration can do wonders in the right hands. Create a detailed script if it's a live demonstration. If it's not something that can easily be replicated, plan a video or scripted screenshots in Microsoft PowerPoint.

>> **Web pages:** Create a few key web pages that tell your story. If your company website doesn't work well for explaining your particular product story, look at what you like in other company's websites to get some more ideas. Then work with your marcom people to implement your company's version of successful websites you've seen.

>> **Videos:** Videos tell your product story visually. A good video will generate traffic from another website, such as YouTube, which increases your site's ranking on search engines. As a bonus, you can embed ads in the video and generate sales or capture immediate interest directly from it. Beware of boring videos, though. Customers who don't desperately need your product will leave quickly if they aren't entertained.

>> **Presentations:** Along with the datasheet, the product presentation is usually the other critical piece of the collateral puzzle. The presentation is used to describe your product to sales, support, outside channel partners, and the press at a range of events before, through, and then long after the launch of a product. If you have funds or an internal graphic designer, it helps to work with a professional to improve the look of it. Refer to *PowerPoint 2016 For Dummies* by Doug Lowe (Wiley) to increase your skill with presentations.

TIP

>> **Updated FAQs:** Capture all the questions you get during your presentations and from talking with customers and use them to create your product FAQs (frequently asked questions). You may have to generate one for internal audiences like sales and support and another one for customers with less sensitive information. Depending on your company, your product and how you sell it, FAQs are emailed, uploaded to internal information databases and posted on websites. As the product manager, you're often the only person who has the answers, so having FAQs you can refer others to will save you a lot of time in answering questions for each person who has them.

>> **Channel collateral:** Channel partners are external companies who sell your product to customers on your behalf. If you rely on channel partners to generate sales for you, you should provide them with collateral to use. Doing so ensures the messaging is consistent and the look and feel of the materials are professional. Talk to your channel partners to find out what they need. Typical requests include sample customer emails, graphics, a presentation that they can add their logos to, and sales training sheets (which are called lots of different names in different industries and companies). By delivering what your channel partners want, you make selling your product easier for them (and cut down on the likelihood that they'll create their own collateral that doesn't match your approach). In turn, they're more prone to sell your product.

>> **Blog and social media posts:** Create a list of possible blog posts and a publishing schedule. (Plan additional time if your company needs to have legal approval on what you write.) Publish the completed posts on the company website, use them as LinkedIn posts, and then post to LinkedIn groups that are interested in the topic. We highlight LinkedIn here because it works well for B2B industries. Blog posts are less valuable for B2C products. Post to social media platforms that your customers spend time using; doing so increases the value and awareness of each post that you create.

WRITING READABLE ENGLISH

English teachers spend enormous effort trying to get students to expand their vocabularies and use complex sentence structures. Writing for marketing means unlearning some of that teaching. Good marketing writing typically contains three elements:

- **Simpler language:** Use simple words to get your point across. To simplify a very long linguistics lesson, English is built on a base of Anglo-Saxon words topped with words of French and Latin origin. You can tell the French words. Usually, they're long and have lots of syllables. Guess what? The kind of English that is most effective in getting to the point and generating action comes from the Anglo-Saxon base of English.

- **Simple, concise sentence structure:** Break up your sentences so that it's more interesting to read. Have both shorter and somewhat longer sentences. Your customers will more easily understand what you write.

- **Humor and wit:** Humor makes the message stick better. If you can't work in gentle humor from time to time, try a good story or example. It will keep your audience's attention.

DIGITAL MARKETING

As more and more marketing activity moves to the digital realm, you also need to know how digital marketing works. This topic goes far beyond the scope of this book; it includes everything from analyzing email and web traffic to targeting ads on various platforms to customer relationship management (CRM) systems for tracking sales opportunities.

Your digital marketing or channel marketing person should be using a dashboard to visualize what is happening with different marketing activities. Ask her to show you the system's capabilities, and look out for opportunities to track what your customers are actually doing. Make adjustments based on what you find. Your job is to work out, in conjunction with your marketing folks, why customers aren't doing what you expect them to do and adjust your marketing programs to improve response rates.

Fitting into the sales and marketing funnel

Instead of approaching a marketing plan as a monolithic set of tasks, break down what you need to do during each phase of the purchase process (awareness, interest, evaluation, commitment, and referral) using a sales funnel as shown in Figure 15-1. If you look over a salesperson's shoulder, you may see this information displayed in their sales software. However, marketing also has a role in the different stages of this funnel.

It's a funnel because a lot of customers start out in the awareness stage. As they investigate product solutions, they start focusing down on fewer options that really seem to meet their needs. They then may evaluate even fewer options before making a final commitment to one solution.

Depending on your product type, the transition between marketing and sales may be simpler or more complex and may happen rapidly or slowly. For example, when was the last time you had a sales conversation to buy a book online? You most likely didn't. You probably completed the sale entirely through a hands-off set of marketing activities that didn't involve a salesperson. If you were buying a new roof for your house, though, you'd most likely go through a complex sales cycle that would include a lot of interaction with salespeople.

FIGURE 15-1:
Sales/marketing funnel by stage and associated activity.

When your marketing plan is taking shape, a good tool to use is the marketing activity by stage in Figure 15-2. For each stage of the sales and marketing funnel, you have a goal and a list of the marketing needed to achieve that goal. The right-hand column is the *call to action* — what the marketing piece specifically asks the customer to do.

Stage of Buying Cycle	Goal	Marketing to Achieve Goal	Call to Action
Awareness	Generate brand and product awareness	Ads: TV, radio, web, social media	Find out more.
Interest	This product will solve my problem	Website, webinar, trade show	Get more specific information.
Evaluation	Let me try it out	Special offers, sales is involved	Do it now!
Commitment	Ok, I'll buy it	Easy buying process (low friction)	You're so close!
Referral	Demonstrate public loyalty	Word of mouth, social media	Like us!

FIGURE 15-2:
Marketing activity by stage.

Here is what to look for in marketing activities at each stage of the marketing and sales funnel:

>> **Awareness:** What activities are generating awareness of your brand and your product? Are they generating awareness in the right places to reach your customer personas (which we describe in Chapter 5)? What do customers need to know to get them to move to the next step? What type of information is overkill at this point? Is your message compelling enough to make potential customers aware of your product?

Another factor is whether your marketing is persistent enough to catch people when they enter the buying cycle. For example, you see a lot of car ads. Most of the time, you ignore the ads — until you want or need to buy a car. Then you find yourself watching intently, trying to decide which car gives you the features you need and matches the image you have of yourself.

>> **Interest:** What will convince customers that your product may solve their problem? How will they find that message? How will they access it? What information do they need to determine that the product is worth investigating? The results of online search engine results can drive potential customers to you directly to this stage.

>> **Evaluation:** After customers have narrowed down their options, they reach out to buy or get more information. What information do customers require to evaluate your product? Do they need a sample? Do they need encouragement to get on and try your product? Many software products successfully use a 30-day free trial option. Other types of products may require a no-risk money-back guarantee.

>> **Commitment:** All of your sales and marketing activities won't matter unless the customer says yes. At this stage, your focus is on what tips the scales for a sale and prevents the customer from backing away.

A key concept here is *frictionless purchasing.* You don't want the customer to need to go through a lot of steps to actually buy your product. You want to make saying yes as easy as possible. Amazon 1-Click is a great example of how a company reduced the purchase process to only one click of a button.

TECHNICAL STUFF

In the digital arena, if customers visit your website, respond to your emails, or click on your ads, you can keep reminding those people about your product for an extended period of time by using a technique called *remarketing ads.* You can set up remarketing ads so they appear as often as you want, reminding your customer to keep considering your product. Unfortunately, these tools don't distinguish between people who bought and people who didn't, so, you may keep reminding people to buy a product that they already purchased.

>> **Referral:** In most cases, companies stop at commitment, but you can create marketing campaigns that focus on having customers refer their friends and colleagues. In an ideal world, customers happy with their purchases tell everyone about them. Instead, most happy customers keep their delight to themselves; the unhappy customers spread their displeasure all over the Internet. A referral from a customer is typically seen as being more truthful than a company's own marketing, so think of ways to use customer loyalty to drive other customers into the sales funnel.

Getting sales the tools to sell the product

Marketing activities are focused on motivating customers to change their behavior (that is, get them to buy your stuff). *Sales enablement* is where you pass the baton from impersonal mass communication to the salespeople. To do their jobs and complete the sale, salespeople need materials that help them communicate the value proposition effectively and easily. A value proposition defines the key reasons that cause a customer to select your product over another offering. The positioning and messaging statements from Chapter 10 for the basis of your value proposition. At a basic level, you need to help sales sell your product by doing the following:

>> Telling them who the target customers are and what their specific needs are.

>> Giving them whatever tools will help make the sale: written documents, spreadsheets that help them calculate the customer's return on investment, demo scripts, competitive selling sheets (how to sell against specific competitive offerings), email templates to use under various scenarios, and much more.

WARNING

These sales tools go much deeper in content and are above and beyond the customer-oriented marketing collateral covered earlier in this chapter.

What you share with sales is sometimes material that shouldn't be given to customers, so you need to be careful. If something is highly confidential and shouldn't be shared (such as a road map of your product's future or a controversial competitive analysis), always mark it clearly so it doesn't get shared inappropriately. In some countries and industries, you aren't allowed to publicly compare your products to the competition. And in many instances, you don't want to draw attention to the competition either.

The big problem with sales enablement is that marketing often builds a one-size-fits-all set of collateral for both customers and salespeople, and not all parts are useful to both parties. To really boost your sales, you need to get proactive and build the most effective tools with a sales enablement improvement plan. A sales enablement improvement plan is a series of changes in marketing and sales activities that leads to increasing sales success. Here's how to put a plan together:

1. **Visit customers who have bought and not bought from you.**

   Find out why they really bought/didn't buy the product. Find out what sales tools influenced their decision and which they find most useful.

2. **Interview successful salespeople and work out the process they use to close the sale.**

   Probe them to find out what they actually use when selling and what they need the most.

3. **Prepare a sales (increase) enablement plan that uses the messaging actual customers have given you and deliver it in the way successful salespeople have told you works.**

   Your customers told you why they bought your product. Take their words and create marketing messages from it.

4. **Train all your salespeople in how to use the sales enablement and tools you've created.**

Becoming marketing aware

In addition to focusing on customer understanding, practice becoming marketing aware. Pay attention to your reaction when you see an ad (or any marketing — even a datasheet) for all the products you're exposed to daily. Gauge your reaction to it. Do you think it's effective? Why or why not? Who do you think the target customer is? Is it the same market segment you're targeting? If you're with others, ask them what they think of the ad. What did they notice about it (if they noticed it at all)? Then ask yourself, "What is the intended purpose and target of this ad or marketing?" Also think about the cost of the marketing, its potential return on investment, and so on. Over time, you'll get better at deciphering the marketing intent behind any kind of communication and at costing marketing material and actions yourself.

Forecasting: A Look to the Future

Forecasting is an integral part of life for many product managers of physical goods; for service and software product managers, it may or may not be a big part of their work responsibility. The reason forecasting is part of the maximize phase is because that's when the need to forecast correctly becomes an ongoing part of tracking the success and failure of your products.

REMEMBER

Learn everything you can about the entire supply chain. Be creative in solving forecasting issues as you come across them. And don't worry about being 100 percent correct – it simply isn't possible. The following sections look at how to become as accurate as possible given the uncertainty surrounding any forecast.

Collecting data for forecasting

Forecasting can be defined as estimating future sales. The first rule of forecasting is very simple: You can't come up with a perfect forecast. It's always just an estimate, and no matter how many techniques and how much analysis you use, the answer you come up with will be incorrect. When you get beyond attempting the perfect forecast, here are a few suggestions for getting better at forecasting.

History has a role to play

Your historical data is a great starting point. If you sold 100 units last month, all things being equal, you should sell about 100 units next month. This point is why one of your first jobs as a product manager is to research the sales data of your product line (including discontinued products) going as far back as possible. Group products to understand the sales trends at the product line level.

If you have no historical data, try a top-down and bottom-up forecast:

>> **Top-down forecast:** For the top-down portion, work from the total market size. Estimate how much of the total market is your target market. Determine how much of the target market you can actually reach, and then decide what a defensible figure for your market share of that reachable market is. Get your salespeople involved in this discussion.

>> **Bottom-up forecast:** For the bottom-up component, define the marketing programs that drive sales and the likely sales results from a certain amount spent on marketing programs. For example, how much awareness will your marketing activities drive, and then how many leads will it create? What percentage of these leads will actually buy the product? How well is the sales channel (overall) able to sell your product depending on what you prime it to do?

Table 15-1 shows a sample top-down and bottom-up forecasts. In each month, choose the lower of the two estimates — June: 500, July: 600, August: 600, and September 800.

TABLE 15-1

Top-Down and Bottom-Up Forecast Results

Top-Down Monthly Sales Result over 6–12 Months	Bottom-Up Monthly Sales Results over 6–12 Months
June: 700	**June: 500**
July: 600	July: 700
August: 600	**August: 600**
September: 800	September: 1,200

TIP

You can also use proxies to generate a forecast. If you sell 1,000 units of a camera, then from total industry sales data and your knowledge of customer buying habits, you expect that 3 percent of your customers also want a wide angle lens.

Quarterly and seasonal variations can impact forecasts

Quarterly sales cycles affect how much you sell, because your salespeople want to make their target sales numbers and will push hard to close deals in the last month of the quarter. Seasonality may also hit. Toy sales are big in November and December, but don't count on those volumes in January after the Christmas rush. Big companies and governmental agencies buy just before the end of their fiscal years to use up budget, which can mean a large spike during this time. The point is that as a product manager you need to have a deep understanding of what drives differences in your product's sales from one month to the next and across longer periods of time. Your historical data (see the preceding section) helps you get a sense of what those drivers are. And your sales, marketing, and operations counterparts often have great insight into the "why" of the numbers.

Forecasting lead times are critical

Physical products are often planned and built long before they arrive to customers. You need to be aware that submitting a forecast often actually drives production at a different time than what you think. You need to be very aware of the length of time that it takes to order parts, plan manufacturing capacity and transport goods. The total of these activities is your *lead time*.

For example, in Figure 15-3, the *forecasting waterfall chart* shows that in December the company submitted a forecast of 1,000 units for the month of July. In other words, in July, the new product will be introduced in the market and in the previous December, the company believes that the unit demand for July will be 1,000 units. This is a complicated concept, so beware of the difference between when a forecast is made (December) and the month that the forecast is for (July). Each month, the company revisits the July forecast number. And it fluctuates between 1,000 and 2,500 units. However, operations and manufacturing stop reacting to forecasting changes after December. They have a lead time for manufacturing of six months (December to June when the units need to be in the warehouse for the July launch). Even if the forecast is changing, the plan for product delivery isn't changing. It's still 1,000 units. Since product managers are aware of their product's lead time, they often control the forecast, especially for the first few months of the product life.

Quantity Forecasted for July Intro

	Dec	Jan	Feb	Mar	Apr	May	Jun
Quantity forecasted each month for July intro	1,000	1,500	2,000	2,500	1,500	2,000	2,000
Operations	Ordered parts for 1,000 units		Parts arrive for 1,000 units				
Supply planning	Book factory capacity for March: 1,000						
Factory				Manufacture 1,000 units			
Shipping					Ship 1,000 units		1,000 Units arrive

FIGURE 15-3: Forecasting waterfall.

Operational constraints may come into play

Operations and manufacturing people can pull off what may seem like miracles if you ask them to. They can ship products faster (at a much higher cost). They can source additional parts if demand spikes and delay production if demand falls.

If you have lead time issues with your product, work closely with your operations partners to see how flexible they can be. A word of warning: When you ask manufacturing partners for heroic measures, your company pays a price in terms of profits and stress. Your manufacturing and production partners may become less eager to do business with you, and they may even raise their prices.

The sell-in cycle may have an effect

You need to understand how fast customers will actually buy new products. The sell-in cycle is a time measurement of how long it takes customers to actually buy a product once they know about it. If, for example, you launch your product in July, big customers may take six months to evaluate the product and start buying in volume. So, six months is your sell-in cycle. Until six months are up, you won't need much volume. How much is enough? Look at historical data for products that came to market before for guidance.

Different POVs provide insight

One other technique for forecasting is to get forecasts from a group of experts, let them each know the others' results, and then ask them to reforecast. Just listening to the differences in points of view gives you insight into a possible forecast. Keep in mind that, generally speaking, experts are more familiar with new product technologies and will assume a faster adoption of new products than that experienced in real life.

Making assumptions

The best way to make sure that your forecast is reliable is to be clear on the assumptions you make. Write them each down and let the operations people and salespeople know what they are. They may have different information, so pulling it all into one place is an incredibly powerful tactic to getting a better forecast.

To practice, look at Figure 15-4, which shows Product A's historical sales data. Answer the following questions:

>> What can you learn from the historical data trends?

>> What would you estimate for the March, April, and May forecasts?

In reading the chart, notice the following:

>> **Quarterly cycle:** There is a three-month cycle to sales. January and February have lower sales than March, and this happens every quarter. One good assumption is that salespeople are pushing product out in the last month of a quarter to make their numbers.

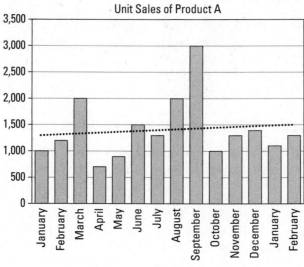

FIGURE 15-4:
Historical
sales data for
Product A.

>> **Annual sales cycles:** Another assumption is that there is a reason for the large spike in sales in September. Is it a market like finance or insurance that doesn't buy after September so that installation is complete by the end of the year? Is the product sold into retail customers who also don't like to make big changes as they go into the Christmas season?

>> **Overall sales trends:** What about the overall sales trend? The dotted line shows an overall annual increase. So another assumption is that the market (or your share of it) is growing.

There are no right answers, but you can make good assumptions and draw some logical, defensible conclusions.

Creating an Effective Marketing Plan

Marketing plans are the ongoing version of the launch plan — often with less time urgency because the "new" product is finished and released for sale. However, your company has to continue to generate market excitement and awareness for your products. Using the marketing concepts discussed earlier in this chapter and the outline of how to create a plan coming up in this section, you can create and maintain a high level of interest in your product, which leads to meeting your sales and profit goals.

Recognizing the importance of a top-notch marketing plan

A great marketing plan considers the customer's decision-making process and also outlines what the most effective communication method or methods are at each particular point in the journey toward buying. Each exposure a customer has to your message is called a *touchpoint.* For example, seeing an ad is a touchpoint. Reading a review is a touchpoint.

Many marketers and product managers make the mistake of assuming that potential customers will only have to hear about their product once to become interested because the product is so good. For less-expensive purchases or items that are purely impulse buys, one may be enough, but for a larger or more important purchase it's likely to be many more. A good rule of thumb is to assume a customer needs at least seven touchpoints to become interested and ultimately decide to purchase your product.

Outlining your marketing plan: What to include

As a product manager, the marketing plan most likely isn't a plan you own or create but rather one that belongs to your marketing department. That said, if you have new product offerings or need ongoing marketing for existing products, the plan should reflect your ongoing requests as part of marketing's overall objectives. Your input should drive the contents of the marketing plan. Here are the main elements of the marketing plan:

>> **Executive summary:** A summary covering the market situation, key objectives, key strategies, and approaches to addressing marketing objectives. What are the risks and the return on investment, and what is marketing's recommendation? Remember that the executive summary is written once all other parts are completed.

>> **Situational analysis:** What is the market landscape? What happened in the past? What is the current opportunity and what marketing resources (money, people) are available?

>> **Marketing objectives and strategy:** What are overall marketing objectives (and product specific ones, if necessary) and key marketing strategies? Which markets does the company or division plan to target? Does marketing need to take any other considerations into account? And product specific information in this section should come from the market strategy and possibly the market needs documents.

>> **Program mix:** In this section, define all your marketing mix components. (We discuss marketing mix earlier in this chapter.)

- **Branding and messaging:** How will marketing support your brand?

- **Advertising:** Document any and all advertising including online ad plans here.

- **Social media plan:** What social media outlets is marketing planning to use? Be specific.

- **Public relations:** What are the public relations strategies? Again, be specific.

- **Direct mail/email:** What are the direct mail and email plans? Does the marketing plan call for sending out a regular newsletter or buy-in lists of potential new customers from list vendors? What activities will marketing undertake to grow email lists?

- **Trade shows and events:** What events does marketing plan to support and how? Will your company be there, or will marketing, product management, and sales support a partner's efforts? What are specific goals and objectives for each event?

- **Channel:** What are sales and marketing's plans for working with the channel? If marketing funds are set aside as a percentage of sales, what is the best use of that money?

- **Timelines:** What happens when? Activities should be spread out so that something is happening over time. On the other hand, marketing should avoid spending money when customers are unlikely to buy.

- **Deliverables:** What are the key deliverables? Videos? Collateral pieces? A new website?

>> **Budget and return on investment (ROI):** What is the budget for marketing activities over a certain period? What are spending plans for each part of the marketing mix? As a result of all these activities, what is the expected ROI?

>> **Governance:** Who are the core marketing team members? Who needs to approve this document? Have a space for each person to physically or electronically sign.

>> **Risks, assumptions, open issues, exhibits, and appendices:** As with all documents, note the risks, assumptions, and open issues and provide appropriate exhibits and appendices.

As a product manager, your focus should be on the following key parts of the marketing plan:

>> What are the marketing objectives and strategy? Does it support what you need it to in order to make the product succeed? The marketing plan may detail activities that support an overall revenue number. Does it align with what your forecast and expectations are?

>> What is the mix of marketing programs? Make sure you understand how the choice of marketing activities helps or hurts your product's overall success. Is there enough online advertising? Not enough focus on public relations or getting good reviews? Make sure the mix supports getting enough touch points to the market you're targeting.

TIP

To get started, have a look at last year's or last quarter's marketing plan for your products or other products in your company. See what the thinking is behind it and how it could apply to your product's plan.

Setting goals

Figure 15-2 earlier in the chapter shows what you should have as a marketing component for each stage. To really succeed, you need to add in another column to cover what the metric of success for each stage is and/or what percentage of people should be moving from one stage to another. Use these numbers to drive specific goals for the marketing plan.

Here are some examples of goals that you can set for each stage.

>> **Awareness:** How many people will be exposed to the product, and how many touchpoints do they need before they take action? Even when people are interested in a topic, they need to see an ad roughly three times before they even register having seen it at all. If the goal is to reach 100,000 people with an ad three times, work with your marketing manager to figure out how to do so and what the costs will be. Marketing professionals are the best placed to flesh out this part of the sales stage.

>> **Interest:** Online search is the way most people investigate their options. Even if they don't know your brand or product, you're likely to have customers come looking if you know their likely search terms and are in the top three options that show up. Make sure that the few words that they see in the search engine results (or advertisements delivered through Google AdWords) deliver a short, compelling message that convinces them to click through. Rely on marketing's expertise to work through the search terms and compelling

messages. These same marketing co-workers will likely know what a good click-through rate is. For example, in some industries a 1 percent click through rate is considered successful. If your awareness goal is to reach 100,000 people, at a 1 percent click-through rate 1,000 people will have clicked through to visit your website.

>> **Evaluation:** The evaluation goal you set depends on your product. For example, software companies can simply allow customers to sign up and try a product for 30 days. This approach dramatically lowers the risk for customers trying the product. And if they aren't paying for it, at least initially, they may just give it a try. But what about larger-ticket items that require complex installation, have high costs, or may be mission-critical for a business? How do you convince these customers to evaluate the product?

Many companies offer a free white paper, with in-depth technical details, or other kind of information. Customers give you their contact info, and then the company can send them a list of informative emails over time (called a *drip email campaign*) or have a salesperson call them. You're always working toward a certain number of touchpoints. If your metric is a 10 percent evaluation rate and your interest stage goal is 1,000 people, your aim here is to get 100 customers to actually make it through to one kind of evaluation or another.

>> **Commitment:** When people evaluate products and have a positive experience, they become increasingly likely to buy. If you assume that 50 percent of the people who evaluate the product actually buy, your commitment goal is to sell 50 units for the original 100,000 people exposed to the product.

>> **Referral**: Referrals are an advanced topic that is addressed in a couple of ways. For larger sales that require salespeople's involvement, the salesperson will ask a customer for a referral or to be a reference on demand. For purchases that don't involve sales, the most common way to move to the referral stage is to ask customers for reviews or ratings. Amazon asks for reviews once you have purchased a product, and smartphone apps are forever asking you to rate them. Product managers are not often asked to participate nor are they asked to track this activity.

TIP

The preceding calculation sets goals from the top down (from awareness and interest through to commitment and referral), but you can also calculate from the bottom up (from commitment to interest and awareness). Start with the level of commitment you're looking for: "I need 50 customers at an average sales value of $100,000. How many potential customers do I need at each stage of purchasing to get to 50 customers?" By using these two approaches and comparing them to the programs in the marketing plan, you can gauge whether the marketing activities will allow you to achieve the overall product goals.

Monitoring Product Success Metrics

Because companies have an overall sales goal they need to meet, keeping an eye on actual sales is where product managers spend a lot of time when they aren't working on the next version of the product.

Keeping tabs on the sales funnel: Leads, opportunities, and conversions

Traditionally, each step in the sales funnel (see Figure 15-1) has a different success rate for each product. Monitor each stage's success rate on an ongoing basis and use the data to alter your product revenue expectations, plans, and forecast. Table 15-2 shows an example of sales tracking (including common terms that salespeople often use for each stage) through a sales funnel.

TABLE 15-2   **Sales Funnel Expected Revenue Results**

Marketing and Sales Terms	Calculated Possible Revenue	Expected Revenue over the Sales Cycle
Interest or leads	$1,000 \times 10\% \times \$100,000$	$10 million
Evaluation or opportunities	$100 \times 50\% \times \$100,000$	$5 million
Commitment or conversions	$50 \times 90\% \times 100,000$	$4.5 million
Expected revenue in the pipeline		$19.5 million

If you believe that your selling cycle is over six months, you should expect to see about $3.25 million in sales per month ($19.5 million ÷ 6).

This figure is sales revenue. Your focus is on spending marketing funds effectively. If you expected an ROI of 100 times what you spend on marketing, you should be spending no more than $195,000 over six months. This approach averages out to $32,500 per month. In reality, marketing budgets are rarely spent evenly. There are peaks and troughs, which is why marketing spends are calculated over at least a quarter.

Examining revenues and profitability

Over time, revisiting the expected revenue and profitability of a product and keeping them up to date with actual data from what has occurred is important. (See Chapter 9 for a detailed analysis of how to figure out those numbers.)

So is regularly reviewing your revenue, overall profitability, and gross margins (particularly for physical goods). If these numbers leave an acceptable range, create a plan of action for addressing and fixing the problem.

Gauging market share

Determining your market share isn't easy. In some industries, there are analysts who follow and ascertain market share for the overall market. If you're in one of these industries, you can buy these analysts' reports and see where you're ranked. *Remember:* These market share rankings often are given in revenue terms. You can check their biases given your known revenue to see whether they're credible sources of information or adjust for their biases.

What happens if you have a very specialized type of product that isn't tracked by analysts? You can use a few approaches:

>> Look at your competitor's publicly released revenue amounts and work the figure back against your known revenue.

>> Ask your distributor for information about how much your product sells versus your competitors. Distributors rarely give you actual sales figures, but they may be willing to give you a total number or a ranking.

>> Compare your overall sales to the total available market (TAM) you calculated as part of the market research into target markets and their size (see Chapters 5 and 10) to see what percentage of the market you've captured.

Unfortunately, there is no magic market share wand to calculate this figure. However, when you've hit on a method that gives reasonable data, keep using it consistently. What you're really looking for is changes up or down.

Benchmarking: Tracking against the business plan

Reading through a business case (see Chapter 9) several months after your product launches can be an exercise humility as you come face to face with how incorrect your initial plans were, but it often provides great insight. Your predictions may have been wildly incorrect, but you can now learn from your past mistakes. Plan a meeting to go over actual versus planned sales results. Collectively list all the differences between the plan and the actual rollout. If possible, attribute percentage amounts to each of the variations.

Once you have reviewed your actual results against your planned business case results, determine any changes that are needed in your marketing plan. Reviewing actual versus planned results means you may avoid some of the mistakes the next time around. The more of these business reviews that you do, the more accurate you get. Finally, write up your findings. Whether you ever look at them again or not, you'll remember it better if you write it down.

Changing Course: Making Adjustments

Your marketing plan will likely need adjustments as it progresses and you get more data. You need to look for ways to optimize what you're spending, focus on what's working, and eliminate what isn't working.

Figure 15-5 shows two different axes of analysis and possible change you can look at:

>> **Margin drivers:** Profitability can change due to a number of factors.

- **Selling price:** Consider changing the price. Because price changes are usually irreversible, this driver isn't the best place for a product manager to make changes.

- **Volume mix:** *Volume mix* is an analysis of how the number of each type of product sold is changing the profitability of the whole product line. Are you selling more of a low-end (less profitable) product or less of a high-end (more profitable) product than expected? Does the value proposition for each specific product make sense to customers or is one product sold more than any others? How does the mix of products sold affect overall profitability?

- **Customer satisfaction:** Are customers not satisfied after they buy your product?

- **Marketing effectiveness:** Is your marketing not delivering the expected leads? Are these leads not very good?

- **Sales effectiveness:** Are salespeople clear on what they need to do? Are they actually doing what is requested of them?

- **Cost of goods sold (COGS):** Did the cost go up? Why, and what can be done about it?

>> **Angle of analysis:** The angle of analysis can be through the lens of the product, the region, a customer segment, or a particular channel. Break down sales numbers and then chart them over time to see what piece of your product delivery system isn't delivering.

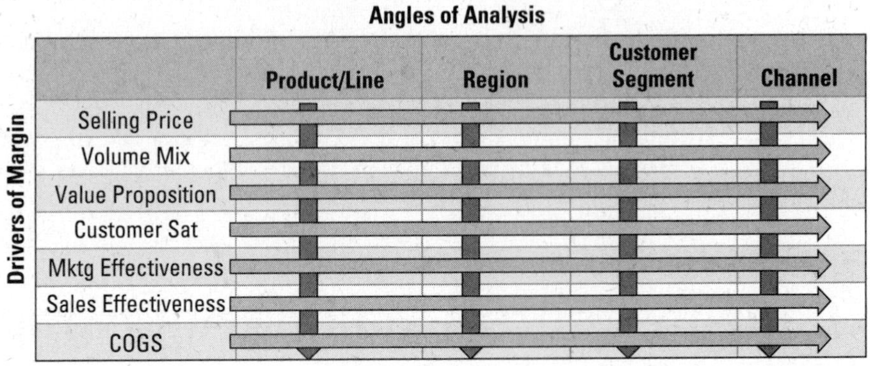

Angles of Analysis

FIGURE 15-5:
Detailed
investigation of
product
performance.

© 2017, 280 Group LLC. All Rights Reserved.

Using Figure 15-5, you can investigate sales of a particular product. You can also compare it to other products or product lines; if those products/lines are performing better, determine why and apply those drivers to your product.

Beefing up sales support

When conducting a product performance investigation, you often discover that the issue is localized to a couple of margin drivers. While you're busy fixing the problems longer-term, you may want to provide better support to your sales folks as a short-term fix. For example, do they need any additional selling tools or information? Can you run a short-term promotion or discount that will fix pricing issues in a particular region? Rely on your salespeople to tell you what may be stalling sales and use this information to react quickly.

Enhancing the product

If your product is failing across the board, you simply may not have gotten the value proposition right. Now you have the tough job of fixing the product, and managing customer and business expectations until you can deliver the right product. This situation takes you back to the conceive phase of the Optimal Product Process (see Chapter 4), where you need to brainstorm and gather ideas for features and additions to the product to make it more attractive to potential customers. If at all possible, talk to prospects who considered purchasing your product but ended up not buying, and get specific reasons as to why they didn't buy your product and what they bought instead.

Trimming costs

Product cost reductions may be challenging to find. However, if you rely on your team members — such as those in operations — you may be able to cut costs which will increase profitability. These cost savings are an immediate boost to the company bottom line.

Here are a couple of ideas:

>> For a hardware product, how can you trim component costs, and how can you build it less expensively? Can you switch parts suppliers? Will your manufacturing facility give you a price break based on the volume you're building with them? Can you increase the number of products produced simultaneously to decrease your per-unit cost? If you build extra units at the same time, take into account the cost of storing extra inventory.

>> For all products, examining the entire product delivery system by using techniques like the customer journey work in Chapter 11 may lead to insights into faster and cheaper ways to get the work done. For example, can you reduce support or warranty costs or shipping costs to the distributors or customers?

Chapter **16**

Retirement: Replacing a Product or Taking It off the Market

Retiring a product (often called *end of life*) occurs when a company decides to exit the market. Sometimes companies make this decision strategically after much thought. Other times, a product may have failed miserably or died out over time, and it becomes obvious that it's time to stop selling it.

Retirement can involve completely pulling the product from the market without replacing it or, in many cases, replacing it with a new version. Products may be retired for a variety of reasons, such as technology changes that make the product obsolete, competitive pressure that make the product no longer viable, or the product simply can't meet the required revenue or profitability thresholds.

Retirement is an area of the product life cycle that companies often ignore. Yet keeping products around that aren't profitable can cost a company a lot of money. Retiring products and determining how best to maximize the corresponding profits isn't glamorous. In fact, most of it is tedious checking and re-checking to make sure that some aspect of retiring a product hasn't been forgotten. However, it's a necessary component of product management. This chapter details why the retire phase is important and how to set up a cohesive retirement plan.

Deciding How to Retire a Product

A lot of thought needs to go into how to retire a product because retirement impacts certain departments, programs, and resources. Customers may have expectations about how long you'll continue to sell and support the product, and if you retire it the wrong way, you can damage your brand or your relationship with them. Retiring a product requires a lot of internal company communication as well as external communication with customers to ensure that expectations are set and met accordingly. Think of it as a launch plan in reverse.

REMEMBER

Spend the time planning retirement. Don't do it on a whim or without thinking things through. If you're going to be replacing the product with a new version, make sure you plan the old version's end of life at the same time you're planning the new version's launch because they'll be highly dependent on each other.

Taking into account internal and external expectations

When retiring a product, you need to look at two distinct points of view:

>> **Customer side:** Who buys it now? How much revenue is dependent on selling this product? Is it related to another product such that this product's removal will cause issues in selling the other one? Your sales and sales operations people are critical to getting this part right. Spend the time to explain the thinking and then give them enough time to break it to their customers and gracefully address the outcome.

>> **Operations side:** Looking at product retirement from an operational point of view as a product manager is completely different. For example, say you're selling only ten units a month of a particular product and should retire it. However, you still have 20,000 units in a warehouse. Scrapping all these units will cost the company $1 million. Your task is to discuss with finance the cost of storage versus price reduction options versus the cost of scrapping. This way, you're giving your company options and a well-rounded view of how to exit the product from the market.

Considering Critical Factors in a Product Retirement Plan

When developing your end-of-life plan, keep the following critical factors in mind.

>> **Loyalty:** How will you maintain customer loyalty?

>> **Negative implications:** Do you encounter any legal or contractual implications if you stop selling the product? Have you promised customers anything that you won't be following through on?

>> **Financials:** Is this product still profitable, or are you losing money on it? If it's profitable, is it worth the opportunity cost of spending resources to keep it on the market, or would these resources be better spent on something newer that may have more growth and profit potential?

>> **Physical concerns:** If it's a physical product, what are the ramifications of discontinuing the product in terms of inventory, channel partners, returns, or customer replacement and support?

>> **Risks:** Are there any other risks associated with discontinuing this product, such as alienating longtime customers or possibly creating a backlash on social media if customers are unhappy that you have discontinued the product?

Breaking down specific end-of-life issues by product type

Not all types of products have the same issues during the retire phase. Here are a few specific issues to look out for depending on the type of product you're retiring.

Physical products

Physical products don't magically go away after you issue an end-of-life notice to your company, customers, and channel. When discontinuing a physical product, keep these concepts in mind:

>> **Closely manage inventory in the pipeline.** Your channel partners often have agreements that allow them to return unsold inventory after a certain amount of time. You may also have a few units in a far-off warehouse. Make a list of every unit you have and decide what to do with it: sell, save for service needs, or scrap.

>> **Reduce price for excess inventory.** For those few units in some forgotten corner of a warehouse consider reducing the price dramatically to encourage sales on a non-returnable basis.

>> **Increase price to drive customers to replacement product.** This no-holds-barred solution is great for getting people to move to a newer product. Increase the price of the existing one, and then consumers will beg you to move to the newer version.

>> **Maintain spare parts availability.** Always, always find your service manager and ask how many units that department will need for service requirements. Service managers have a magic formula known only to them that tells them that if the company sold x units over y years and needed to repair one percent of them, then the service department needs to keep z units in reserve. Transfer that many units to their department and say, "Thank you."

Software

Software products have their own unique set of issues. Since there is rarely a physical package that the customers purchase, inventory issues are usually minimal. However, many customers will continue to use the software products for many years, and things like how long support will be provided for the retired version must be determined. Here are some additional considerations:

>> **Waiving new-product costs for recent purchasers:** If you're a business to consumer (B2C) software provider, you can't tell your customers that you're introducing a new/improved product in the next month. Those who just invested in the current version aren't going to be very happy. Instead, you give the customers who purchased the software in, say, the last three months the new version for free, providing them with what's known as *upgrade-protection pricing*. Business to business (B2B) customers are often protected by contracts which give them the right to upgrade at no cost through their support contract.

>> **Working with developers to support the existing product:** If you have (loyal) external developers who build on top of your software, ensure that you can give them bug fixes and patches to known issues for a certain amount of time after the new version becomes available. Make sure to specify how long you can reasonably give them to make the transition. (Two days, for example, is too short a time.) This task shouldn't be difficult; as part of your end-of-life plan, you would've asked your developers how long moving to the new version would take and incorporated that information into your plans.

>> **Ensuring compatibility with prior versions of the product:** Nothing is more annoying than having created a document in one format and then being unable to open it when the new version arrives. Make sure that the new and old versions provide compatibility with each other so that you don't upset customers. It's time consuming to spend development time on, but without it, you'll lose customers quickly.

Services

Retirement of services also has its own unique challenges. Following is a list of additional considerations.

>> **Downloads and technical information:** A few years ago, we checked out products that we'd launched ten years before. To our surprise, the software downloads and support materials were still live. The actual company had been sold off, but the website still supported customers many years after the last units were sold. Plan to maintain old service databases or websites for existing users long after sales or enrollment has stopped.

>> **Data continuity:** Every few years, a company will migrate to a new database or website. Remember that farsighted product managers arrange to transition the data and information over to the new system. We have been pleasantly surprised by a retailer who kept our data (and discounts) live for over ten years. Our loyalty will long remain with this company.

Distinguishing a product's various end-of dates

The discussion about end of life often seems like it's just one fixed date in time, but the reality is that a product has many end-of dates. The last day the product is sold isn't necessarily the last day it's serviced or supported. When developing your plan, make a list of all these end-of dates and estimate how much notice you need to give for each step. Microsoft, IBM, and Cisco are organizations that clarify the end-of schedule extremely well. In fact, most large companies have written policies so that customers are crystal clear on what to expect. Table 16-1 spells out what each end-of date represents.

TABLE 16-1   **End-of-Life Date Terminology**

Term	Definition
End-of-life (EOL) announcement date	Day company notifies customers that a product will be retired
End of sale	Day orders are no longer taken for a product
End of build	Day a product is no longer manufactured
End of contract	Day company no longer supports a product except by time and materials (if available)
End of service (also known as shutdown)	Day service is no longer available because technical or maintenance service contracts have expired

Checking out parts of a product retirement plan

A product retirement plan has many sections. Check out Figure 16-1 for an example of the components of a product retirement plan. Because the retire phase offers many options, you may not actually need to fill each and every section.

TIP

Check out the 280 Group Product Management LifeCycle Toolkit (included as a free download with this book; see the Introduction, page 4, for details) for an end-of-life plan template.

Introduction	
Product description	
Parties affected by retirement	Internal groups at the company
	Resellers and channel partners
	Customers
Retirement alternatives	Sell off product to another company
	Spin out product
	Continue sale for limited time
	Shut down product in near term
Chosen alternative and reasoning	Sell off product to another company. The product no longer is a good strategic fit for where the company is headed.
Announcement plan	Critical dates
	Manufacturing plan
	Spare parts supply plan
	Upgrade assistance
	Customer support options
	Technical support plan
	Compatibility
	Recycling/disposition guidelines
	Trade-in or upgrade options
Critical success factors for retirement of product	

FIGURE 16-1: Components of a typical end-of-life plan.

Following Best Practices when Retiring a Product

There are a number of best practices to be aware of and implement when deciding to retire one or more products:

>> Consider creating a standardized end-of-life process so you can minimize and more easily predict the impacts to different groups within your company and to resellers and customers.

>> Communicate early and often so that stakeholders know what to expect when.

>> Get the support and backing of all responsible groups and executives well beforehand so that things go smoothly.

>> Plan for continued support, warranty servicing, and so on for a stated time period to meet your stated policies to customers.

Make the retirement phase of a product just as important as the launch phase. When you successfully retire a product by keeping to a plan, you keep internal groups and external customers updated and happy.

4

Becoming a Phenomenal Product Manager

Enhance your people skills to advance your career.

Communicate with all your stakeholders to keep them focused on your goals.

Recognize how to influence the people who don't report to you but are necessary for your product to succeed.

Map out your career success plan step by step.

Chapter **17**

Cultivating Your Product Management Leadership Skills

Your role as a product manager may be a tactical role where you do lots of detail work with the team and make meaningful contributions to the team's effort. Alternatively, you may step up to be a product leader, creating and driving the strategy while inspiring and guiding the team. For some product managers, the former is what they enjoy best and what leads to a rewarding career. But for other product managers, their passion is leading the team and the overall effort. Stepping up to do so takes a combination of courage, tact, and skill. Although cultivating leadership skills can enhance both career paths, this chapter is particularly targeted toward product managers aspiring to a leadership role with expanded responsibility. The chapter provides some insights into what it takes to develop into a leader.

Identifying Traits of an Effective Product Management Leader

A number of characteristics and abilities turn great product managers into great leaders. Following are the most important ones for you to develop in yourself:

- » **Vision:** *Vision* is the propensity to see where the market, competition, and industry are going and to create a strong vision for where the product needs to be to win the market and satisfy customers. Enhancing vision includes both short-term and long-term thinking; it often requires defying what others in the company may believe because they don't have as much information or customer and market insight as you do. With a strong and compelling vision, you can attract others to follow.

- » **Boldness:** Boldness means to stand up for what you believe in. If you have great ideas but don't make the effort to fight for them, you may never break out of your comfort zone and achieve a higher leadership role. Create opportunities for yourself by thinking outside the box and turning ideas into realities.

- » **Ability to influence:** A product management leader must be able to use both logic and emotion to win over wide ranges of audiences as she is implementing the product vision and strategy she believes in. For example, if there is a particularly important feature that needs to be included with your product, can you find a way to use both data (to appeal to the logical side) and personal stories about customers (to appeal to the emotional side) to persuade your engineers to include the feature?

- » **Expertise:** Being an expert in both the field of product management and the market segments your product targets is critical. If you aren't an expert about the customers, markets, technology, and trends for your product, getting others to follow you will be difficult, if not impossible. For example, do you routinely spend time reading available articles about your market, competitors and customers online?

- » **Enthusiasm:** Enthusiasm is contagious. An enthusiastic product manager brings people together. When you project enthusiasm, you get yourself and your team to aim for a higher level. You get others excited to be involved with your vision. *Note:* The opposite is even truer. A jaded and negative product manager will ultimately fail with both products and career advancement.

- » **Tenacity:** The ability to keep going despite facing difficult people and circumstances is critical. As a product manager, you encounter situations that seem insurmountable, and tenacity is the key to breaking through. The effort isn't a one-time activity or meeting. It's succeeding in the long-haul with a vision and campaigning to achieve your goal.

Hiring managers instinctively look for tenacity in product managers. When faced with an obstacle, did the PM give up or work through it? One great approach if you have what appears to be an insurmountable challenge is to break it down into smaller steps and affect as much change as you can.

>> **Commitment to excellence:** This characteristic includes excellence in both the work you do and deliverables. Your presentations, market requirements documents, and business cases should read well and look amazing. Your product details should shine. The product manager is at the center of all aspects of the product. If you don't own delivering excellence for all aspects of the product, no one else will.

Developing Your Leadership Style

Leadership style is a very personal thing. It is highly dependent on your own personality and what you are good at. Anyone can be a great leader: introvert or extrovert, highly analytical and detail oriented or big-picture thinker. The key is to be authentic about who you really are rather than trying to be someone you aren't. This section covers two different leadership styles as well as handling stress and communicating like a leader.

Reaching for results and motivating people

There are two primary factors to consider when determining your leadership style: concern for results and concern for people. Leaders often tend to be stronger and more focused on one than the other. The result is that their leadership effectiveness varies quite a bit. Look at Figure 17-1 to understand how people perceive leaders depending where their leadership focus is.

>> **Fear:** If you're more concerned with results than you are people, you may get short-term results; however, in the longer term, your team members may leave, choose to not cooperate, or even turn against you. A results-only focus leads people to fear you. This path can cause them to behave passive-aggressively and build up resentment and may contribute to nasty corporate politics that hamper your product success or even limit your career.

>> **Like:** On the other hand, if you're only concerned with making people happy, you may have a team that likes you as a person but doesn't do what's required to achieve the business results that the company demands. As the product manager, you're still accountable for the overall results, so if product success doesn't happen, you get the blame from the executive team.

>> **Not noticed:** If you don't focus on results or people, from a leadership perspective, you become irrelevant. People don't notice what you say and don't take your opinion into account. By all means, avoid being a product manager who people don't notice.

>> **Trust:** A true product management leader finds a way to walk the fine line and focus on both results and people. The outcome is that the team and stakeholders trust the product manager. Trust means that they are willing to support his vision and work hard to achieve it. In some instances the trust and respect that you earn mean that you sacrifice popularity. Your stakeholders' trust in you comes from their understanding of the balance you strike between results and making people happy. Look back through your career, and you'll most likely uncover leaders who cared about both results and people and achieved highly successful outcomes. These leaders may not have been liked, but they were trusted to take teams on challenging journeys. Make sure you become one of these leaders.

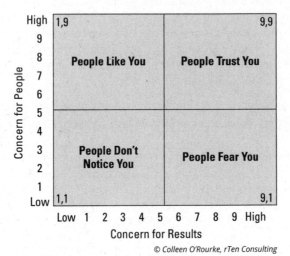

FIGURE 17-1:
Leadership grid.

Handling stress

Product management is a stressful job. You have conflicting demands. The path forward to success isn't always clear, and you often have to go back to your stakeholders and ask them to make changes. Change can induce stress in them and you. This section covers how to deal with stress within yourself and with others.

Turning a negative into a positive

Because doing your job often means making stakeholders' jobs more stressful, over time, your arrival in someone's office or even your name on an email can induce a stress response. To counteract that, you must become the most positive and complimentary person in the office. A 5:1 ratio rule can help you overcome the stress deficit that you create in others. The basic rule is that five positive interactions can offset one negative interaction. Both this chapter and Chapter 18 frequently reference taking people to lunch; that act counts as one positive interaction. Here are just a few other ways to get to five:

» Congratulating and thanking someone for a job well done

» Telling a joke

» Showing interest in employees' children and hobbies

» Smiling at team members in the hallway

What other ways can you think of?

Managing stressed-out stakeholders

Humans are hard-wired to react to danger, stress, or conflict (real or imagined) with one of three instincts: fight, flight, or freeze (see Figure 17-2).

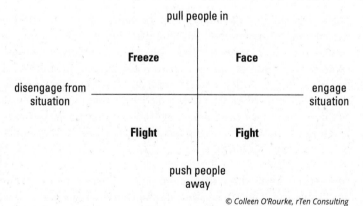

FIGURE 17-2:
The three modes of reacting to challenges.

© Colleen O'Rourke, rTen Consulting

Because you can't stop the stress process from happening, your goal is simply to acknowledge that it's going to happen and work through each stage until your harried stakeholder gets back to a calm state where you can both deal with the new challenge in front of you.

Following are of the top ways for calming down stakeholders:

>> Tell the people involved that you understand their disappointment. Just accurately naming their emotion at this point takes the sting out of the emotion.

>> Give them time to work through their anger (fight), withdrawal (freeze), or non-acceptance (flight) of the new information. For big changes (or team members especially sensitive to change), offer to come back to discuss the change further when they've had time to digest the information. If the calming process just takes a minute or two, hang tight. Practice your active listening skills and keep using them as you collectively develop a path forward. Active listening skills are covered in Chapter 18.

Reducing your own stress

You aren't immune to stress reactions. Plan for them. If you feel your blood boiling, are stunned into silence, or find yourself walking away, tell people that you're trying to digest the change and ask them to give you a few moments to compose yourself. Work out exactly the steps that work for you, and then put your plan in place. Over time, your co-workers learn that you have a certain way of dealing with stress and respect that you can manage your way through the situation.

Building confidence

The key to building confidence is to recognize that your emotional reactions are part of your human nature. Building confidence is discovering how to work with your natural tendencies to turn each of these situations into an opportunity to exercise your courage muscles. Instead of giving in to your first instinct of fight, freeze, or flight, work on a deliberate and conscious approach to facing difficult situations. Your solution to facing difficult situations combines both sincere and genuine concern for the people involved and the results you're trying to achieve. When you do both, you'll be practicing true leadership. The results you can achieve over time may astound you.

TIP

You weren't born with a manual on how to handle the tough situations that can hit at any time and without warning. Know that at any particular time you may be called on to deal with a situation you believe is far beyond your ability to cope. When you find yourself standing in an impossible situation, remind yourself that you're enough — that you have enough compassion, knowledge, toughness, and smarts to get through whatever the world throws at you. Remember that you're *always* good enough, and you will be.

Thinking, acting, and communicating like a leader

The old axiom that people perceive you based on how you perceive yourself is highly applicable in product management leadership. If you think of and view yourself as a leader, you're more likely to project the qualities of a leader. Similarly, others sense when you don't think of yourself as being capable of leading.

As a product manager, you need to practice thinking, acting, and communicating like a leader at all times.

>> **Act decisively.** Don't waffle when you communicate or take action. Make decisions and lead others by using your business analysis skills, market and customer expertise, and don't be afraid to make mistakes.

>> **Ask for help.** Don't be afraid to ask for help if you aren't sure or need more information. The best leaders know that they don't have all the answers and that the teams they're leading often do. In fact, people are flattered when you ask for their advice.

>> **Give credit, take blame.** Leaders are the ones that give themselves permission to give others credit for what has gone well. They also take the blame when things didn't work out as planned. Leadership doesn't come with a red hero cape. It comes with a huge dose of humility.

TIP

If you think giving others credit makes them the leader, try this exercise: Next time something good happens in the group, be the first person to give someone else credit. Since leaders are the ones that are supposed to give credit to others, over time, you become perceived as the leader.

REMEMBER

Leadership is earned, not taken. Thinking of yourself as a leader doesn't mean that you can order people around. It means that you've developed a deep inner awareness so that people will, over time, respect and follow you based on your consistent actions.

TEAM LEADERSHIP

One of the primary roles of a product manager is to work effectively with their engineering teams. Sometimes you're the junior party in the room, and sometimes you're the leader. Here are a couple of tips for dealing with team situations to make sure that they're well led:

- **Keep it psychologically safe.** Studies show that team members participate when they believe it's safe to do so — that is, when everyone is able to speak for about the same amount of time. We're not suggesting you break out a stopwatch; however, if a few individuals dominate the conversation, talk to them and ask them to back off to allow for wider participation. And as a balance, ask for quiet team members for their opinion. Both the team's participation and performance increase when each member is psychologically safe.

- **Engage remote teams.** Remote teams and individuals can feel very left out. Keep them engaged by turning the video on. Periodically do fun things as a virtual team. We've heard of one team that held virtual team events monthly in pajamas (the team members all worked from home) or odd shirts or funny hats. What can you think of to engage your virtual team members?

Chapter **18**

Mastering the Art of Persuasion

Persuasion and influencing are the skills where the rubber meets the road as a product manager. You can do all the excellent work to create a great product strategy and a credible plan, but if you can't get others to support your efforts, you won't succeed. Because virtually all product managers are individual contributors and the people they depend on to deliver products don't report to them, being able to influence without authority is a critical link to your success.

This chapter gives you solid tips on how to be your best persuasive self as well as how to specifically influence the executive board, your development team, and the sales force.

Brushing Up on Persuasion Basics

The foundation of persuasion as a skill is knowing what outcome you want to achieve and then putting together your best arguments and communicating them as effectively as possible. In this section, we cover three core basics of effective persuasion: active listening, convincing, and asking for what you want. Master these tools, and you're well on your way to getting the end result you want.

TIP

We highly recommend that you pick up a book like *Persuasion and Influence For Dummies* by Elizabeth Kuhnke (Wiley) to supplement this section and continue to increase your skills. We also suggest you look into a training course that teaches in-depth people skills for product managers and allows you to learn and practice in an immersive environment.

Active listening

Before you can find a solution, you first need to have a deep understanding of the situation. Active listening is a very popular and highly effective technique that helps you get a handle on another person's point of view. When you're trying to influence a team member regarding a new product, you need to be able to listen first and speak second. Also, using active listening can diffuse challenging situations where others are insistent or argumentative. Many times conflict arises simply because the other party doesn't feel heard and doesn't believe that you deeply understand its point of view and opinions.

To practice active listening, do the following:

1. Allow the other person to talk and state his complete case.

Don't cut him off or try to respond. Let him speak his piece so that he has been able to voice everything he needs to. If he talks a long time, give him verbal cues like "uh huh" so he knows you're still listening.

2. When he's finished, say, "It seems that. . ." or "What I heard you say is. . .", and then repeat back what you think you heard.

If you got it right, he'll automatically respond with "yes." If you didn't get it right, he'll correct the part you missed or even say "no." If you're the least bit unsure about whether your understanding is correct, ask him whether he feels you have an understanding of his point of view. If you don't feel comfortable paraphrasing what he just said, simply repeat the last three words.

REMEMBER

Deep down, the need for active listening is only partly in making sure that you understand the facts. Acknowledging the feelings behind the argument is equally or maybe more important. Here's the difference: "I hear that you want to go to the store." Fact, no feeling. "I hear that you're frustrated because you want to go to the store and can't figure out how to get there." Practice the second kind of response.

3. Repeat Steps 1 and 2 as necessary until both parties are convinced that you thoroughly understand the other's point of view.

If you hit a wall in this process, you may need to ask open-ended questions to get more insight from the other person about what you're misunderstanding. Try starting your open-ended questions with "what" and "how" for more informative answers.

The interesting thing about active listening is that after going through this process, you often don't need to explain your point of view to the other person. When he feels heard and knows that you understand (but don't necessarily agree), he may drop the subject altogether. And sometimes when the other person believes he's been heard, you can let him know that you now understand and will factor his opinion into the decisions you make about the product.

TIP

The usual role of a product manager is as an arbiter and decision maker. Active listening can be very frustrating because you simply can't tell someone what to do. Imagine that in most of your activities, you lean forward to drive the conversation forward. If you're in an active listening situation, change the forward stance and physically lean back onto your heels or into your chair. It gives you a different physical sensation and reminds you that you're in listening mode. Practice this skill often, and you'll be amazed at the results.

Convincing with the three reasons method

After doing some active listening to get the other party's point of view (see the preceding section), you may still need to do some convincing to sway him to agree with you. One of the simplest and most effective methods is the *three reasons method*.

Here's how it works for a conversation that you plan in advance:

1. **State what you believe should happen and that you have three reasons.**

   Plan out your three reasons.

2. **Provide your first reason, using any data or real-world examples you have.**

   Use as many facts as you can because facts and data are difficult to argue with.

EFFECTIVELY REDUCING CONFLICTS

Conflict resolution also uses active listening. If someone is energetically expounding on his point of view or frustration, respond with more energy in your voice. We don't mean start shouting; we just want you to match the other person's energy. Think about speaking with an excited child who just discovered a bug. You wouldn't say, "Calm down." You'd be excited with him at first and then take your energy level down slowly as the conversation proceeds to model how the child should respond. The same principle can apply to adults in conflict; because you matched the other person's energy to start with, he'll follow your lead as you take the conversation down to a calmer state.

SPUR-OF-THE-MOMENT CONVERSATIONS

Not all conversations are planned. You run into a colleague or manager in the hall or start talking over lunch. You can still use the three reasons method. When you're unprepared, you're likely to run out of reasons after two reasons. Don't worry. Say that you have three reasons, and then if you can't think of a third reason, simply state that you lost your train of thought and can't remember the third reason.

3. **Repeat Step 2 with your second reason.**

   Again, use facts and examples wherever possible.

4. **If the first and second reasons don't convince your audience, you can present a third reason.**

So why does this method work so well? Regardless of whether you have a well-thought-out argument upfront, using this approach gives the other person the impression that you're confident about what you're saying. Anyone who claims three good reasons for an opinion most likely has a reasonable stance to argue, so declaring you do puts you in a strong position right out of the gate. Does it work every time? No, but if you aren't able to come up with three reasons your opinion and argument are right, you may need to rethink your position in the first place.

Asking for what you want — concisely

One of the keys to getting people to listen to you (or read what you have sent) and then do what you ask is to keep things as brief as possible. For example, if you need to influence your team to change the schedule to add a crucial new feature, having a long conversation or writing a three-page email stating every reason you can think of simply won't work. Chances are that your audience will tune out after the first minute or no one will read the entire email. Instead, your information will simply be ignored or dismissed.

In all your communications, be as short and to the point as possible. In emails, use bullet points if possible. Many times, your response to an email can simply be one or a few words, such as "Agreed" or "Approved." In fact, short communications can, in many cases, be more effective than longer ones. Product managers who go on and on endlessly, whether via email or in conversation, tend to be far less effective than those who can get their points across rapidly and efficiently.

Figure 18-1 outlines a good method for concisely presenting your case to get what you want. You sketch out the situation in a few sentences, give a few pieces of vital information to make your argument, and then clearly tell the other party what you want and why giving it to you is good for both sides. The key to this method is to not try to present a long, drawn-out case. Make any communication short and compelling.

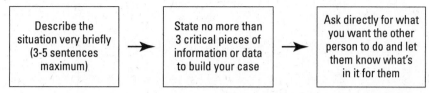

FIGURE 18-1: Three-step method for quickly getting support.

TIP

If you think you have a tendency to being long winded — or even if you don't — time yourself the next time you give an explanation. See how close you can get to a sufficient (not exhaustively complete) explanation in 30 seconds. In emails, shoot for no more than two or three short paragraphs.

Getting Your Executive Team on Board

As a product manager, your ability to influence executives, sell them your ideas, and get them to back you up is critical. Often, executives don't know the ins and outs of the market or the intricacies of a product. It's then your job to build their confidence that you're a product and market leader, and that your understanding of the right strategy and execution is going to help them succeed.

Drawing up an influence map

One tool to use when influencing executives (and other stakeholders) is an influence map, as shown in Figure 18-2. An influence map helps you determine who is on your side and how much they can help or hinder your efforts. An influence map can also give you a sense of what kind of politics may be going on behind the scenes so that you can build the relationships and have the conversations you need to ahead of time to get support for your efforts.

To create your influence map, list all the executives who have any influence on your work. Map them into how supportive they are for your product efforts and then how influential they are in the organization. You are looking for those who have a lot of influence and are very supportive. Target your key influencers with more information and ask them to support your cause with other executives. For executives with lots of influence who don't support your product efforts, list issues they consider to be more important and then how you can link your product to their key interests and goals. Enlist executives who are on your side to take up your cause with the others who don't support your cause. Use the relationship building techniques in the next section to explore resistance to your product ideas and build as much positive perception of your product at the executive level as possible.

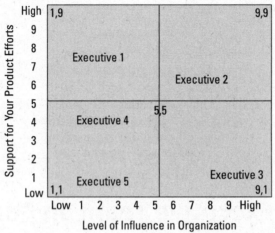

FIGURE 18-2:
Influence map for executives.

In rare cases, every (or almost every) executive is mapped as not supporting your product efforts. If you don't have the support you need and you don't believe you'll be able to change the situation, your best bet may be to move on to a situation where you'll have a better chance of success. For example, if the CEO or several senior-level executives don't believe in your product or strategy and aren't willing to fund it, you'll have an uphill battle as the product manager. The alternative is to remain on the job and become frustrated and negative, and that is truly career limiting.

Building relationships with the key players

One helpful technique for influencing executives within the organization is to determine the top five key players that you'll need support from. Fostering relationships with these people early on, without any agenda, is important. By getting to know them on a personal level while showing them that you're the market and product expert, you'll be setting yourself up so that when you do need support in a critical situation, they have confidence in you.

Building these personal relationships is also a great way to help move your career along. Find out what the executives are interested in and what motivates them.

Take them to lunch or stop them in the halls to ask their advice. If you can, get them to agree to be your mentor. These steps all seem like common sense, but the product managers who succeed actually follow through with doing this stuff.

Here are a few ways to build rapport:

>> Mirror executives' language — both verbal and body as you communicate with them. Note how they dress and dress in a similar style. Don't go out and buy the same sweater that the CEO wore last week, but do keep to the same general corporate look. Women should emulate the same or slightly higher level of dress formality, and not, for example, adopt collared shirts and slacks (if that is the male corporate uniform).

>> Find opportunities to share experiences by either working on a tough assignment at work or, if you travel for work, doing something together during non-work hours.

>> Share information and assistance with them freely. Be helpful, cheerful, and always positive. Share your successes with them.

>> Remember that they also need down time. Don't pester them. Let them guide the level of interaction that is comfortable for them.

Talking the talk: Executive-speak

In order to influence executives, you have to learn how they think and speak their language. For example, product managers are often very interested in the minute details of how their products work. They have to be in order to make sure they deliver a polished product that delights customers.

Executives, however, don't generally know or care about the in-depth details of product features. They're much more concerned with the big picture and things like how to accelerate the growth of the business and whether they're allocating resources the right way to maximize the company's return on investment. Thus, presentations for executives that have 20 (or more!) slides about the details of the product will lose their interest (and hurt your credibility). Keep things short, sweet, and focused on what they care about.

TIP

Keep these guidelines in mind when communicating with executives:

>> **Keep it short and to the point.** Don't waste their time.

>> **Focus on what's in it for the company and for them.** Be specific on the benefits that the company and the executive are interested in. Learn what successful talking points have worked with executives and then use similar

ones. For example, one company may focus only on profitability. In another one, it's all about engaging customers.

>> **Provide a summary, but have the details and data on hand in case they want to dive deeper on a topic.** Put non-essential slides into an appendix.

>> **Be succinct and to the business point in all your conversations.**

Winning Over Your Development Team

Being able to influence and work effectively with the development team and individual engineers is a huge part of whether you'll be successful as a product manager and satisfied with your job. Your success depends on your ability to get your engineers to build the product that you believe meets customer needs and moves forward on your vision.

Building your credibility

Credibility in product management is everything. Your challenge is going to be to build credibility despite what development considers your role to be or not be. You need to show engineers what you're doing and why you're doing it and make sure they view you as an expert in a range of areas. Areas to show your credibility in include the following:

>> **Technical:** Establishing yourself as a technical expert with your development team members is absolutely critical. Otherwise, they simply may not respect or work with you. Your ability to influence them will be negligible. Follow the trends in your area of technology and know the acronyms and terminology. You don't necessarily have to be a complete expert and understand all of the underpinnings of the technology, but you do have to prove to your team that you have the *ability* to understand. Check out Chapter 2 for more details.

TIP

If you don't have technical expertise in your new area of responsibility, ask a lead engineer to brief you on the product. It is common to have an engineer brief a product manager on technology topics, so don't be shy. At each stage, remember to look for the customer significance of each of the technologies or features that developers are telling you about. Take good notes because you need to get up to speed quickly.

>> **Product management:** Everyone in your company — not just your engineering team — needs to view you as someone who understands product management inside and out. You wouldn't want to hire a chief financial officer or an accountant if you didn't know the candidate knew finance inside and out, and product management is no different.

TIP

Certainly, any training you can go through and any certifications you can get increase your credibility. If you become a certified product manager through the AIPMM (Association of International Product Marketing and Management), for instance, and you hang your certification in your office cube, your team will see it and understand that you truly have studied this discipline and are excellent at what you do.

>> **Best practices:** You need to be able to confidently say, "This is the wrong approach. Most companies do it the following way." You also need corresponding skills for tasks like creating business cases, prioritizing product backlogs, writing user stories, and creating personas.

>> **Market:** You have to know more about your market than anyone in your entire company. You need to understand growth rates and competition, and you need to be able to have facts and data ready that you can bring up in discussions.

>> **Customer:** You want to be viewed as the person who is the true voice of the customer. You'll know you've established yourself as the real expert who has a finger on the pulse of the customer when your development team proactively comes to you to ask, "We can solve this issue this way or that way; which way do you think the customers will want it?"

To attune yourself to the customer's needs, make lots of customer visits. Write up a summary of what you found at each visit. Include stories about what happened and information about the customer environment. Then share your report or email with your development team. Do this for each and every visit summarizing information into bullet points where possible. Continually bring up the customer in your conversations to remind engineers that you've spent significant time with them.

Another good tactic is to occasionally bring your engineers along on customer visits. Taking them out in the field and having them observe what kinds of questions you ask and what environment your customers work in is always extremely valuable. For example, one engineer saw a customer actually cry when faced with a difficult-to-use test interface and adapted it overnight for the next round of customer feedback. When engineers meet real customers, they share their experiences with their development team back at the ranch, and it becomes a lot easier to get the team to adopt your ideas later on.

Assessing your team and adjusting

You need to analyze the development team you're dealing with and then adjust accordingly. You may have a great team or a difficult team that may or may not respect you (or anyone else who is a product manager).

In some cases, you'll have a great team where you can easily establish yourself as a leader. When you're in the upper-right quadrant of Figure 18-3 is when your job in product management is really, really fun.

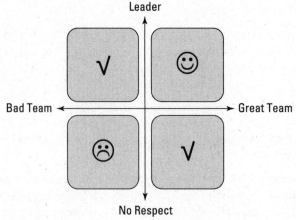

FIGURE 18-3:
Sizing up your development team.

If you're in either of the check-marked quadrants, you can definitely make it work and can move toward the upper-right quadrant. In most situations, that's where you'll be as a product manager. Brainstorm with the team or your manager about how to move toward the upper-right quadrant by building teamwork and increasing your respect within the team.

In the worst case, there's nothing you can do with some teams and situations. You may be in that bottom-left quadrant, and you may seriously need to think about whether you want to move on to a different product or move to work with a different team. Before you utterly give up hope, talk to the team's manager (or HR, if the manager is part of the problem). See whether a coach can be brought in or whether HR can facilitate an intervention with the team to its improve relationships and internal workings. In some situations, there is simply no way to win. Don't let yourself get stuck for a long time in one of these — it's a career-limiting move.

Sizing up different types of developers and how to handle them

Understanding the personalities of the individual developers and how to deal with each personality type is just as important as working with the development team as a collective unit. The following sections break down common developer personality types and give you tips on working with each.

Types of personalities

There are three major types of developer personalities (see Figure 18-4):

» **Prima donna:** These developers are absolutely brilliant and insist on having an argument about everything to make sure that they get to the truth (though usually they've already made up their mind about what the truth is). They may be excellent at what they do, but they don't necessarily know or care about the role of product management.

» **Coder:** Coders are people who don't have strong opinions but rather say, "Tell me exactly what to build. Give me a specification; I just write code. I'll add any feature you want. Just be very clear and very specific."

» **Team player:** In between the coder and the prima donna is the third type, which is the team player. Team players understand the value a product manager brings, and they really want to work with you interactively to build a product that customers love.

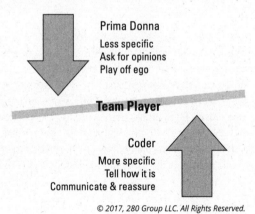

FIGURE 18-4: Developer types.

Coping with different personalities

Each developer personality outlined in the preceding section requires a different approach to achieve your desired result. Follow these tips to get the most out of each relationship:

» **Be less specific with prima donnas.** For instance, when you deliver a market requirements or product requirements document or specify some features, suggest possible solutions instead of handing down *the* solution. Put a recommendation in that says "Customers need to be able to do the following. Here's one way you can do it, but this is just an idea." Let the prima donna solve it; in fact, challenge him to come up with a great solution. Ask prima donnas for their opinions and justifications. "Is this really the best way to solve the problem?" Play to their egos.

Your job in working with prima donnas is to make them hungry for real-world data only you can provide about customers and the market. And if you can present arguments such that they draw logical conclusions that they believe they've come to on their own, so much the better.

» **Be open to creativity from team players.** Give team players information about customer needs and pain points and an idea of the requirements and allow them to creatively come up with a solution. They'll often amaze you with the elegance and creativity they display.

» **Be more precise with coders.** Tell coders exactly what you need: "The following feature needs to be implemented this way. Come back with a design, and I'll approve it." Keep in close communication as they're creating the solution and reassure them that they're on track in delivering what you want.

The challenge here is that if you aren't specific, you may end up with something very different from what you originally envisioned. You often find coders among remote development teams. Because distance increases their uncertainty, they're afraid to make mistakes, and then work progresses very slowly. A great approach with coders is to write more specific requirements and then work very closely with coders to execute them so the coders don't get too far down the wrong path. In an ideal world, coders grow up to be more experienced developers. In reality, they often move onto another job before they can build confidence in bringing their ideas to the team.

Fostering rapport with the team

Building good rapport with your team is a critical component of winning over your development team. Otherwise, you can't count on team members' support when you need a favor in a difficult situation.

The key to creating real rapport is sincerity. You can sincerely develop connections in a variety of ways, both subtly and overtly:

>> **Feed them.** Obviously, grabbing lunch or coffee together is a good thing. When was the last time you had lunch brought in for your whole engineering team or took some engineers out after work to get to know them? If you can bring doughnuts to your weekly team meetings, attendance will likely go up dramatically, and you'll develop a better working relationship. (Who doesn't love doughnut day?) This approach sounds too simple to be true, but small things add up.

>> **Remember them when you're picking up event freebies.** If you go to trade shows, pick up giveaway items such as thumb drives for your team. Engineers don't get the chance to go out on the road and attend trade shows, so bringing them back some of the swag can go a long way.

>> **Always have the coolest new gadget.** Ask your team for their opinions on which one you should get, what the best features are, and so on. If you talk about games, gadgets, and cool new technology, many of your engineers will suddenly view you as more than just that business-oriented product manager.

>> **Don't be Chicken Little.** As a product manager, you constantly get frantic requests from sales or a large customer about "urgent" changes the product "needs" because of changing market environments or some other impetus. If you rush to your team like the sky is falling every single time one of these requests comes through, team members may eventually come to feel like you don't have their backs. Instead, be very careful about how you filter any change requests for the development team. That's not to say you can't go back and ask for changes, but focus on the major changes that need to be made.

When you really build rapport and get to know your team, you then have the ability to occasionally play a chip and ask for a change that may otherwise seem unreasonable. Done correctly and sparingly, using this leverage can be very effective.

Getting Sales on Your Side

A product manager's sales team can be his best ally or worst nightmare. When armed properly, rewarded correctly, and enthused about your products, sales can make the difference between failure and massive success. In the following sections, we discuss many tactics for getting your salespeople on your side and enlisting their help.

Making it easy for sales to sell your product

Following are a few tactics that help make a salesperson's job much easier. And if sales is happier, your job becomes that much easier. Keep these factors in mind as you work through how to structure your product for sales success.

Discovering what motivates salespeople

The first tactic is to make sure you understand the motivation of a salesperson. Money and being successful in their position are key motivators for salespeople. Here are a couple of others:

>> **Finding a great solution to fit the customer's needs:** As a product manager, your job here is to make sure the salesperson understands how your product solves the customer need. If you can easily link the product to the customer and let sales know how best to succeed at completing the sale, sales can get on with their job without asking you to participate in every sale call.

>> **Competing and winning:** Many salespeople thrive on doing sales for a living because it gives them the chance to compete against other companies to win the business from customers. Show your sales folks how your products help them win this fight, and they'll help you hit your revenue goals.

Highlighting what's in it for them

Another tactic for leveraging your sales team is to be incredibly crisp and clear about "What's in it for me?" or WIIFM. Make sure you can tell team members in less than one minute why focusing on your product is worth their while and why you're making it easy to sell. Include info on how they can easily cross-sell and upsell customers with other products. Create opportunities to add on consulting, support, and other ongoing revenue streams. Convince salespeople that the solution is ideal for their customers. Then, when it's sold, they don't have to spend time fixing problems and instead can focus on closing new deals.

Identifying the target for them

Make sure your salespeople understand who the target is and that they're selling to the right customer. You want to paint them a picture about the size of the market and its potential for them so that they're excited. Teach them about the buyers and the buying process so that they can be as effective as possible.

Give them the persona for the user, decision maker, and purchaser and tell them what the motivation is for each and why your product is a perfect fit. This information lets them understand the customer pain points and the motivation for purchasing. (Flip to Chapter 5 for more on personas.)

Creating great messaging

All your messages should be right on target. You have to have a compelling elevator pitch (that is, be able to explain the product in an elevator in ten floors or fewer). You need to nail your product positioning. You should be able to get it all across in literally 30 seconds — and teach sales how to do it in less than 2 minutes. Salespeople won't be as concise as you are, and they also add in sales related language on top of your key selling points. Check out Chapters 10 and 15 for the best way to create these impactful statements.

REMEMBER

Having compelling messaging that your sales reps can easily repeat goes a long way to making them more successful. Ideally, every rep should be able to sit down with any customer and very quickly convey why that customer should be interested in purchasing the product. If you can get your messaging to that point, the salesperson will have a much higher chance of success.

Giving them excellent sales tools

Your sales tools (or the ones that product marketing creates for you) have to be simple and effective, and they have to make it incredibly easy for the rep to make the sale. If sales constantly asks you to be involved with customer visits or to provide additional information, you probably don't have good sales tools in place. If you did, the sales reps would be able to tell the whole story without having to get you involved. For particularly complex sales scenarios, sales engineers get involved to bring in technical expertise. Your sales tools may never be technical enough for these folks, so plan specific technical training sessions for them.

Check out Chapter 15 for a complete list of sales tools.

Capturing their feedback

One of the big challenges that product managers face is that sales reps generally have far too many feature requests that they consider urgent. They may have fallen into the habit of coming back from a customer site convinced that they could close the sale if the product just had features A, B, and C. You could simply ignore the request, but then sales may not work hard to sell your product.

Proactively share your process for capturing feature requests so that salespeople feel like their feedback is being taken into account and being put into the product planning process. Ideally, you'd set up a web form to get the details and the justification for the request, as well as the associated revenue and customer name.

TIP

Don't stop at showing sales the process for gathering requests from all over the company: sales, tech support, the team, customers, and other stakeholders. Let them know how you prioritize feature requests, explaining that you'll use their provided justification during the process. When your extended team believes it's being heard, it's more likely to be influenced when the time comes.

Chapter **19**

Getting to the Next Level in Product Management

Over a long career, product managers can work on many different products in vastly different fields. One product manager we know started in computer hardware and is now vice president of product management at a health insurance company. The great news is that the process for remaining employable and up-to-date in skills and your domain knowledge is the same for any product manager. In fact, over time and with practice, you can make the transition from one industry to another relatively painlessly if you have to or want to. This chapter shows you how to set appropriate product management career goals and achieve the best career results possible.

Mapping Your Career Path: Setting Goals and Target Dates

It used to be that companies would create career paths and development plans for their employees. These days, very few companies do this, so you as a product manager need to take the initiative and be responsible for your own career advancement. By setting goals with target dates, and creating a specific plan for where you want to go and how you want to get there, you increase your odds of success dramatically.

Establishing goals

The first step in setting your career goals is to determine where you want to go. Do you want to become a CEO, general manager, or vice president? Or do you want to become a great product manager and spend your career working with innovative teams building great products? Are you interested in managing people and helping your employees become great at what they do? Or do you prefer being an individual contributor?

There is no right or wrong answer here. It really comes down to what motivates you, what you enjoy, and what you're good at. Many product managers thrive without ever moving up into management and becoming corporate executives. And you can find many examples of people who started as product managers and became CEOs, such as former Microsoft CEO Steve Ballmer; Scott Cook, founder and former CEO of Intuit; and Yahoo! CEO Marissa Mayer.

Product management is a great training ground for moving up because it requires you to learn, interact with, and understand all parts of the business. Figure 19-1 gives you the stepping stones of the base level of product manager to CEO.

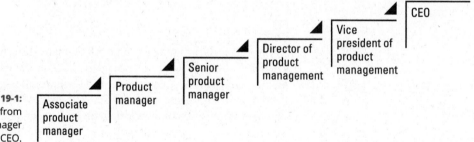

FIGURE 19-1:
Career path from product manager to CEO.

When you set your goals, make sure that they're ambitious yet achievable. If you're a brand-new product manager, you won't be a vice president of product management in one or two years unless you work for a very small company. In a larger company, you may be able to achieve that transition within five to seven years. Your goals have to inspire you and at the same time be completely believable and achievable.

TIP

The SMART goal approach is one that many people find effective. It helps you get clear about how you'll achieve your goals. SMART stands for the following:

>> **S**pecific

>> **M**easurable

>> **A**chievable

>> **R**ealistic

>> **T**ime-bound

Here's an example of a SMART goal: Within one year (time-bound), I will attend a product management training class (measurable) that addresses every step of the product life cycle (specific) to increase my skill level as a junior product manager. I am prepared to attend the class regardless of whether the company pays for it (achievable and realistic).

Building a career plan

When you've set your goals, you're ready to build the plan for how you're going to get there. Figure 19-2 shows the components of a typical career plan for a product manager.

FIGURE 19-2:
Elements of a
product
management
career plan.

© 2017, 280 Group LLC. All Rights Reserved.

Here is a breakdown of the career plan components:

>> **Finding mentors and coaches:** Choose three people who have accomplished what you hope to achieve and ask them whether they'll mentor you. A mentor is someone who is more experienced and can help guide someone else. By choosing mentors that have achieved what you are hoping to achieve you can show them your plan and get their advice about how best to proceed.

Professional coaches can also be very helpful. They're able to give you an external, unbiased perspective on your situation. They evaluate your plans and keep you accountable to your actions. Coaches are a great way to keep you on track to accomplish your goals. Once you have chosen a mentor or a coach, select specific goals that you want to work on and ask them to help you break down what it takes to achieve the goal. Plan specific meetings approximately every two weeks to meet with your mentor or coach.

» **Getting training:** Start by checking out training to become a more effective product manager, excelling at the position you're currently in. According to a 2015 study by the 280 Group, less than 2 percent of product managers ever receive training, so going through foundational training that teaches you all the skills across the entire product life cycle gives you a huge advantage over other product managers. Then add some advanced training courses (such as leadership skills) and more specialized courses (such as Agile and people skills), and you'll have even more of a leg up on your fellow product managers. These skills differentiate you from others and allow your resume to stand out from the rest. A bonus: You become more effective at work, and your job is more enjoyable.

» **Building your network:** Creating a solid network gives you a basis for showcasing your skills to varied professionals to help with earning promotions and changing careers or companies. The better your network is, the more job security you have. Join a local product management group to extend your network. For example, in Silicon Valley, you can check out www.svpma.org.

» **Becoming active online:** Having an online presence and participating in online activities are important for staying current in product management and keeping your name in front of colleagues. A good place to start is by creating a LinkedIn profile (if you don't already have one) at www.linkedin.com. You can check out *LinkedIn For Dummies* by Joel Elad (Wiley) for help with creating a profile. After your LinkedIn profile is in good shape, start to connect with as many people as you can, beginning with the other product managers and executives at your company. Then every time you're at an event or are networking, invite the people you meet to connect.

Become part of product management groups on LinkedIn, such as the 280 Group: Product Management & Product Marketing group, which has over 35,000 members and hosts great discussions. These are great places to learn best practices and ask others about how to solve difficult challenges that arise. Join the Association of International Product Marketing and Management (AIPMM) at www.aipmm.com and participate in its monthly webinars.

» **Volunteering as a way to get your name out there:** You have many opportunities to volunteer in the product management community. One way is by attending product management associations' events and offering to help out. As your product management experience grows, consider sharing your knowledge at association events. Product management events are great for making connections, beefing up your resume, and increasing your resume differentiation.

>> **Earning a certification:** Becoming a Certified Product Manager, Agile Certified Product Management and Product Owner, and/or a Certified Product Marketing Manager through AIPMM is another way to show that you've mastered product management skills and knowledge. Such certifications stand out on your resume and LinkedIn profile. *Note:* If you choose to get certified, make sure that the company who administers the exam is independent and different from the company that trains you in the material. Companies that train and administer their own certifications often have very easy exams and 100 percent pass rates, so the certifications aren't worth as much as those from an independent testing organization like AIPMM.

Writing one-, three-, and five-year action plans

You can take your career plan and turn it into an action plan. By writing it down, you can mark specific steps and make yourself accountable. Break your plan down into three milestone points one, three, and five years out. Here's an example of such a plan:

>> By the end of year one, I will accomplish the following:

- Find one mentor or coach, with whom I review my plan and meet at least once a month to check in on my progress.

- Attend a foundational product management training course to ensure I have the basic skills to manage any product at any phase in the product life cycle.

- Confirm my LinkedIn profile is up-to-date, has high-quality information about my product management skills and experience, and features a great picture. Make at least two LinkedIn connections per month with people who are in my industry.

- Find a local product management association or product camp and attend the sessions to become familiar with it.

- Join a product management LinkedIn group and actively participate, asking and answering questions and reading discussions that will be helpful in doing my job.

» By the end of year three, I will accomplish the following:

- Have three mentors and one coach that I am working closely with at least once a month.

- Attend additional advanced courses to increase my skills in areas that are relevant to my career advancement, such as people skills, working more effectively with Agile development teams, or leadership.

- Continue to build my LinkedIn network to include at least 100 quality connections and keep my profile up-to-date.

- Volunteer at my local product management association or product camp.

- Join several more LinkedIn product management groups, answer questions in discussions, and start discussions of my own.

» By the end of year five, I will accomplish the following:

- Continue working with my mentors and coaches and start to mentor others.

- Earn at least one advanced product management certification credential from a highly-respected organization.

- Build my LinkedIn network to at least 200 meaningful connections that I can rely on if/when I want to find my next job.

- Volunteer for a highly visible position at my local product management association or product camp and/or join the board of directors.

Remembering the favors

An important success factor in moving forward in your career is to genuinely care about others and to help them out without hesitation. People who are willing to go that extra mile for someone else find that the reward always comes back tenfold. For example, if someone you know is looking for a job and you connect him with an opportunity he lands, chances are he'll go out of his way for you in the future if you need help.

Mastering Your Market and New Technologies

In addition to becoming great at product management skills, it is also important to increase your knowledge of your market and any technologies that your products will rely on. These need to be part of your goals and career plan. For example, are you going to pursue a growing market and make your mark in terms of your career in that particular market? If so, you'll want one of your goals to be to learn more about that market than anyone else.

Becoming the market and customer expert

Mastering the foundational and advanced skills of product management is critical to being a successful product manager. But that's only half the equation. To build your credibility and become a product leader, you also have to become the de facto expert in your market, and you've to have enough technical knowledge to be credible.

Here are some tasks you can work into your routine to increase your expert status in terms of your market and customers:

>> **Visit customers often and make sure you summarize and share your findings.** Nothing builds your credibility more with your team than taking a trip to see customers and sharing what you've found. Over time, team members and executives in your company will view you as *the* voice of the customer, and your ability to influence what they're creating will increase.

>> **Determine which, if any, analyst firms (such as Gartner, Forrester, or IDC) cover your particular market.** Scour their available research for free articles and data and consider having your company sign up for the firms' services. Also subscribe to their newsletters and follow their blogs. Many times analysts can provide you with data and insights that have valuable additional perspective. As the market expert in your company, being aware of prominent analysts and using them in your work to strengthen your arguments and bolster your product decisions increases your credibility significantly.

>> **Set up Google alerts with terms specific to your market as well as your competitor's names and products.** Google will scour the web every day and send you an email notification anytime something new comes up so you're among the first to know. When your team or executive points something out, you have the advantage of already being aware of it.

>> **Leverage any internal resources and groups that you may have.** Some companies have competitive analysis and market research departments. Become familiar with what they have to offer, and use their expertise and help.

>> **Gather and track any quantitative data you can find about your product and your competitors.** Information about market share, spending, costs, hiring, marketing activities, and so on can prove very valuable when you're planning out your own strategy. Having this knowledge positions you as the market expert with your team and your company executives.

>> **Prepare and share a market update either once a quarter or every six months.** Some companies will require you to create and present this report to management, but doing it proactively even when you aren't required to positions you as the true market expert in the minds of your executives and your team. Make sure you share this information; visit staff meetings to present about your market and informally share the results with a wide range of people who are involved with your product.

Increasing your technical expertise

For some product management jobs, you don't need to have technical expertise. If you're working on a nontechnical consumer product, a service that requires no technology development, or other products and services that have no technology component, you may be able to do the job without establishing a base level of technical competence. You should, however, be known as the subject matter expert in the area that your product serves.

REMEMBER

However, if you're working on a software or hardware product, you need to have enough technical competence for your team members to respect you. They'll be making highly technical decisions that directly affect the feature set and experience for your customers. Not having any technical credibility significantly reduces your ability to influence what decisions the team makes.

No, you don't need to have an engineering degree or know how to write software. But you have to understand enough about the underlying technology, standards, jargon, and acronyms being used to be able to talk intelligently with your engineers.

You can get up to speed in these areas in many ways. You can take courses at a local college or junior college or look for free online courses from organizations like Coursera. You can read books on the most important technologies for your product. One great idea is to ask your engineers to explain the basics of how the technology works. Engineers like being experts and are often more than happy to help you, but take good notes. They won't want to do it on a weekly basis.

TIP

Keep on the lookout for new technologies and trends. Any time your engineers or others bring up something, be curious and go learn as much as you can about it. Most of the time, engineers are very aware of which future technologies are going to be game-changers, so stay aware of what they're talking about and following. The engineers love new technology and will want to use it as soon as possible, perhaps earlier than the market needs or wants. You need to be ready to have any new technology discussion with them sooner rather than later.

5

Part of Tens

Product launches are complex. Avoid the most common errors to save a lot of time, money, and work (and possibly your professional reputation).

Road maps can be powerful and effective tools for a product manager. Expand your knowledge and proper usage of road maps to keep everyone on board and the entire project on track.

Identify the most common failures that product managers encounter so you can sidestep them!

Chapter **20**

Ten Common Product Launch Mistakes to Avoid

Companies invest millions of dollars each year in developing new products and trying to increase their revenues and profitability. Some of these are good products, and some aren't. Nonetheless, they all have one thing in common: Without appropriate launch and marketing activities, they'll most likely fail. In fact, many inferior products have won in the marketplace simply because the company's launch and marketing were more effective than those of their competitors with the superior product.

The key to an effective product launch is to create and execute a plan that is appropriate to meet your goals given your resource, budget, and time constraints. This chapter covers the ten most common mistakes that occur in product launches so you can avoid making them.

Failing to Plan Early Enough

Many companies wait to plan their product launch until they're just a few weeks away from the product being ready. Effective launches take much more time and effort than many people realize. Build your launch plan a minimum of four months prior to product availability. This time frame gives you enough opportunity to plan for and execute extensive public relations activities and marketing programs and to get all the positioning, messaging, collateral, and pricing finalized. It also allows enough time to communicate to your partners (and internal groups, if your company is large) so that they can prepare for and support your efforts.

You can pull off product launches in a matter of weeks, but doing so is extremely stressful, leads to miscommunication and poor execution, and ultimately usually results in less-than-optimal results and lower revenues. Do yourself and your company a favor and start early — it will dramatically increase your chances of success.

Not Having a Sustaining Marketing Plan in Place

One of the biggest launch mistakes, particularly in high-tech fields, is that companies assume that the launch is an event unto itself and that the initial buzz generated, combined with the excellence of the product, will be enough to generate ongoing sales momentum. If the product is exciting and the company achieves a lot of initial press coverage and revenues, the company often becomes convinced that it has hit the magic revenue generation formula and that all is well.

Unfortunately, what often happens is that after an initial post-launch spike in sales and excitement, revenues quickly drop to a much lower level. The company is then baffled. After all, it had clear indications that things were going well at and just after launch. The company forgot that customers need to be reminded on an ongoing basis that a product exists and solves their problem or they stop buying.

Effective marketing programs take several weeks (and sometimes months) to plan and execute, so the company is now in a bind. Getting adequate programs going takes quite a bit of time, and in the meantime revenues will continue to miss expectations.

The key to avoiding this situation is to plan realistic sustaining marketing programs well in advance of launch to ensure that you meet your key goals, such as lead flow and revenue generation. Sustaining marketing programs are ongoing marketing activities such as web ads, short-term promotional pricing, and webinars that remind customers to buy your product. Figure 20-1 shows the difference in sales when sustaining marketing is planned as an immediate follow on to launch activities. Don't wait until the product is already in the market to get your sustaining marketing planning and execution going.

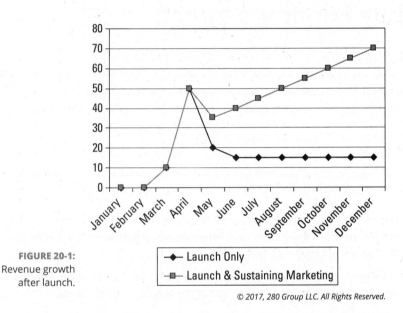

FIGURE 20-1:
Revenue growth
after launch.

Shipping a Poor Quality Product

Letting a poor quality product out the door is a potentially deadly mistake because it can sometimes be impossible to recover from. If the press gets hold of your product and it doesn't work as promised, or if customers have a bad experience with it, the product image and brand may be tarnished permanently. During the dot-com boom, you could find literally thousands of examples of products that customers tried once and then were never willing to try again.

The best way to avoid this problem is to set quality goals early and gain consensus on their adoption among all the key stakeholders, including the executives involved. If you're a start-up, wanting to get first version of the product out is tempting.

If you're a public company, you may be under immense pressure to meet quarterly goals. And there is always the temptation to ship a product that isn't quite ready but that can be "fixed" with downloads from the Internet by the time it's in the hands of many customers. Set concrete goals quality goals early (see the Chapter 13) and be diligent about sticking to them. After all, your team has worked hard to create a product that can be successful. Don't jeopardize it by releasing it too early.

Inadequately Funding Launch

Companies often believe that they have such a compelling product that for a small amount (a few thousand dollars), they're going to be able to launch a wildly successful product. This situation is particularly true with products that have a viral marketing component. Companies overestimate how viral the product will actually be and whether customers will really care about it. The reality is that viral products and wild successes are few and far between.

One way to avoid this mistake is to do a return on investment (ROI) analysis. *ROI* is the profit you make based on the money you spend. Follow these steps:

1. **List all the ways you're going to reach customers: announcements, product reviews, marketing programs, word of mouth, online advertising such as Google AdWords, and so on.**

2. **Roughly estimate how many impressions you plan to make to your target market and how many of those you can expect to turn into leads.**

3. **Estimate what you think your close rate will be for those leads.**

   For example, do you believe that 10 percent of them will actually buy your product and pay you money?

4. **Calculate your ROI.**

   The formula for return on investment is $ROI = Net\ Profit \div Total\ Investment \times 100$. In Figure 20-2, $ROI = 376,800 \div 500,000 \times 100 = 75$ percent.

Calculating ROI helps build a reality-based picture so you can make more informed decisions about what an adequate spending level really is.

Program	Cost	# exposures	# leads	# sales	profit
PR Program	120,000	500,000	2,500	500	$200,000
Adwords/Online Advertising	5,000	N/A	10,000	250	$100,000
Print Advertising	250,000	450,000	2,250	450	$180,000
Collateral & Demo	25,000	-	-	-	$ -
Trade Show/Launch Event	30,000	1,200	480	192	$ 76,800
Email Blasts	20,000	100,000	1,000	400	$160,000
Channel Mktg Program	50,000	N/A	1,000	400	$160,000
TOTAL	500,000	1,051,200	17,230	2,192	$876,800

Total Profit	$ 876,800
Less Total Cost	$ (500,000)
Net Return	$ 376,800

ROI	75%

FIGURE 20-2: ROI calculation for a product launch.

Underestimating the Required Marketing Exposure

Studies show that potential customers need an average of at least seven exposures to your marketing message before they have enough awareness to take action. This need for repetition is one of the reasons that marketing after the product launch is so critical. Don't assume that reading about the product once or clicking on an ad one time is going to create enough awareness and desire for the product that people will purchase it immediately. Have a look at Chapter 15 for how to create customer exposures to your product through different marketing activities. Unless your product is life-changing or is so simple and compelling to try, you're better off being realistic about just how much exposure and marketing it will really take to drive sales.

Driving Customers to Buy Your Competitor's Products

Nothing is more disappointing than launching and marketing a product only to have prospective customers purchase your competitor's product instead. You're essentially educating the market and creating awareness in order to lose a sale (and potentially the lifetime relationship with that customer) to a competitor who is trying to put you out of business.

How do you avoid handing customers to your competition on a silver platter? First, make sure your product is widely available at launch so that customers can find it and, more importantly, won't accidentally stumble across another alternative. Second, make sure you set the competitive argument in your positioning, messaging, packaging, collateral, and anywhere else possible. When you set the competitive argument, you describe the problem in a way that gives your product the advantage in any comparison. Unless your competitors are completely unknown and customers have no chance of finding them, you want to make sure you have the proof points and messages in place to present your product as the best solution and the only logical choice. Since search engines ensure even the smallest competitors can be found, part of your messaging should address either your experience (for established companies) or your cutting-edge advantage (for new companies pushing into exciting new product areas). And finally, don't announce your product too early (as we discuss in the next section).

Announcing Too Early

If you announce your product too early, you run several risks:

- ❯❯ You're playing your cards publicly, so any competitors can respond before your product becomes available. They can change their marketing to reset the competitive argument, for example.

- ❯❯ The announcement may drive customers to investigate other options and become aware of or even purchase your competition.

- ❯❯ When your product does ship, you may not be able to get any press coverage because your item is old news.

Announcing products early is tempting for a number of reasons. You may have a great idea you want to be able to share with the world early on so you get credit for coming up with it. Or a competitor may already have an offering you're scared will grab all the mindshare and leave you with no opportunity when your product is available.

TECHNICAL STUFF

Large companies sometimes use an early announcement to prevent customers from considering smaller company alternatives. The common term for this tactic is *FUD*, which stands for fear, uncertainty, and doubt. Customers who are loyal to a large company brand often prefer the safe route of waiting for the large company solution rather than take the risk on a smaller, unproven company. If your company is big enough, consider pre-announcing to keep space for your alternative in the market place.

REMEMBER

You may also announce the product too early because your confidence level in your development schedules is too high. You should typically assume that the launch is going to happen 30 days later than the planned date. Deciding on how early is too early is related to your sell in cycle (see Chapter 15). For B2B customers, launching early would be a time period greater than 25 to 50 percent of your sell in cycle. The idea here is that being just a little bit late with an excellently executed product launch is better than announcing a product that then isn't available. Nothing is more frustrating and decreases potential revenue than driving lots of customers to seek out your product based on your announcement only to have them never return again.

Not Having a Dedicated Product Review and Public Relations Program

Product reviews can be your greatest ally or your worst nightmare. Good reviews validate your product with an external source and provide much more credibility than your own marketing or advertising ever could. Poor reviews, on the other hand, can stop customers in their tracks during the purchase process.

The choice you must make is whether you want to proactively manage the review program or reactively respond to it if a problem occurs. Proactively managing a review program means creating supporting documents (reviewer's guides) and having ongoing conversations with reviewers as they review your product. Your goal is that they recognize and report on valuable aspects of your product. And hopefully, spend less time on the weaker parts of your product. Of course, if a problem occurs during a review, it's usually too late to do damage control. Even if a publication prints a retraction to clarify the facts, the majority of the people who read the bad review will never see the revision. They'll believe your product isn't good.

Few companies understand how much time and effort running a full-scale proactive product review program takes. However, product review programs conducted correctly and with the proper amount of resources, can greatly improve product reviews.

Larger companies have public relations (PR) folks in house who work with specialist public relations firms outside the company to target specific publications, bloggers, and industry influencers and analysts. Smaller companies hire a PR consultant or keep one on *retainer* (pay them a small monthly fee). Press or PR takes a lot of communication framing and coordination work, and product managers are not specialists in this area. PR work includes generating interest in your product by getting press and analysts excited about your product, having great attendance at press and analyst briefingss and, more specifically, asking for publications to review your product. Customers rely heavily on press reviews when making product decisions as the reviewer is perceived to be an unbiased information source.

Industry analysts, more commonly referred to simply as *analysts,* are specialist firms that develop secondary research about your product and industry. See Chapter 6 for further reading on secondary research. At launch, you are setting the stage for secondary research firms. Figure 20-3 shows the timelines and activities for analyst and press programs. We recommend planning press and review activities from four to six months prior to launch.

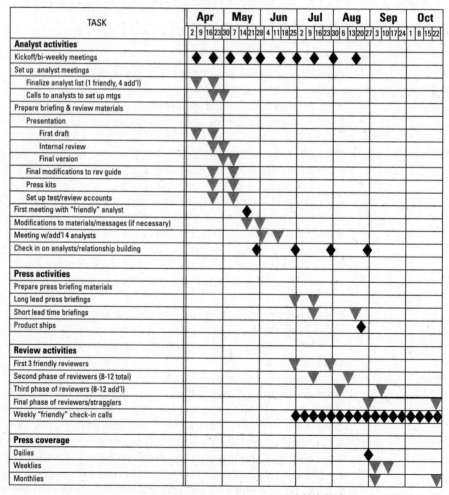

FIGURE 20-3: Typical timeline for a product review and public relations program.

Delaying Communication

One mistake that can hamper launch success is failing to brief and inform the key constituents early enough. The key constituents are internal, channel partners, and press and analysts. When you aren't in contact with these specific internal or targeted audiences ahead of time, here's what can go wrong:

» **Internal marketing and sales:** In a big company, you may lose opportunities to take advantage of events, sales opportunities, or marketing programs that other groups are running.

» **Channel partners:** If you don't give your channel partners enough advance notice, they may take quite a bit of time to work your new products into their plans.

» **Press, bloggers, and analysts:** You want to brief these folks far in advance so that positive announcements, news, and reviews about your product run concurrently with product availability. *Note:* Briefings are given under non-disclosure agreements (NDAs) and are subject to embargos so that news about the product isn't made available to the public until the day of launch.

WARNING

Communicating early to your key constituents does have some risks. Your competitors may get wind of what you're doing. Your salespeople may stop focusing on selling the current product and sell future products instead. And if you miss your date by a substantial amount, you may lose credibility for future launches. For companies where the risk of leaks is too high (one example is Apple), the solution is that no internal communication (other than to the people that absolutely need to know like a small marketing team) is made until the day of launch and then the planned communications roll out happens very quickly.

Considering International Markets as an Afterthought

The international market is often a significant revenue opportunity, but it's one many companies fail to plan for because they're so focused on the domestic market. Make sure you communicate to your international divisions (within your company) and international partners (outside your company) early enough so that they can make plans accordingly. Ask your international product managers, marketing, and sales to find out just how long before launch bringing in international partners is appropriate. Three months isn't uncommon; however, the type of product you work on and the markets you work in change a lot of timing.

TIP

To save time and energy and ensure your messaging is coherent on a worldwide basis, design all your launch materials (collateral, marketing pieces, packaging, and so on) so that they can be used in international markets with little or no adjustment. If your material needs to be translated (the official term is *localized*), your materials have to be ready even earlier than for the domestic market. Delivering coherent messaging and delivery of information within localization lead times reduces the time required to generate international revenues by three to six months.

Chapter **21**

Ten (Plus One) Road Maps to Help You Succeed

roduct road maps can be a highly effective tool for a product manager. They help to organize and plan out the future of products, show the team and others how the product will achieve its vision, and serve as a way to communicate with internal and external stakeholders. In this chapter, we present the 11 most commonly used road maps for product managers.

TIP

When sharing product road maps both internally at your company and externally with others, make sure to use the following best practices:

» **Share selectively and carefully.** After people see something on a road map, they'll consider it to be a plan of record.

» **Never publish or share road maps in PowerPoint format.** Use Adobe PDF format and apply passwords so that others can't change the road map details. If you share road maps in electronic formats across the company using wikis or other storage software, make sure they are marked confidential so that they won't be shared outside the company.

>> Always mark your road maps with "Confidential — Do Not Distribute" so that others don't accidentally send them to someone who shouldn't see them.

>> **Use code names for projects rather than the actual names.** That way, if the road map ends up in the wrong hands, your plans will be less obvious.

>> **Keep road maps to be used outside your group higher-level and more generic.** Remove many of the finer details from road maps shared with customers, channel partners, press, analysts, and other groups in your company. For example, you may share a road map that shows the themes for your next three major releases but doesn't include the actual details about what features those releases include.

>> **When you're creating your road maps — and any plans for your product — make it a highly-collaborative process with your team.** Get team members' feedback and buy-in early so that everyone is on the same page as opposed to creating and presenting a finalized road map that may surprise them.

TIP

In this chapter, there are a lot of references to technology. What if you don't work in a highly technical industry? No problem. Replace "technology" with "legal" or "regulation." The beauty of road maps is that they illustrate change over time for any product manager.

TIP

There are lot of suggested formats in this chapter. If none of them work to tell your product, technology, or market story, use these ideas as a starting point for illustrating what you have to say. Have fun!

Theme-Based Product Road Maps

You create this road map by grouping your potential prioritized feature list into themes. Figure 21-1 shows what an internal theme-based road map looks like. For example, a theme could be performance, usability, or competitive parity. The beauty of a theme-based product road map is that it makes creating marketing messages and plans for communicating clearly with customers easier. Without a theme, you may be delivering customers a bunch of features and then leaving them to decide why they should buy.

Theme-based road maps are useful because they help keep your product from experiencing *feature creep*, where stakeholders constantly want to add new features. Using themes allows you to decide whether to add a feature based on whether it's related to the theme. If it isn't, you can defer it to a later release. Theme-based road maps can be for just the next one or two releases over a period of a year or can have much longer time frames including several years and many releases. These versions are a great way to paint a longer-term picture of how your product will fulfill its vision over time. Figure 21-2 is a sample of a theme-based road map over five years.

One-Year Theme-Based Internal Product Road Map

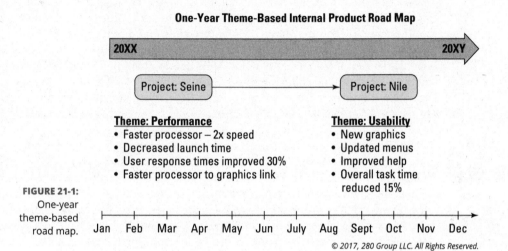

FIGURE 21-1: One-year theme-based road map.

Five-Year Theme-Based Internal Product Road Map

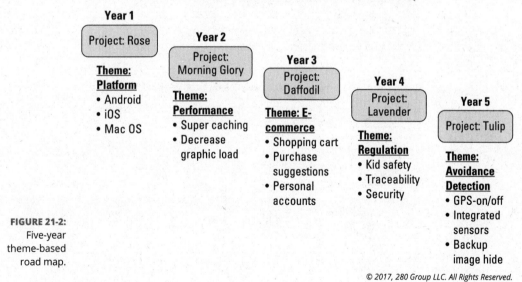

FIGURE 21-2: Five-year theme-based road map.

Timed Release Product Road Maps

Timed release road maps are based on the concept that new versions of the product will be released on a consistent schedule that doesn't change. For example, a new product would be released every six months — no matter what. To create this road map, you list your features in priority order for the next release, estimating what can be done in the time frame. If a feature slips and doesn't make it into this release, it simply goes into the next release. A consistent release cadence like this one works well if your team is doing Agile development and is either releasing after every sprint or combining every few sprints and releasing on a regular schedule. (Chapter 12 has more on sprints.) Have a look at Figures 21-3 and 21-4 to see the difference between a quarterly and yearly timed release road map.

TIP

When deciding on the cadence of a timed release product, take into account the rate at which your customers can integrate new products into how they work. For many corporate accounts, the process for accepting new software is slow and deliberate. They may not want to accept new or revised software any more than once a year. In the consumer market space, the cadence is much faster. For example, Facebook updates its app every two weeks. In some instances your software is released to customers the moment that it's written and tested. This is called *continuous deployment*. Products using continuous deployment or those released more frequently than once a quarter still benefit from a road map. Product managers focus on creating themes that are developed over a quarter. You then have a road map which shows all the features that will have been developed by the end of a particular quarter. And your customers only get the full benefit of all the changes at the end of the quarter.

Quarterly Timed Release Road Map

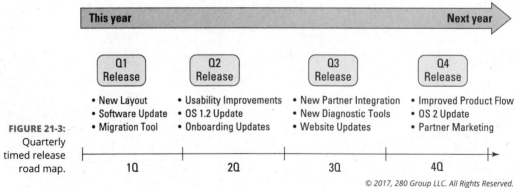

Q1 Release	Q2 Release	Q3 Release	Q4 Release
• New Layout	• Usability Improvements	• New Partner Integration	• Improved Product Flow
• Software Update	• OS 1.2 Update	• New Diagnostic Tools	• OS 2 Update
• Migration Tool	• Onboarding Updates	• Website Updates	• Partner Marketing

FIGURE 21-3: Quarterly timed release road map.

1Q   2Q   3Q   4Q

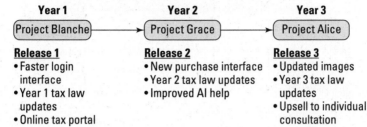

Three-Year Timed Release Internal Product Road Map

Year 1	Year 2	Year 3
Project Blanche →	Project Grace →	Project Alice

Release 1
- Faster login interface
- Year 1 tax law updates
- Online tax portal

Release 2
- New purchase interface
- Year 2 tax law updates
- Improved AI help

Release 3
- Updated images
- Year 3 tax law updates
- Upsell to individual consultation

FIGURE 21-4: Three-year timed release road map.

Golden Feature Product Road Maps

Golden feature road maps use a simple concept: Choose one overriding important feature for each release; the product can't be released until this golden feature is completed, and only very minor other features can be added. This approach can be a good strategy because it provides focus for product development and makes marketing messaging very clear.

Of course, the downside is that stakeholders may become impatient if their pet feature isn't on the next release (or on the road map at all). Figure 21-5 is a sample of a golden feature road map.

Quarterly/Yearly Golden Feature Product Road Map

Redwood	Sequoia	Cherry	Oak

HiRez Display
- Minor Feature 1: processor upgrade

Amplified Touch
- Minor Feature 1: Faster storage access

Voice Activation
- Minor Feature 1: processor upgrade

Professional Camera
- Minor Feature 1: storage upgrade

1Q   2Q   3Q   4Q   Year 2   Year 3

FIGURE 21-5: Quarterly and yearly combined golden feature product road map.

Market and Strategy Road Maps

Market and strategy road maps help you paint a picture of what markets you'll be pursuing and how you'll do so. They can help you align resources across the company and obtain funding for all the work that needs to be done. Figure 21-6 shows you a sample of a market and strategy road map. You'll notice that certain rectangles are blank. If no activity takes place in year one, for example, on acquiring a company, then leave it blank.

Market and Strategy Road Map

	Year One	Year Two
Markets	Healthcare	Financial Manufacturing
Partner	XYZ Company	
Build In-House		2.X release
Acquire		Data analytics

FIGURE 21-6:
Market and strategy road map with sample data.

Visionary Road Maps

Visionary road maps allow for painting a broad-brush view that shows industry trends and how they fit into the long-term vision for your product or products. This type of road map provides few details but links industry trends to your product's evolution over time to create a picture of where you're headed. Visionary road maps are great to create before developing a particular product road map because the visionary road map gives the context and reason for particular product choices. Look at Figure 21-7 for an example of a visionary road map. You can see how the future vision is linked to particular industry trends.

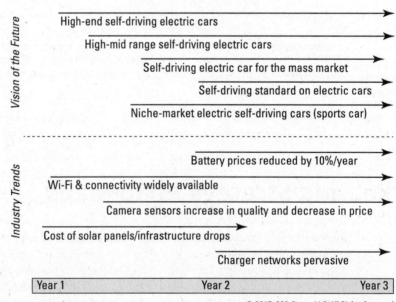

FIGURE 21-7:
Visionary road map for electric and self-driving vehicles.

Three-Year Visionary Road Map

Vision of the Future

High-end self-driving electric cars

High-mid range self-driving electric cars

Self-driving electric car for the mass market

Self-driving standard on electric cars

Niche-market electric self-driving cars (sports car)

Industry Trends

Battery prices reduced by 10%/year

Wi-Fi & connectivity widely available

Camera sensors increase in quality and decrease in price

Cost of solar panels/infrastructure drops

Charger networks pervasive

Year 1 — Year 2 — Year 3

Competitive, Market, and Technology Trends Road Map

This type of road map is helpful to create when developing and communicating your overall strategy. It provides a holistic view of the forces surrounding your product over the next few years and how your product and strategy fit in so that you win in the marketplace. Try using the example in Figure 21-8 to create your own high-level context. What you discover may change what you decide to do next.

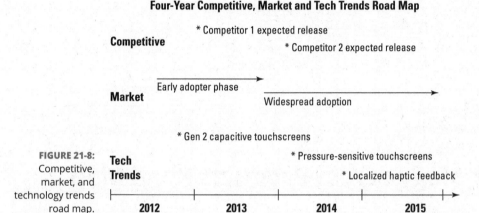

FIGURE 21-8: Competitive, market, and technology trends road map.

Technology Road Maps

Technology road maps are useful for capturing what's happening in the overall world of technology and linking it to what you're developing internally. The top part gives you an idea of what technology your internal team needs to develop for, add to, or build on top of. Industry technologies are great because they set standards so that your products can leverage the work that has been done outside. On a side note, large companies have groups that influence industry standards boards to gain competitive advantages by putting in features that make product development easier for the company doing the lobbying.

Develop a technology road map along with your chief technologists to make sure that you capture all the technological inputs. Figure 21-9 gives an example of a technology road map.

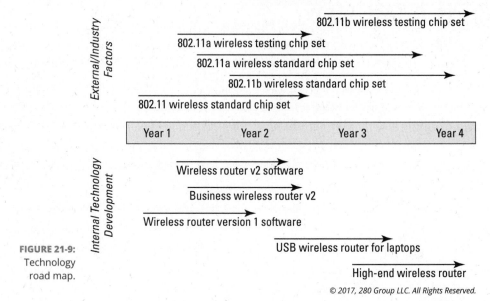

**Four-Year
Technology Road Map**

*External/Industry
Factors*

802.11b wireless testing chip set

802.11a wireless testing chip set

802.11a wireless standard chip set

802.11b wireless standard chip set

802.11 wireless standard chip set

| Year 1 | Year 2 | Year 3 | Year 4 |

*Internal Technology
Development*

Wireless router v2 software

Business wireless router v2

Wireless router version 1 software

USB wireless router for laptops

High-end wireless router

FIGURE 21-9:
Technology
road map.

Technology across Products Road Map

This type of road map gives you a quick view about how the company will share technologies across a variety of products. It gives you a glimpse into what kind of cross-product technology leverage you can create and what each of the products is dependent on.

The technology across products road map in Figure 21-10 is a great way to coordinate the discussion of technology platforms across a large organization. The signed-off version clarifies to all departments, divisions, and business units what the schedule and interdependencies are.

Technology across Products Road Map

	2010	2011	2012
Product 1	Codec		New Architecture
Product 2		Codec X-platform UI	
Product 3		X-platform UI	New Architecture
Product 4	Codec		New Architecture

FIGURE 21-10:
Example of
technology
across products
road map.

Platform Road Maps

Platform road maps like the one in Figure 21-11 are critical when creating a software platform that other developers will be using to build solutions. Examples of platforms include Microsoft Windows, Apple MacOS and iOS, Google Android, and others.

TECHNICAL STUFF

The world of product management can intersect that of engineering more often than not. In the platform road map and the technology across products road maps, the term *Codec* is used as a way of compressing or reducing data in a smart way so that performance is increased. Less data moves faster than more data. The terms *B1*, *B2*, and *FCS* are used to refer to the versions of software as it's being built. B1 and B2 are beta versions 1 and 2. FCS stands for *first customer ship* or the first version of the software that is good enough for customers to use.

Platform road maps communicate your plans to your customers, press, developers, and other stakeholders so that they can plan accordingly. They need to know what to expect in terms of the platform releases as well as development tools so that they can plan their activities. See Figure 21-11 for an example. Don't be surprised to find information from your platform road map on their road maps next time they brief you on their plans.

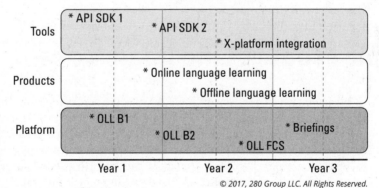

FIGURE 21-11: Example of a platform road map.

Matrix Product Road Maps

Matrix product road maps like the one in Figure 21-12 allow you to communicate information about many products and the corresponding details. They show what will be released when, the target market, and competitor and technology trends.

If you're briefing marketing, or even the entire company, the matrix product road map allows everyone involved to understand the context of how a set of products comes to market. Each department is more capable of doing its job when it understands the whole picture of how and when a product is coming to market.

Quarterly and Two-Year Matrix Road Map

	Q1 2010	Q2 2010	Q3 2010	Q4 2010	2011	2012
Code Name or Product Name						
Target Market						
Major Features or Theme						
Technology Trends						
Competitor's Products						

FIGURE 21-12: Matrix product road map.

Multiple Product Line Road Maps

When you need to convey what will be released across multiple product lines during a given time period, this is the type of road map to use (see Figure 21-13). Use this road map to communicate to management and other stakeholders what to expect with a range of products at a high level. In the example, the exact detailed features are not discussed. Managers and executives want to understand when product changes are planned so that they can prepare the rest of the organization for what will happen.

Some highlights of this road map are that it can show when too many products are launching at the same time. A multiple product line road map can also illuminate interdependencies. If you are counting on a product to be available as part of a multi-product solution and it's delayed, the organization as a whole needs to make difficult decisions. For example, delay all the products or give the delayed product more resources. You can also add the expected revenue value to each of the products to understand the relative importance of one product versus another.

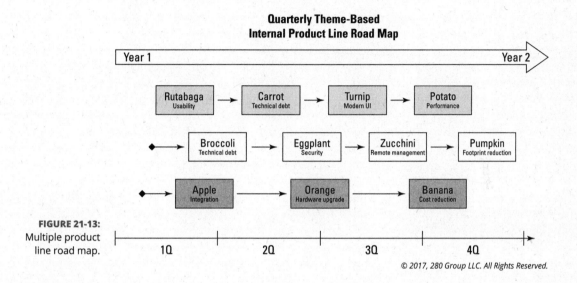

Quarterly Theme-Based Internal Product Line Road Map

FIGURE 21-13: Multiple product line road map.

Chapter **22**

Ten Ways Product Managers Fail

The chapters throughout this book focus mostly on ways to make your product and your product management career successful. This chapter is a more tongue-in-cheek look at things we've seen product managers do that have caused them to fall short.

Talking More Than Listening

REMEMBER

If you're a product manager and you aren't accustomed to being quiet and listening to what customers, engineers, salespeople, and executives are really saying, you're in trouble. If you talk too much, you may miss the nuances behind what team members are saying, and you may be intimidating fellow colleagues out of talking altogether. Who wants to disagree with the product manager who thinks she is smarter than everyone else in the room?

If this scenario describes you, start practicing active listening constantly. If you still have trouble giving others the floor, take a people skills class to learn how to better communicate, negotiate, and influence. Remember, silence is much more powerful than chatter.

Focusing Only on Features

Product managers love products. They live for products. And their tendency, particularly those who come from a technical background, is to spend every opportunity on sweating the small details with their friends, the engineers. That's what's comfortable.

Don't make the mistake of zeroing in on the trees and missing the forest. Of course, you need to spend the right amount of time making sure the product is right, but you also have to step up and be the strategic leader for the product to ensure its success. Be in contact with all the groups involved with making the product a success. Go find customers to talk to. Reach out to salespeople. If you don't do the long-range work of a product manager, who will?

Not Continuing to Learn

Product managers come from all different backgrounds, bringing varied skill sets to the job. Though one whose history is in sales may excel at communication, another from an engineering background shines at developing product features. Both may lack certain product management skills because of the focus of their prior occupations.

Knowing you have gaps in your skill set is fine; just continuing with what you know and not enhancing all the skills that build a successful product manager isn't. Because many companies don't offer training in the product management arena, it's up to you to improve your skills (which you're well on your way to doing by buying this book — bravo!). Look into taking a product management training course that covers the entire product life cycle. No matter where you are in your product management career, this kind of training boosts your product management skills.

Reinventing the Wheel

Product managers spend a huge amount of time doing things like creating their own templates, starting documents from scratch, and even attempting to create a product management process from scratch for their company.

Remember that these documents and templates are all things that others have done already. Leverage those people's efforts and save your energy for other parts of the job. A great place to start is the Product Management Office Professional from the 280 Group.

Avoiding Seeking Help

If you don't have a coach or a mentor (or at least a supportive boss who's willing to teach you), then you're going to make the same mistakes that many other product managers have made. Instead of forging ahead blindly, tap into the insights of others that have gone before you and get a direct link into what works and what doesn't.

TIP

Hire a coach or enlist a mentor to guide you, and you'll put your career on an upward trajectory. With a mentor, someone's always got your back, and you have a sounding board whenever you have questions or want to break in a new idea.

Digging In and Refusing to Compromise, Ever

One of the most common situations between product management and other departments is where one side refuses to give any ground in a disagreement. We know; you have to stand your ground and insist things be a certain way some of the time. But if you do it all the time, the other side will realize that you aren't a reasonable partner to work with. If you're not prepared to compromise, why should others? Eventually, you're liable to end up with an unpleasant and unsuccessful stalemate.

If you find yourself digging in, start using your active listening skills. Make sure you really understand the situation and, if necessary, get advice from your manager on the best way to tackle the difficulties you face so that both parties can feel somewhat successful. You need to win the whole war and get a winning product to market. Winning one battle with an internal department won't get you there.

Never Visiting Customers

If you aren't getting out to see customers, holding a customer council, or communicating with customers by phone or email several times a month, then you're going to be out of touch with the reality of the market. And your credibility with your team members will be much lower. They won't see you as owning the voice of the customer, and you won't be the true advocate for what customers need.

Set specific goals like talking to customers twice a week. When you get out of the meeting or off the phone, summarize your conversations. Then send your notes to the engineers and extended team. You'll know you've succeeded when your engineers come to you to find out what customers will value the most in terms of features or implementation. What a win for both the engineering team and you.

Not Owning the Whole Product

No one in your company has the complete 360-degree view of your product that you do. You know everything about it: competitive environment, strategy, challenges, support and warranty policies, pricing, how salespeople are representing it, and more. As such, no one else can drive to ensure that the whole product offering is in place. This is far beyond just the product's feature list.

Creating the whole product offering means moving beyond the comfort zone of your strict job specification and challenging others outside the traditional sphere of influence that the organization has set for you. Challenge them to join you and deliver on the whole product solution by adding special support and training products, for example. Then your customers will truly love your product. Once you own this larger whole product responsibility, you'll be perceived as a leader.

Adopting Agile but Losing Overall Business Focus

Agile development has huge benefits and can be great for the right products. However, most product managers are thrust into an Agile environment without knowing how this approach dramatically changes their jobs or how to be effective.

In this situation, take a course on doing great work with Agile development teams and learn the skills of both an Agile product manager and product owner. This training is especially important if you're also assigned as the product owner in addition to the product manager. When you're in your new role as a product owner, don't end up focusing all your time and effort on the product development process. Your responsibilities extend far beyond the Agile process, backlog, and sprints. You have to own all elements of product success. Remember that you own product and market strategy, business cases, market needs, effective launches and marketing, and end of life. Having a dual focus isn't easy, so be clear on how and why you're deciding to spend your time — whether time should be spent on an Agile task or a more business focused task. (Chapter 12 has more information on the Agile process.)

Being a Product Janitor Rather Than a Product Manager

One of the traps that many product managers fall into is that they don't learn how to say "No." They end up doing mostly low-level tactical work rather than having a strategic focus in their jobs. Any product being developed will always have an endless number of small tasks and cleanup. If you aren't careful, you can become a product janitor, cleaning up the mess that others have made.

REMEMBER

Delegate and prioritize so you can rise up to be a strategic product leader.

Glossary

A/B testing: Also known as split testing. Used to compare two different versions of the same web page and determine which one is measurably more effective at achieving results. Results are usually measured as click through, purchase, or download.

active listening: The process of listening and responding by echoing some of the talker's words to ensure understanding.

Agile: An iterative and incremental approach to, typically, software development that involves short phases of work followed by checking that the work achieves the agreed upon goals and adapting to new information given market changes.

alpha: The very first version of the software that works, sort of. Term mostly used in waterfall development.

application program interfaces (API): A set of definitions, protocols, and tools used to build software. Especially important to define when different software parts need to work together.

assumption: Unproven business supposition used to make rapid progress toward a conclusion.

business-to-business (B2B): A business model where a business primarily supplies its product to other businesses.

business-to-consumer (B2C): A business model where a business primarily supplies its product to consumers.

barrier to entry: A set of obstacles that prevent or slow down a business from conducting business.

benefit: A description of a product advantage written from the perspective of the customer. Often includes emotional aspects.

beta: The almost final version of the software. Term mostly used in waterfall development.

beta plan: A plan to validate whether a product meets or does not meet customer expectations. A beta plan is created and executed prior to product launch.

beta program: A program to execute the beta plan.

brainstorming: A problem-solving meeting with specific rules intended to generate a wide range of ideas.

brand: A name, term, design, or symbol that identifies a company or product.

break-even: The financial point at which the total cost, including investment, of all products sold is the same as the profit generated by the same product.

business case: A financial and business justification to support investment in a particular product or solution.

business model: The specific way in which a business is organized to generate revenue and profits in a sustainable manner.

channel partner: A company that works with the provider of a product to sell it onto other channel partners or end users. A channel partner usually sells products from many different product providers.

conversion rate: In the digital marketing space, the percentage of all customers or website visitors who act in the way that the company wants at that point in time. For example, converting a website visit to a sale.

customer development: A process for bringing customers to the point of choosing your product through a deep understanding of their needs and the way that they purchase products.

customer panel: Groups of selected customers who provide feedback on a company's strategy, plans, and specific product offerings. Customer panels can be strategic or tactical, but not usually both.

DACI: A decision-making matrix developed to ensure a company can make decisions more quickly and that the process is transparent to all parties. D stands for Driver, A for Approver, C for Contributor, and I for Informed.

daily standup: In Agile, a very short daily meeting where everyone stands up. Each participant quickly answers specific questions.

design thinking: An integrative process involving a small inter-disciplinary team to analyze problems from all sides including logical, empathetic, and systemic points of view.

differentiation: An aspect of developing products and solutions that ensures customers can distinguish different offerings on a basis that is meaningful to the customer.

distribution channel: A chain of businesses through which a product passes until it reaches the end user. Different industries use widely varying terms for distribution partners.

embargo (press): A press embargo is a request that the information not be made public until a specified date.

feature: A distinctive factual attribute of a product or service.

frequently asked questions (FAQs): A list with answers of the most commonly asked questions about a company, product, solution, or service.

gate: In the context of a phase-gate process: a decision point as to whether a product or project should proceed, be held back, or cancelled.

Golden Master (GM): The final released version of software.

head count: The number of people allocated to a particular project or department. A *fully loaded head count* is the full cost including all personnel and business expenses of having the person employed.

ideation: The process of generating, fleshing out, and prioritizing product ideas.

inbound marketing: Marketing efforts that bring customers to you as a result of their searches for information on a certain topic. White papers, ebooks, blogs, and social media are examples of inbound marketing.

kanban: In software development, a method for developing software on a just-in-time basis. Kanban removes the scrum time boxed method to track work, which is useful when your development team members have specialized skills.

key performance indicators (KPIs): A set of business metrics used to determine whether a person, product, group, or division is successful.

landing page: Landing pages are officially any web page that a customer is directed to via a hyperlink. For large websites, landing pages are used to direct customers quickly to a more specific topic of interest.

Lean: A methodology for approaching problems by delivering quality with speed and customer alignment. Usually followed by a descriptor of Lean: Lean startup, Lean UX. The goal is not to create anything unless it adds value.

market: A space where buyers and customers can interact to exchange money for products. In product management terms, often used to mean a group of customers who interact with the company in the same way.

market analysis: An analysis of specific markets with the goal of determining relative attractiveness of addressing a product to a particular group of customers.

market needs document: See *market requirements document*.

market offering: A combination of products offered to a market to satisfy a particular need.

market requirements document (MRD): A document that defines the high-level market need for a product. An MRD is written from the point of view of the problem space and the customer.

market research: The process of gathering, analyzing, and interpreting information about customers and markets to determine their preferences.

market segments: A unique group of customers who share similar characteristics in the way that they react to marketing.

market share: The portion of the total market sales that accrues to one company.

minimum viable product (MVP): The smallest and most tightly defined product that will generate initial sales. Customer feedback is then gathered to inform the next version of the product.

mockup: A model of a final product used to guide product development and gain customer feedback.

new product development (NPD): The process of conceiving a product until it is finally delivered to market.

non-disclosure agreement (NDA): A formal agreement or contract by which two or more parties agree not to disclose confidential information that they share with each other.

opportunity cost: The cost of not pursuing a different alternative instead of the one chosen.

outbound marketing: Marketing that reaches out from the company to the customer. This includes but isn't limited to direct mail, email, and advertising.

payback time frame: The period of time needed to recover all the costs of the project.

persona (market and product): An archetype of a customer, decision maker, or influencer that defines its role, attributes, behavior, and any other insights pertaining to its perception of your product or the way that the person perceives marketing messages.

phase: A time period during the product life cycle when certain prescribed activities are completed by different departments with the goal of completing specific tasks before the next gate. Also referred to as a *stage*.

phase-gate process: A project management technique where phases of prescribed work are punctuated by decision gates. Also known as *stage-gate* process.

pivot: In the Lean start-up world, a pivot is a structured, often rapid, course correction on the basis of new market, customer, and development information.

positioning: The marketing objective of a customer having a clear, unique, and advantageous understanding of a product.

product line: A group of products related to each other under the banner of a brand.

product line extension: An additional product added to a product line that prevents revenue decline or increases overall revenue for the overall product line.

product portfolio: A range of products sold by a company. Many products and product lines can be part of a product portfolio.

product requirements document (PRD): A document that contains at least all the high-level product-specific requirements or features for that product to be developed and ready for market.

profit: In financial terms, the difference between the price that a product is sold for and the total cost to provide and sell the product.

prototype: The first model of a product. In software, it's the incomplete product used for testing and validation before final development.

public relations (PR): The development and maintenance of a positive public image of the company by an internal department very often in conjunction with external PR specialist firms.

RACI: A tool for identifying roles and responsibilities within and between organizations. R stands for Responsible, A for Accountable (to whom R is accountable), C for Consulted, and I for Informed.

requirement: A market need for the customer or product feature in a product that needs to be addressed for a customer problem to be solved.

return on investment (ROI): A numerical financial calculation used to compare different investment opportunities. ROI = (net profit/cost of investment) × 100.

revenue: The amount of money a company receives from operations during a specific period.

risk: The chance of a negative thing happening.

road map: A time-based visual representation of future scenarios for products, technologies, and market forces.

scope: The features and characteristics of a product. *Scope creep* occurs when additional features are added during development.

scrum: An iterative and incremental time-boxed method of developing software using small, self-directed teams. The goal of scrum is to flexibly develop what customers find valuable.

scrum master: In software development, the person who facilitates the work and decisions of a scrum team.

segmentation: For product managers, mainly market segmentation where different markets are divided so that choices can be made as to which markets to address.

sprint: In scrum, the defined period of time during which an agreed upon list of tasks should be accomplished.

sprint goal: The goal of a particular sprint communicated to all team members.

sprint planning meeting: A collaborative meeting facilitated by the scrum master during which the plan is developed and clarified for the upcoming sprint. Product owners participate to clarify user stories for the team.

sprint retrospective: A meeting held at the end of each sprint to evaluate the previous sprint and decide on changes that the team agrees for the next sprint.

sprint review: A meeting held at the end of a sprint to demonstrate the work that was completed during the sprint and get feedback for upcoming work.

stage: See *phase*.

strategy: A plan for achieving major objectives under conditions of uncertainty, usually over an extended period of time.

SWOT analysis: An analysis of the company's strengths and weaknesses compared to the opportunities and threats in the market place.

target market: The markets selected for the product to be sold to because they are the ones most likely to achieve positive company outcomes.

technical debt: In software, refers to code that should be reworked to improve it for a variety of reasons. Typically arises when shortcuts are done in development to get to market more quickly.

unique selling proposition (USP): The unique reason that a customer should choose your product over other offerings.

user experience (UX): The entirety of the customer experience with your company and product including purchasing, look and feel, functionality, and support.

user interface (UI): Anything that the customer interacts with and gets information from your company or about your product. Primarily, but not exclusively, used in software development.

user story: Description of the functionality that a product should have, written from the perspective of the user. A very simplified and focused requirement description.

value proposition: A statement of the value that your product brings to your customer. The main reason that a customer should buy from you.

vision: In product management, the description of the future that will exist when your product is developed. Used to provide a "true north" description to bring all stakeholders on board.

voice of the customer (VOC): The in-depth process of capturing customer needs, which includes market research and customer visits.

waterfall development: A linear and sequential development methodology where, for the product development part, product managers define all aspects of the product before it is given to engineering to create. There is no official role for feedback loops and flexible changes in waterfall development.

wireframe: In software development, a visual guide to the information hierarchy in the software as users follow a flow from screen to screen.

Index

A

A/B testing, 125, 343

ability to influence, as a trait of good product managers, 282

acceptance criteria, 189

accountability, ensuring, 235

Achievable, in SMART goal approach, 307

action plans, writing, 309–310

active listening, 290–291, 337, 343

advanced products, in development budget, 124

advertising, in marketing plan, 262

Agile development

about, 24–25, 27, 128, 131, 340–341

avoiding errors with, 181

compared with waterfall development, 203–213

creating backlog in, 207–211

defined, 343

key principles of, 210–211

phase-gate approaches and, 43–44

Plan phase documents for, 132

product launch under, 231

scrum and, 212

testing with, 220

trade-off triangle in, 214

Agile Manifesto, 210–211

AIPMM (Association of International Product Marketing and Management), 14, 52, 308

alpha, 218, 343

Amazon web services (AWS), 61

analysis

angle of, 267–268

as a component of market strategy, 173

product launch and, 323

as a product manager skill, 13

analyst firms, 311

analytics, 122

angle of analysis, 267–268

annual sales cycle, 260

Ansoff's opportunity matrix, 153–155

API (application program interface), 343

appearance, for visiting customers, 78

appendices. *See* exhibits and appendices

application program interface (API), 343

applying scoring models, 110–114

architectural vision

in product description, 195

in product description document, 198

asking for what you want, 292–293

Association of International Product Marketing and Management (AIPMM), 14, 52, 308

assumptions

in business case, 135, 143

as a component of market strategy, 175

defined, 343

in launch plan, 241

making about forecasting, 259–260

in marketing needs document, 191

in marketing plan, 262

in product description, 195

in product description document, 199

attitude

competitive intelligence and, 94

as a persona attribute, 183

in persona descriptions, 72, 73

attributes

defined, 70

of personas, 183

awareness

goals for in marketing plan, 263

in sales and marketing funnel, 252–253

AWS (Amazon web services), 61

B

B2B (business to business), 16–17, 70, 71, 343
B2C (business to consumer), 16–17, 70, 343
background
  as a persona attribute, 72, 73, 183
  in problem scenarios, 184
backlog
  creating in Agile, 207–211
  defined, 208
  prioritizing, 207–209
Ballmer, Steve (CEO), 8, 306
barriers, in business case, 140
barriers to entry
  in business case, 139
  as a component of market strategy, 174
  defined, 343
BCG (Boston Consulting Group) matrix, 150–151, 155
behavior, as a persona attribute, 73, 183
benchmarking, 266–267
benefit, 343
best practices
  building your credibility with, 297
  Development phase, 215
  for planning, 115–117
  product retirement, 277
beta
  defined, 343
  testing mistakes, 220–221
beta agreements, 224
beta plan
  creating, 219–220
  defined, 343, 344
  putting in place, 221–225
Beta Plan document, 55
blame, taking, 287
blogs and bloggers
  as collateral pieces, 250
  product launch and, 323
Blue Ocean Strategy, 67–68
boldness, as a trait of good product managers, 282

Boston Consulting Group (BCG) matrix, 150–151, 155
bottom-up forecast, 257
brainstorming
  in Conceive phase of product life cycle, 63–65, 66
  defined, 344
brand
  as a core competency, 47
  defined, 344
  in marketing plan, 262
  prioritizing and, 102
  product and, 245
brand promise, as a component of market strategy, 157
breakeven
  in business case, 142
  defined, 344
brochures, as collateral pieces, 249
broken product promise, 11
budget
  as a component of market strategy, 169, 175
  in marketing plan, 262
  for product launch, 229
building. *See also* creating
  career plans, 307–309
  confidence, 286–287
  networks, 308
  personal relationships, 294–295
  sales support, 268
  technical expertise, 312
  your credibility, 296–297
business acumen, as a trait of product managers, 32–33
business canvas, 104–108
business case
  about, 133–134
  assumptions, 135, 143
  competitive landscape section, 139–141
  conclusions and recommendations, 135, 144
  defined, 344
  documenting, 136–146
  executive summary, 135, 136–137, 138
  exhibits and appendices, 144

financial and resource impact analysis, 135, 141–143

getting buy-in for your, 146

governance, 144

importance of, 134–135

information gathering for, 136

market landscape section, 139

for new products/services, 134–136

open issues, 135, 144

outlining, 135–136

problem and opportunity section, 137

profit and loss (P&L) statement, 145

risks, 143

Business Case document, 55, 130

Business Case template, 133

business expertise

as a core competency, 47

as a product manager skill, 16

business focus, losing, 340–341

business model

defined, 344

in product-market fit triad, 102–104

business model canvas, 126–127

business plans, tracking against, 266–267

business to business (B2B), 16–17, 70, 71, 343

business to consumer (B2C), 16–17, 70, 343

buyer personas, 77, 188

buy-in, getting for your business case, 146

buying features, 114

C

call to action, 252

calmness, 291

cannibalization, in business case, 142–143

capturing feedback, 303–304

career goals and plans, 305–309

case histories, as collateral pieces, 249

CEO/MD, on organizational chart, 19

certifications, 309

CFO (financial decision maker) persona, 188

change-tracking, in living documents, 117

channel, in marketing plan, 262

channel collateral, as collateral pieces, 250

channel expertise, as a core competency, 47

channel partners

as a component of market strategy, 173

defined, 344

product launch and, 323

chasm model, 152–153, 156

Cheat Sheet (website), 4

CIO (technical decision maker) persona, 188

clarity, in discussions, 180

coaches, 307–308

codec, 333

coder personality type, 299–300

COGS. *See* cost of goods sold (COGS)

Coke brand, 157

collateral materials, in launch plan, 239

commitment

to excellence, as a trait of good product managers, 283

goals for in marketing plan, 264

in sales and marketing funnel, 252–254

communication

as a component of market strategy, 174

for product launches, 229, 323

as a product manager skill, 13

company background, in business case, 139–140

company culture, planning requirements for your, 120–122

company performance claims, as a component of market strategy, 174

company web pages, in launch plan, 239

compatibility, 189, 197

competencies

core, 47

prioritizing and, 102

competing products, in business case, 140–141

competition, Porter's five forces in, 155, 156

competitive, market, and technology trends product road maps, 331

competitive analysis. *See* competitive intelligence

competitive intelligence. *See also* market research

collecting, 93–98

identifying competitors, 93

importance of, 83–87

tracking the competition, 98

funding
  in business case, 143
  competitive intelligence and, 94
  for product launch, 318–319

G

G&A (general and administrative), 145
gate, 42, 345
general and administrative (G&A), 145
geographical segmentation, 71
GM (Golden master), 345
GM (gross margin), formula for, 145
GM% (gross margin percentage), formula for, 145
goals
  in business case, 137, 139
  career, 305–307
  as a persona attribute, 72, 73, 183
  setting, 221–222
  setting for product launch, 230
  setting in marketing plan, 263–264
  validating launch plan against, 241–242
golden feature product road maps, 329
Golden master (GM), 345
Google Alert, 98, 311
Google online forms, 225
go-to-market strategy, 149
governance
  in business case, 144
  in launch plan, 241
  in marketing plan, 262
gratitude, showing to customers, 79
gross margin (GM), formula for, 145
gross margin percentage (GM%), formula for, 145
grouping ideas, for brainstorming, 65
Growth, in four-phase cycle, 45
growth strategies, 154–155
guerrilla marketing activities, 234

H

headcount, 345
Heineken, 161

help, asking for, 287, 339
Hiam, Alexander (author)
  Marketing For Dummies, 23, 243
high-context methods, of market research, 92
high-level scope
  in product description, 195
  in product description document, 198–199
highlighting competitors, 319–320
high-value strategy, 159
horizontal launch, 232
"How Competitive Forces Shape Strategy"
    (Porter), 96
HR/Legal, on organizational chart, 19
hybrid, Plan phase documents for, 132

I

icons, explained, 3–4
ID number, 189
ideation, 345
identifying
  competitors, 93
  target, 302–303
ill defined, 122
implications, negative, 273
inbound marketing, 345
incentives, 223
Independent, in INVEST acronym, 210
in-depth planning
  about, 127–128
  compared with Lean planning, 118–119
  estimating time investment, 132
  key documents for, 130–132
  whether to document, 128–129
industry knowledge/expertise, as a trait of
    product managers, 33
influence, as a product manager skill, 13
influence map, 293–294
influencer persona, 77–78
information delivery, product life cycle and, 42
information gathering, 136, 183–187
in-person interviews, 91
insights, as a persona attribute, 73, 183

operational constraints, forecasting and, 258–259

operations
  on organizational chart, 19
  point of view of, for product retirement, 272
  role of, 30–31

OPP. *See* Optimal Product Process (OPP)

opportunities, weighing, 108–109

opportunity cost, 346

opportunity matrix, 153–155

Optimal Product Process (OPP)
  about, 52
  core documents, 54–55
  how it works, 52–54

organizational chart, 19–20

outbound marketing, 346

overall sales trends, 260

overall strategy, as a component of market strategy, 169

overview, in business case, 139

P

packaging and distribution needs, 191, 245

participants, recruiting, 222–225

payback time frame
  in business case, 142
  defined, 346

people, concern for, 283–284

people skills
  as one of the additional P's, 247
  as a trait of product managers, 34

performance, 190, 197

performance feature (Kano model), 110

personableness, for visiting customers, 79

personal relationships, building, 294–295

personalities, 299–300

personas. *See also specific types*
  about, 72, 189
  attributes of, 183
  creating, 183–184
  defined, 346
  description components, 72–73

developing, 74–76
  in market needs document, 188
  in problem scenarios, 184
  validating, 74

persuasion
  about, 289–290
  active listening, 290–291
  asking for what you want, 292–293
  of development team, 296–299
  influencing executives, 293–296
  of sales team, 301–304
  three reasons method, 291–292

PESTEL (political, economic, social, technological, environmental, and legal), 96–98

phase, 346

phase-gate approach, 346. *See also* waterfall development

physical concerns, process of and, 273

physical evidence, as one of the additional P's, 247–248

physical products, product retirement issues for, 273–274

pivoting, 120, 127, 346

P&L (profit and loss) statement, 145

place, as one of the four P's, 246

Plan phase, of product life cycle
  about, 44, 47–48
  best practices, 115–117
  in-depth, 128–132
  Lean approach, 124–128
  quantity of, 117–124

planning
  for brainstorming sessions, 63–64
  for product launch, 229
  product launches, 237–241
  product retirement, 273–276
  product road map, 199–200

platform product road maps, 333

point of view
  forecasting and, 259
  for product retirement, 272

political, economic, social, technological, environmental, and legal (PESTEL), 96–98

Porter, Michael (author)
  five forces in competition, 155, 156
  "How Competitive Forces Shape Strategy," 96
portfolio, of products, 171
positioning
  as a component of market strategy, 161–165,
    169, 172–173
  defined, 346
  prioritizing and, 102
positioning statements
  creating, 162–165
  format for, 162
positives, turning negatives into, 285
PR (public relations), 261, 321–322, 347
pragmatists, 153
PRD (product requirements document), 182, 347
presentations, as collateral pieces, 250
press
  as a component of market strategy, 173
  in launch plan, 239
  product launch and, 323
press releases, in launch plan, 239
price fixing, 171
pricing
  about, 30
  based on market position, 158–159
  based on quality, 159
  as a component of market strategy, 157–158,
    169, 171
  in Lean process, 127
  as one of the four P's, 245–246
pricing stacks, 159–160
prima donna personality type, 299–300
primary goal, in problem scenarios, 184
primary research, 85–86
print surveys, 92
prioritization matrix, 112–113
prioritized backlog, 208
prioritizing
  about, 101–102
  applying scoring models, 110–114
  backlog, 207–209
  business canvases, 104–108

detailed features, 192
market needs, 192
product-market fit triad, 102–104
weighing opportunities, 108–109
priority, 189
problem
  in Lean process, 127
  in product-market fit triad, 102–104
problem and opportunity, in business case,
    135, 137
problem scenarios, 184–185, 188, 189
problem statement, 137, 184–185
problem-solving aptitude, as a trait of product
    managers, 35
process
  inefficiencies of, as sources for new product
    ideas, 61
  as one of the additional P's, 247
ProdBOK (Product Management Body of
    Knowledge), 52
product and problem quadrant, 108–109
product backlog, 208, 209
product demonstrations, as collateral pieces, 249
product description document, 55, 130–131,
    195–199
product descriptions
  about, 168
  creating, 178–180, 193–199, 194–195
  in launch plan, 238
product development
  as a growth strategy, 154
  on organizational chart, 19
  role of, 29–30
product evaluations, in launch plan, 239
product features
  in Agile, 207–208
  compared with market needs, 178–180
  as constraints, 210
  defined, 345
  focusing on, 338
  prioritizing, 192
  product and, 245
  in product description, 194–195
  in product description document, 196–198

remote teams, 288

requirement, 347

research and development (R&D), 145

resellers, pricing and, 160

resource impact, in business case, 142

resources, in product description document, 198

respect for people, as a core concept of Lean planning, 118

response rates, 223–224

Responsible, Accountable, Consulted, Informed (RACI), 38–39, 40, 347

results, concern for, 283–284

retainer, 321

Retire phase, of product life cycle, 51–52. *See also* product retirement

return on investment (ROI)
  in business case, 142
  defined, 347
  in marketing plan, 262

revenues
  about, 30
  defined, 347
  formula for, 145
  monitoring, 265–266

rip-off strategy, 159

risk analysis
  in business case, 135
  as a component of market strategy, 175
  in launch plan, 241
  in product description, 195
  in product description document, 199

risks
  in business case, 143
  as a component of market strategy, 170
  defined, 347
  in marketing plan, 262
  process of and, 273
  in product description document, 196

road maps, 347. *See also* product road maps

Road Map document, 55, 131. *See also* product road maps

ROI. *See* return on investment (ROI)

roles and responsibilities
  during Development phase, 211–213
  of finance department, 30
  of legal department, 29
  of marketing department, 29
  of operations, 30–31
  as a persona attribute, 72, 73, 183
  of product development, 29–30
  of product management, 9–12
  of product managers, 15–40, 212–213, 291
  of product marketing managers, 22–23
  of product owners, 24–25, 213
  of sales department, 28
  of scrum masters, 25
  of service and support, 31–32

running product launches, 234–237

S

SAFe (Scaled Agile Framework), 27

saga, in Agile, 207–208

sales and marketing
  basics of, 244–256
  competitive intelligence and, 95–96
  digital, 251
  in Lean process, 127
  on organizational chart, 19
  planning and, 121
  for product launch, 229

sales and marketing funnel, 252–254, 265

sales and mkt, 145

sales department, role of, 28

sales effectiveness, profitability and, 267

sales enablement, 254–255

sales engineer, 28

sales operations, 28

sales process, 28

sales representative, 28

sales support, increasing, 268

sales team
  persuading your, 301–304
  for product launches, 236–237

sales tools, 303

Salesforce.com (website), 220

'saying no,' 341

Scaled Agile Framework (SAFe), 27

scope

  defined, 347

  in product description document, 196

scoring models, applying, 110–114

scrum

  about, 205

  Agile and, 212

  defined, 347

Scrum For Dummies (Layton), 212

scrum master

  defined, 347

  roles of, 25

seasonal variations, in sales forecasts, 257

secondary research, 85–86

security, 189–190, 197

segmentation

  as a component of market strategy, 161, 169, 172

  defined, 70, 347

self-assessment, conducting, 32–37

sell-in cycle, 259

selling price, profitability and, 267

service and support

  about, 191

  on organizational chart, 19

  in product description document, 198

  role of, 31–32

services

  product and, 245

  product retirement issues for, 275

setting

  career goals, 305–307

  goals, 221–222, 230, 263–264

  goals for product launch, 230

  goals in marketing plan, 263–264

  target dates for career, 305–307

shipping, decisions about, 226

shutdown, 275

Sinek, Simon (author), 181–182

situational analysis

  in business case, 141

  in marketing plan, 261

Small, in INVEST acronym, 210

SMART goal approach, 306–307

social media plan

  in marketing plan, 262

  posts as collateral pieces, 250

soft launch, 231–232

software, product retirement issues for, 274

Specific, in SMART goal approach, 306

spending, competitive intelligence and, 94

sprint goal, 212, 347

sprint planning meeting, 212, 347

sprint retrospective, 212, 348

sprint review, 212, 348

sprints, 205–206, 347

spur-of-the-moment conversations, 292

stage. *See* phase

stage-gate process. *See* waterfall development

stakeholders

  for product launches, 236–237

  stressed, 285–286

sticky notes, for brainstorming, 64–65

story mapping, 207

strategic alignment and business value, in business case, 137

strategy, 348. *See also* market strategy

strengths, in business case, 140

strengths, weaknesses, opportunities, and threats (SWOT) analysis, 96–98, 348

stress management, 284–287

subconscious mind, 60

success criteria, in marketing needs document, 191

success stories, as collateral pieces, 249

summary, in business case, 141–142

support. *See* service and support

supporting sales, as a component of the product marketing manager role, 23

SurveyMonkey, 225

surveys, 92

About the Authors

Brian Lawley is the CEO and founder of the 280 Group, the world's leading product management consulting and training firm. He is the author of five best-selling books: *The Phenomenal Product Manager* (Happy About), *Expert Product Management* (Happy About), *42 Rules of Product Management* (Super Star Press), *42 Rules of Product Marketing* (Super Star Press), and *Optimal Product Process* (280 Group Press). He's the former president of the Silicon Valley Product Management Association (SVPMA) and received the Association of International Product Marketing and Management (AIPMM) award for thought leadership in product management. He has been featured on *World Business Review* and the *Silicon Valley Business Report* and is the editor of the Optimal Product Management blog and newsletter.

Prior to founding and running the 280 Group, Brian spent many years working on innovative products at world-leading companies, including Digidesign (acquired by Avid), Apple (as product manager for the MacOS human interface), Claris, Symantec, and Whistle Communications. Brian is a Certified Product Manager (CPM) and Certified Product Marketing Manager (CPMM) and has a bachelor's degree in management science from the University of California at San Diego with a minor in music technology and an MBA with honors from San Jose State University.

Pamela Schure is director of products and services with the 280 Group. Prior to joining the company, she worked for many years in U.S. and international roles in product management, product marketing, and marketing for Apple and Adaptec. She has launched over 40 software and hardware products and managed teams of product managers from all parts of the world. Along the way, she also received two product patents. Pamela ran her own businesses in the United Kingdom and South Africa. Pamela is a Certified Product Manager (CPM), Certified Product Marketing Manager (CPMM), and Agile Certified Product Manager (ACPM). After attending two years of French *lycée* secondary education, she earned a bachelor of science degree in applied mechanics from the University of California at San Diego and an MBA from Columbia Business School. Pamela speaks English, French, and some Italian and learns other languages as a hobby.

Dedication

Pamela: I dedicate this book to Jane Burley, without whom I never would have begun this incredible journey.

Brian: I dedicate this book to my late wife, Sarah, my incredible kids, Taylor, Matt, and Sarah, and to my parents, Gail Lawley and Ken Lawley. Without you all and your support for my dreams, my world would be very empty.

Authors' Acknowledgements

We as authors want to thank the many people who had the patience and kindness to help us learn what we have learned so that we may pass it on. Our apologies if we forget anyone on this list!

Brian: I would like to thank many of the people I worked for who believed in me, taught me the craft of product management, and gave me the opportunity to practice it, including Charlie Oppenheimer, Jim Stoneham, Bill Campbell, John Zeisler, Mike Holm, Peter Gotcher, John Atcheson, John Mracek, Gordon Ritter, John Hamm, Jim Li, Marci Reichelstein, and hundreds of incredible peer-level product managers and other folks I had the privilege of working with.

In addition, the entire 280 Group team deserves a huge amount of credit for helping create both the Optimal Product Process methodology and one of the most amazing companies in the world. The 280 Group folks include (in random order) Will Iverson, Dave Dersh, Melissa Holtzer, Jillian McLaughlin, Cynthia Petti, Aaron Hyde, Mira Wooten, Aaron Canales, Duncan Gilmore, Mimi Salman, Phil Burton, Chuck Myers, Jim Reekes, David Fradin, Rosemary Yates, Bill Haines, Colleen O'Rourke, Tom Evans, Dan Torres, Eric Krock, Alyssa Dver, Bill Pieser, Jen Brecheen, J. F. Ouellette, Hector Del Castillo, Leslie Bixel, Linda Merrick, Rick Bess, John Cook, Megan McNamara, Michael Gonzalez, Ken Feehan, Greg Cohen, Roger Snyder, Matthew Lawley, and, of course, my co-author, Pamela Schure. A huge thanks to AIPMM, Therese Padilla, Paula Gray, and Chris Frandsen for their immense contributions to the profession of product management.

And last but not least, a huge thank you to the tens of thousands of product managers and product marketing managers who have helped move the profession forward, have purchased the 280 Group's products and services, and have inspired me to want to help others deliver incredible products to market that delight customers!

Pamela: I would like to first thank the product management team at Apple U.K.: Jane Burley (now Pearce) for putting me in the role and teaching me the ropes — and so much more; Jan Edbrooke for keeping me in product management once I left the United Kingdom; Clive Girling, Nigel Turner, and Neil Holland for being amazing colleagues (among many amazing colleagues at Apple U.K.) and Bianca Walker for taking over once I left; and Marc Jourlait for being part of the team that reinvented our European roles. The team at Adaptec, starting with Jean-Eric Garnier, who thought I'd make a good software product manager — thank you; Rob Griffith, who gave me the space to discover what customers really wanted;

Long Huynh and Scott Chambers, who started me off as a manager of product managers; David Manner and David Stokes, who taught me an amazingly collaborative way of managing teams; and Greg Agustin, Joel Lardizabal, Jason Ivan, Naser Mgariaf, Mia Giannotti, and Vadim Sigalov for reinventing product delivery and launches in record times.

A big thanks to the team at the 280 Group, who are amazingly interesting and thoughtful to work with. I am truly lucky to work with you every single day.

A big shout out also to my children, Adair, Aidan, and Amara. Definitely my A team. Finally, last, but certainly not least, Joe Bailey for being the loving ballast in my life.

Publisher's Acknowledgments

Acquisitions Editor: Tracy Boggier
Project Manager: Linda Brandon
Development Editor: Linda Brandon
Copy Editor: Megan Knoll
Technical Editor: Greg Cohen

Production Editor: Antony Sami
Cover Photos: © Peshkova/iStockphoto

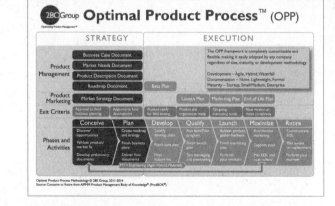